DISCOVERING KHAO LAK

R. Kobi

ISBN Paperback: 978-3-033-07595-5
ISBN e-Book: 978-3-033-07594-8

R. Kobi, 4132 Muttenz, Switzerland
E-Mail: Ruco.kobi@gmail.com
Texts by Rudolf Kobi
Cover, pictures and maps by C. Kobi

Disclaimer:
The contents have been carefully researched or derive from personal experience of the author. However, the author is not liable for consequences of possible errors in the text. R. Kobi does not assume any responsibility for the persistence or accuracy of URLs for external or third-party Internet websites referred to in this publication and does not guarantee that any content on such websites is, or will remain, accurate or appropriate.
Designations used by companies to distinguish their products are often claimed as trademarks. All brand names and product names used in this book and on its cover are trade names, service marks, trademarks and registered trademarks of their respective owners. The publishers and the book are not associated with any product or vendor mentioned in this book. None of the companies referenced to have endorsed the book.

CONTENTS

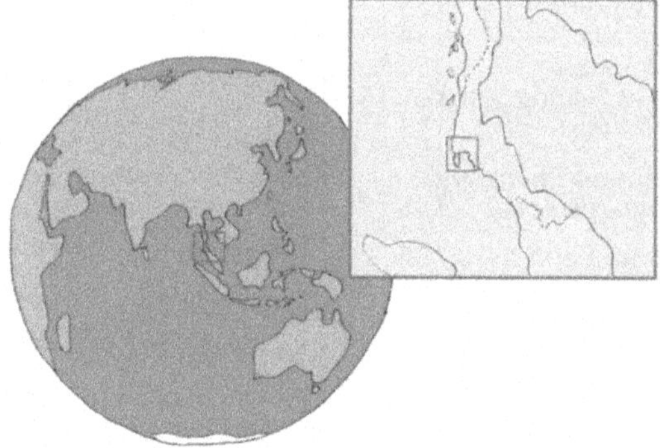

1-Location of Khao Lak in Thailand, Southeast Asia

FOREWORD BY THE AUTHOR

Thailand is – and rightly so – a popular tourist destination. It has a lot to offer for everyone, from backpackers to tourists to families. It has everything from fine dining to clean beaches, fantastic landscapes to pleasant weather and cultural places. You could say that it is the ideal holiday destination! In most travel guides Khao Lak was only mentioned in passing. A real deficit. Our travel guide has addressed this shortcoming since 2016 and describes Khao Lak and surrounding areas in detail. Not like the AI-generated books that have been flooding Amazon since 2024. The content of this book has been revised, corrected, and expanded annually (except for the enforced Covid-break in 2021 and 2022).

In this guide you will find more than 500 attractions and tips just for Khao Lak and its vicinity. We give an overview of Khao Lak and the surrounding areas, show the common attractions in Thailand (which, of course, also exist in Khao Lak); the attractions specific to Khao Lak; the tours offered as well as ideas for self-drive tours and excursion destinations. I mostly do not go into individual tour operators, since many offer the same, or at least similar tours. That also applies to hotels and accommodations, of which there are countless beautiful ones. The restaurant recommendations have been expanded, though we are still far away from the over 200 restaurants in the area. In addition, the book contains general, useful information about visiting Thailand, how to avoid a culture shock, some history of the area, a short list of do's and don'ts, information about traffic, health, customs regulations, emergency addresses, and a little bit of Thai for tourists. If you're looking for inspiration, you'll find it in the chapter "What for whom?"

On what kind of basis did I write this guide? I have been visiting this wonderful country yearly for over 30 years now. In the last years we were mainly in Phuket and Khao Lak. While I was initially travelling alone, I now travel with my wife and my (now teenage) child.

I hope this guide proves useful. Since it is a work in progress I look forward to your feedback and suggestions at ruco.kobi@gmail.com

Save travels and happy holidays!

Ruedi

Khao Sok

Similan

Phang Nga

KHAO LAK – AN INTRODUCTION

Khao Lak is not *one* place, but rather **a string of small towns** along the Highway 4 in the Takua Pa district of the Phang Nga Province in southern Thailand. Each of these places has different characteristics and at least one associated beach.

Today Khao Lak lives off tourism. But compared to Phuket it is not nearly as overrun by mass tourism and it still retains its Thai charm in many places and has a lot of places yet to be discovered.

The name "Khao Lak" means "Mountain Lak", which is the main elevation in the otherwise rather hilly region. But even this "mountain" only has a height of 1050 meters. It is in the Khao Lak Lam Ru National Park. There are **seven national parks** (those at sea included) within an area of 70 km around Khao Lak, more than anywhere else in the world. The coast with its **golden sandy beaches** belongs to the most beautiful ones in Thailand. In the hinterland there are **rainforest-covered hills**. There are **Mangrove forests** close by and **rocky steep hills** with incredibly spectacular views both at Khao Sok and the Phang Nga Bay. Off the coast there are the **coral reefs** of the Similan and Surin islands where you can dive with turtles and manta rays.

Khao Lak is renowned for its **quiet atmosphere** and is the **starting point for diving and snorkelling trips** to the Similan and Surin Islands. It is located ideal for excursions to the **animal-rich Khao Sok National Park** or the **culturally interesting town of Takua Pa** or the **fantastic Phang Nga Bay**. It differs from Phuket with its quiet hotels of higher class, less overcrowded beaches, family-friendly nightlife, and a local building code that prohibits the construction of buildings higher than a coconut palm tree, so Khao Lak only grows horizontally, not vertically.

Orientation

If you say "Khao Lak" you could mean any of these beaches – even if they extend over a total of 25 km along the coast. This sometimes makes it difficult to communicate where to go. You need more precise directions: Which beach? Which town? Even the addresses of hotels or restaurants are not very meaningful. Somehow, all of them have Phangnga and Moo something in it, and, oddly enough, most addresses also contain Khuk Khak (probably because of the county administration there).

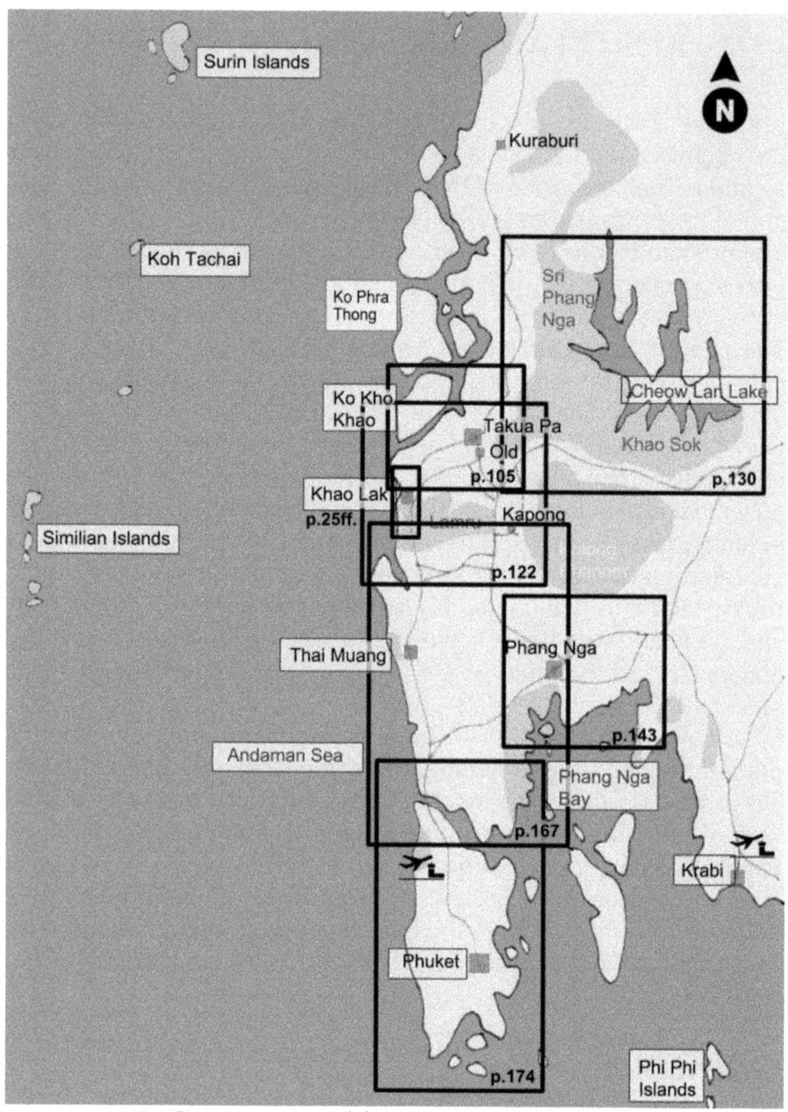

2 - Overview Map of the surroundings of Khao Lak

The rectangles show the detailed maps in the book: **The villages of Khao Lak p.25ff. Takua Pa and Ko Kho Khao p.105**., Kapong p.122, **Khao Sok and Cheow Lan Lake, p.130**, **Phang Nga p.143**, **Between Khao Lak and Phuket p.167**, **Phuket p.174**

At the End of the Book is a touristy map of the Phang Nga Area p. 234

For this reason, I do not use the postal addresses of the attractions here, but rather the descriptions to get there and in addition to that the coordinates in decimal degrees (DG provided by Google) and in GMS (in degrees, minutes, seconds). You can **use them for your satnav or app**.

Type Latitude / Longitude

DG 8.65112 / 98.25252

GMS N 8° 39′ 4.032″ / E 98° 15′ 9.072″

Since the **place names** are phonetic translations from Thai to English, there are quite some variations. For example: Tab Lamu, Tap Lamu, Thap Lamu or even Tublamu all refer to the same place. I've used the most common versions in the book, but you should be open to very variable names when you're searching the web and on the road.

Maps

The QR code (or link **bit.ly/klentdecken**) links to our **Google map** with all the attractions mentioned in the book and a few more that haven't made it yet into the travel guide. Underneath the individual chapters, you'll find additional Google Maps linked with marked route suggestions and attractions.

For local navigation without roaming charges, you can download the Google Maps for offline use. Instructions for the less tech-savvy (like me): Open the Google Maps app on your smartphone. Click on your Google profile in the top right corner. From the list, select: Offline maps. Custom map. Select the map section and download it. If you're there and don't have internet, Google Maps will automatically switch to offline navigation.

Most tourist maps that you get for Khao Lak are very rudimentary and sometimes just plain wrong - because they want you to use the tour operators. We therefore created new ones for the book.

Time

Thailand is 6 hours ahead of Central European Time (CET) and 5 hours ahead during summertime.

Climate and Weather

The temperature in Khao Lak remains fairly consistent throughout the year with only minor seasonal differences. The temperature typically ranges from around 25 degrees Celsius at night to 32 degrees during the day on a sunny day. Khao Lak is influenced by two monsoons that occur seasonally: the southwest monsoon and the northeast monsoon. The southwest monsoon begins in April, when a current brings warm and moist air and thus rain from the Indian Ocean. It ends in October, which is the wettest month in Khao Lak. The following months are under the influence of northeast winds from China and are much drier. Therefore, the time from November to March is considered the dry season. March is the hottest month.

	Jan	Feb	Mar	Apr	May	Jun	Jul	Aug	Sep	Okt	Nov	Dez
Max. Temp. (°C)	33	34	35	34	33	32	32	31	31	32	31	31
Min. Temp. (°C)	21	22	23	24	24	24	24	24	23	23	23	22
Precipitation/ Niederschlag (mm)	33	36	68	205	527	406	452	478	582	476	250	48
Rainy days / Regentage	4	4	7	15	24	23	21	23	24	22	16	6

Klima Khao Lak / Climate Khao Lak

From a tourist point of view, the **dry season** (between October and April), is perfect to visit Khao Lak. But even on a "rainy day" it is not bad at all. It usually rains in the late afternoon or early evening and even then, just briefly most of the times. The rain can also just occur very locally – which falsifies the statistics, so the indication of the number of rainy days is misleading. Weather apps usually show this as a whole day of rain and are therefore notoriously unreliable.

In **low season** – (the rainy season May to October), you often get flight and accommodation at a bargain price, but regardless of the weather, some otherwise busy places may be either deserted or even closed. This applies to restaurants and shops as well as tourist destinations. For diving and snorkelling trips during these months it is advisable to ask the providers in advance.
Still, there's plenty to do (and enjoy) even when it's raining – tips about this can be found later in the book.

On the website of the Thai Meteorological Department (💻weather.tmd.go.th) there is a weather radar for Phuket and Khao Lak, which is more useful for getting an idea of the current weather than the classic weather apps.

Money and Currency

The currency in Thailand is the Thai baht (THB). 100 baht are approximately £ 2.26 or $ 3.0 (exchange rates as of April 2025). For current exchange rates, use currency converters in apps or search engines. Credit card payments are not accepted in many places. In hotels, yes, but most restaurants, small shops, and even gas stations accept (only) cash. See also the sections on exchanging money, tipping and bargaining.

A word about **prices**: Thailand is cheaper than Europe and the USA, but Khao Lak is definitely not a backpacker's paradise anymore. Take the prices for **food and drinks**, for example. In simple soup kitchens you can still eat and drink for around 200 baht per person. In Khao Lak's restaurants, prices per dish range from 150-300 baht (£4-8), and drinks between 50-150 baht (£1-4), so you'll pay around 400-700 baht (£11-19) per person for two courses plus drinks. In the better hotel restaurants, you would pay two to four times as much.
Water is available at 7-Eleven and other markets for 15-20 baht per bottle (€0.50). In restaurants, soft drinks and fresh juices cost between 50-100 baht (€1.50-€3), while cocktails and alcoholic drinks range from 80-180 baht (€2-€5).
Transportation: Taxis usually have flat rates depending on the destination, ranging from short trips (150 baht for two people, approximately €4) to long distances (such as to the airport, around 1500 baht, approximately €40). Tours cost between 900 baht (short trip, approximately €25) and 4000 baht (day trip, approximately €100) per person, depending on the type of excursion, services included, and duration (children are usually cheaper or free).
Accommodation: Hotel prices per room with 2 people occupancy: cheap hostel rooms are available from 20 euros per night, in luxury hotels up to over 200 euros per night.

How to get there

Khao Lak is located about 80 km north of Phuket and you would usually reach it after arriving at Phuket airport and a one–hour transfer via the Sarasin Bridge on Route 4. Highway 4 – one of the main routes through Thailand – is currently being widened (up to Bangkok, according to government plans). On the route between Phuket and Khao Lak, construction work has now been completed.

Phuket Airport

Phuket Airport is one of the busiest in Thailand and, after opening the new building in September of 2016, consists of two terminals. The old airport building is used for domestic flights and called Terminal 2, the new airport is used for international flights and called Terminal 1.
The place where the airfield is located is remarkable: it lies directly behind *Mai Khao Beach*, over which the flights in the high season come in (when the wind blows from the east). They then start over the wonderful Phang Nga Bay. In the rainy season it is the other way around.

Arrival: After the immigration, where a photo is taken of you, you will find five luggage carousels, various information desks, currency exchanges, ATM machines (both not with the best exchange rates) and stands where you can get local SIM cards in the long hall. The car rental companies Avis, Alamo, National and Hertz have counters in the arrival's hall. Budget and others have their offices still in the old airport terminal.

Departure: Be there early enough when departing: 2 hours before an international flight is the absolute minimum, 3 hours are highly recommended. For domestic flights, (in the old terminal) be there 1-2 hours before departure. In case you are not certain from which terminal you depart (especially for flights via Bangkok), you should look at your ticket before arriving at the airport or inquire with your travel agency. Terminal 1 is the new airfield; Terminal 2 is the old one.

From the airport to Khao Lak

If you have booked a hotel, transfer to it from the airport is sometimes included. Of course, you can also book a taxi or transfer by yourself.
A taxi from the airport to Khao Lak costs around 1700 baht, around 2000 for a minibus for more than 3 persons.
There are several **taxi apps** in Thailand that you can use to order a taxi online. In the tourist hotspots, these are Grab, Bolt and inDrive. Uber is no longer available in Thailand: the business has been taken over by Grab. Grab is very active in Phuket, less so in Khao Lak. Grab is not always the cheapest option. Sometimes it is cheaper to take the hotel bus or call a taxi. According to the app (in Feb 2024), a Grab from Khao Lak (Nang Thong Supermarket) to the airport was 1581

baht. The hotel transfer was 1200 baht. Conversely, transport from Phuket airport to the hotel is easily possible with Grab (faster than a minibus and cheaper than a taxi). After arrival, organize a Grab transport via the app, go to exit 7 and then turn left about 30 - 40 meters towards the domestic hall. The Grab is usually already there and waiting.

Of course, there is also **public transport**: public buses operate between Phuket Town and Khao Lak. Thailand has a good public bus system, which is operated by the *Transport Company* 💻 transport.co.th. Unfortunately, the airport is not connected to it. You must get to Highway 4 – and that is 5 km from the airfield. Taxi or motorbike taxis may take you there, but need a bit of persuasiveness, as short trips to cheaper transportation are not happily agreed to.
On Highway 4 take a bus towards Takua Pa, Ranong or Surat Thani. All of them stop on request in Khao Lak or (wherever you want) along the road. A bus ticket from the airport to Khao Lak costs between 80-100 baht and you cover about 80 km.
The buses from the airport only go to the larger towns on Phuket itself. However, some of them (like the *Phuket Airport Bus Express* (phuketairportbusexpress.org) make a first stop on the main road. It costs 50 baht to Muang Mai station.

Cars can be **rented** at the airport. Getting to Khao Lak is easy: from the airport, take the 402 road north. Stay on the Highway 4 and always keep left at the junctions (along the coast) – except for this one junction in the village of Thai Mueang: there the road goes to the right, even if it looks like you should go straight ahead. Once you have crossed a hill over curvy roads you are in Bang La On – the heart of Khao Lak region.

Khao Lak itself lies along **Highway No. 4**, which is called Phetkasem Road here. The villages lie between the coast and the wooded backcountry. Not exactly ideal for excursions you should think – but you are wrong!

Getting Around in Khao Lak

Pedestrians

As a pedestrian, you may encounter some problems in Thailand –and Khao Lak is no exception here. Many sidewalks are in poor condition, so you have to be alert to avoid holes, (semi-) open sewer lids or loose and protruding stones. Electricity pylons, signal masts and other things may be mounted right in the middle of the sidewalk. The walkway edges vary in height and are often considerably higher than in Europe. So, concentration is called for if walking here and – if you have a stroller – it is even a bit more strenuous, but still feasible. Crossing the street can be adventurous. For most of us, the cars approach from the wrong side (from the right) and pedestrian crossings (zebra crossings) seem to only serve as decoration – only a minority of drivers will stop to let a pedestrian cross. They are mandatory in front of schools, but there police officers and helpers make sure that drivers stop. Otherwise, as a tourist, you must be aware that this cannot be assumed!
Especially on the main road, Highway 4, you really must be careful. Accidents, some of them serious, happen every week and are often caused by the carelessness of western tourists.

Highway 4 is now a multi-lane thoroughfare. The median has been replaced by a continuous, approximately 1-meter-wide grass strip, with high guardrails in parts. This makes crossing the road difficult and only possible in certain places. In La On, in front of the Orchid, where there was previously only a pedestrian crossing, a traffic light has now been installed, as well as in Bang Niang, just after entering town. One can only hope that the new traffic lights will be better observed than the pedestrian crossings.
We found the countdown here amusing, which shows the time until green. The counter starts as soon as a pedestrian presses the button. At 0, the traffic light man (used instead of the green "walk") on the sign starts running – and you better do too! You don't have much time left. When you reach the median, you have to press a button again because the other side is still on red / don't walk!

Taxis / Songthaews and Minibuses

Those who do not rent a car but want to explore Khao Lak and the surrounding area, depend on taxi drivers or tours.

Although prices went up in the past 15 years, they are still moderate. Taxis are a little more expensive here in the South than in Bangkok, but they do not drag you from gift shop to gift shop or try to change the desired destination with statements like "temple closed today" (which by the way is never true). The taxi drivers here are numerous and friendly and not very intrusive. A simple shake of the head is enough when you are asked if you need a taxi. In front of the big hotels, there is normally a taxi rank, even (or especially) if the hotel is quite isolated.

Most Taxi drivers have **fixed prices posted** for frequently visited destinations and routes. No haggling necessary. You pay upon arrival. The prices listed are for up to two people; additional passengers pay a small surcharge, so it's worthwhile to pool and book excursions with a group. Below you'll find two price lists: one for excursions departing from La On/Bang Niang and one for those departing from Khuek Khak/Bangsak.

100 Baht is approximately 3.1 $ or 2.31£ (exchange rate April 2026). So, we're not talking about very expensive trips here (especially when I think about what I usually pay in Switzerland/Europe...).

Taxi prices Khao Lak (from **La On**, Bang Niang) 2023/2024
For 2 people, one way. 2 more people in the taxi pay 50 baht each.

To / Nach	**Price (Baht)**	**To / Nach**	**Price (Baht)**	**To / Nach**	**Price (Baht)**
Nang Thong	200	Small Beach	300	Sea Turtle Conservation	450
Bang Niang Markt	150	White Sand Beach	350	Ban Nam Khem Tsunami Memorial	650
Chong Fah Waterfall	350	Happy Beach	450	Suwan Kuha Temple Phang Nga	1200
Sai Rung Waterfall	450	Memories Beach	450	Samet Nangshe	1200
Ton Prai Waterfall	750	Poseidon Beach	450	Khao Sok Ntl Park	1200
Lam Pi Waterfall	750	Pakweep	350	Phuket Airport	1500
Khuekkhak Temple	300	Bangsak	450	Phuket Town	1700
Takua Pa Old Town	750	Khuk Khak	350	Patong, Karon, Kata (Phuket)	1700
Thai Muang	800	Mini Golf	200	Krabi Airport	1700
Tap Lamu Pier	500	Fresh Market	200		
Ko Kho Khao Pier	650	Bamboo Rafting	450	From La On/BangNiang	

Taxi fares Khao Lak (from the JW Marriott in **Khuek Khak**) 2025
Prices are for one way, for 1 to 4 people. (= 1 taxi)

To / Nach	**Price (Baht)**	**To / Nach**	**Price (Baht)**
Khaolak Center (Bang Niang or La On)	300	Ban Nam Khem Tsunami Memorial	700
Bangniang Market	300	Lampi Waterfall	800
Pakarang Beach / Apsara	400	Takuapa Old Town	800
White Sand / Coconut Beach	300	Khaosok National Park Office	1500
Memories Beach / Elephant Home	400	Samet Nangshe Sky Walk	1500
Bangsak Beach	500	Phuket Airport	1500
Sairung Waterfall	500	Krabi Airport	3000
Chong Fa Waterfall	500	Kamala Beach (Phuket)	2500
Sea Turtle Conservation Center	600	Phuket Old Town	2500
Ko Kho Khao Pier	700	Suratthani Airport	3500
Tublamu Similan Pier	700	Pier nach Ko Samui	4500

For longer trips, there are **2 pricing models** that you can arrange with the drivers:
Hourly Rate: for example, 2000 baht for 4 hours, then 500 baht per hour – depending on the distance.
Fixed price for the whole trip: for example, 2500 baht for the 3 Temple Tour. – Keep in mind that pre-existing tours often include drinks, eating and a (English or German or French-speaking) guide in the quoted price.

Songthaew

A Songthaew is a kind of public taxi, which is used by many locals to get around. They are pickup trucks in various colours with two rows of seats at the back of the loading area, covered with a roof of a thin metal or wood. During the day they can be seen driving up and down on Highway 4. If you want one, you just signal them to stop. Tell them your destination and the driver says if he goes there. You can also find them in front of bigger hotels or restaurants on the side of the road. You pay on departure. If you want to stop on the way, you press the "buzzer" or hit the roof with your hand. You should agree on a price beforehand. Take care if you negotiate a total price for all, or per person. Songthaews operate as "public transport" from morning to afternoon and become regular taxis in the evening. Songthaews that park on the side of the road or in front of the hotel are normal taxis – you only pay after you arrive at your destination.

By the way: **Tuk Tuks** serve the same purpose in Thailand. These are 3-wheel motor vehicles found in Bangkok and some provinces.

Hotel buses

Many hotels (especially the larger, isolated ones) offer free transportation at certain times – ask at the front desk. In addition, some restaurants offer pickups for free if you eat with them (but only if you do not stay too far away).

Public buses

You can easily travel Thailand by bus: either in the simple public buses by the *Transport Company* that stop in many places along the highway if you sign them, or in the well-air-conditioned VIP buses with sleeper seats. The VIP buses can be booked at *Baw Khaw Saw (BKS)* bus stops. These air-conditioned buses only stop if they have seats available or if you have booked a ticket (available at the travel agency). It is therefore necessary to buy these in advance and reserve your seat on the bus.

The BKS bus stop in Khao Lak is located north of Bang Niang behind some buildings on the Khao Wang Road at the fresh market. The buses here go to Phuket or Morchit Station in Bangkok and make numerous stops on the trip: in Takua Pa, Khuraburi, Ranong, Chumphon and in many more places. VIP costs about 900 baht and takes 12 hours, first-class about 600 baht and 13 hours, and 2nd class costs only about 450 baht and takes 15 hours.

The bus stop for the public buses is located south of Khao Lak Beach at Thap Lamu Pier. The buses to Takua Pa and Phuket stop here and take passengers in each direction every hour. It costs 40 baht to Takua Pa and takes 35 minutes, to Phuket it costs 80 baht and takes about 1.5 hours. These buses run between Takua Pa or Phuket and Bangkok on Highway 4 through Khao Lak and you can stop and board them anywhere by signalling.

There is also a **railway** in Thailand, the network has its center in Bangkok. Unfortunately it does not reach Khao Lak. The nearest station is at Khiri Rat Nikhom in Surat Thani Province – just over 2 hours' drive from Khao Lak.

Longtail Boats

The longtail boat (Thai Ruea Hang Yao) is a typical Southeast Asian water transport vehicle. It is between 14 to 18 meters long and less than 2 meters wide. A pivoting engine is mounted at the rear. The longtail boat is steered with the long propeller shaft on the engine, there are no rudders. Longtail boats can be found on the sea as well as on lakes and larger rivers. They serve as a water taxi, snorkelling station and for fishing.

Renting a vehicle

I recommend renting a vehicle if you want to be truly flexible and independent and if you dare driving on Thai roads. Motorcycles and scooters can be rented without difficulties at many places in Khao Lak. Those who book from home can get their car at the airport and drive up to Khao Lak by themselves.

Cars

Several international car rental companies have rental stations in Phuket; Budget in Khao Lak itself.
Especially in high season, it may well be that cars are not available on short notice or must be brought up from Phuket, therefore it is sometimes cheaper to rent them prior to arrival or down in Phuket.
Budget Car Rental: The rental station is at the gas station in Khuk Khak. 💻budget.co.th

I would caution you not to rent a car on the roadside, as they are privately rented cars – and thus not insured. This also applies to private tour guides and transfers without registration: hit-and-runs may happen, and the tourist is left behind, having not only to explain to the police how he got into the car, but also to pay for the accident (material and personal injury).

Scooters

Scooters can be rented in the tourist resorts in many places, sometimes at the hotel itself. Prices vary depending on location and length of rental – the longer the time, the cheaper the rent is usually. Daily rates are about 250 to 300 baht. Petrol is sold at filling stations and on the roadside – the bottles with the red content on the wooden racks.

Most tourists underestimate the risks of riding a scooter or motorbike in Thailand. Thailand's traffic can range from unpredictable to dangerous, and as a motorcyclist you have no crumple zone. Accidents and injuries among tourists are very common, partly because they often ride lightly dressed and in sandals. Anyone with no experience and no motorcycle license should probably avoid riding here. Most rental companies won't check your license, but the police will. Those who have an accident and end up in the hospital without a valid license for the correct category of motorbike often find themselves faced with high medical bills and an insurance company that refuses to pay.

5 Star Motor Bike Rental at the Highway 4 near Bang Niang Market is recommended. The German expat offers well-maintained scooters and services such as street maps and apps for orientation.
💻 5-star-motor-bike-rental-khao-lak.business.site
No.1 Motorbike Rental Khao Lak. The station is in La On on the 4th. Book locally or online. They deliver to the hotel.
💻 no1motorbikerental.com.

Bikes / Bicycles

Biking provides you with a better insight into the country and local life than driving a car, but it is more strenuous in the heat. Many hotels offer rental bikes as a good way to explore the area because Khao Lak and the whole stretch along the coast is mostly flat. The hinterland is hilly and in the south there is the "mountain" Lak. Where there are hills, there is also forest. Do not go off-road through the forest: there are often snakes there, so even Thais do not just trudge or bike through the bushes. However, crossing the forest on the roads is safe. Those who do not yet know what to go and see, can book one of the guided bike tours. They visit various points of interest: waterfalls, villages, beaches. Some are combined with kayak trips or bathing in a river.
The *Green Biking Club* is a tour provider for bicycle tours and other environmentally friendly excursions. 💻 greenbikingclub.com

Rental bikes are available in many larger hotels, or from the local bike shop and mechanics.
Chak Ka Bike on Main Road 4 between La On and Bang Niang (seaside) rents and repairs bikes from 100 baht per day.

E-bike rental Khao Lak: There is now a rental company for the motorised bicycles. It is located near Memory Beach about 2 km from the gas station. Since only 6 bikes are currently rented out, it is recommended to book in advance. Rent is by the day, week or month. Prices start at 250 baht per day in the cheapest category. The bikes can also be brought to the hotel.
Contact via e-mail and Whatsapp: (in german, english and thai) ✆+66 920 927 456 💻monaplus@hotmail.com, e-bike-khaolak.com

Tips for renting a vehicle:

If you rent a motor vehicle in Thailand, you need an **international driver's license**. Even if the rental company does not always check the validity of the license, this could be a problem with police controls or insurance later.

Occasionally, the deposit of a passport is required for the rent. This should not be done in any case. On the one hand because you may need to present it upon police checks and on the other hand because the rental agency could really cause you problems in the event of damage – you need it for your departure. It is better if the rental agency requires a cash deposit or deposit via credit card. Often a copy of the passport will do.

Insurance of the car will cover damage to person and vehicle, but usually only with an excess of up to 50'000 baht. Check vehicles for damage before you leave the station and have them written down – otherwise you may have to pay for repairs later. If you take a digital photo with a timestamp, this may help later in the case of possible claims.

Insurance for mopeds only covers personal injury, not vehicle damage, which you must pay yourself. At least the repairs here are often way cheaper than at home.
Tip: Note the number of the insurer and let the rental company give you a phone number which you can contact in case of an accident.

Songthaew

Hauptstraße 4 durch Khao Lak

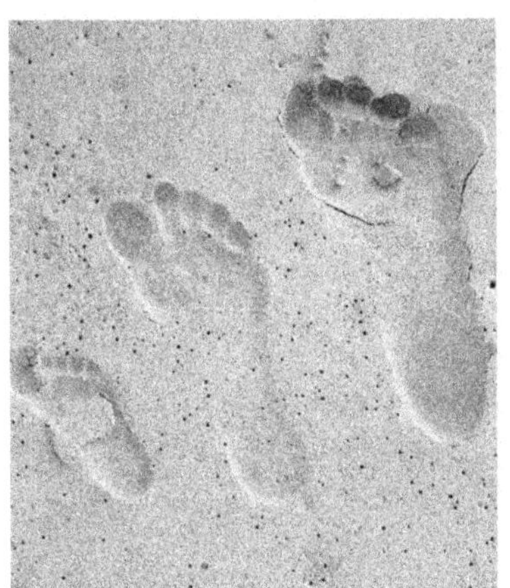

Longtailboat

Beaches and Places

Khao Lak is a series of small towns stretching from Khao Lak Village in the south to Bang Sak in the north. Each of these places has different characteristics and one or more associated beaches. There is no continuous road that runs along the beach. From the main road, Highway 4, smaller streets branch off to the beaches and the hotels.

Here is an overview of the different beaches of Khao Lak, starting in the south. Some are located in front of the towns and are correspondingly busy, others in front of isolated hotels, others are almost completely lonely. There is something for every taste here – and since Khao Lak is often considered a typical beach destination, the chapter here is intended to help you find the right place to stay – or to offer ideas for excursions for a day at the beach.

All these beaches are public (like all beaches in Thailand). The hotels have infrastructure such as parasols and deckchairs, but the beach strip is mostly free of them and open to everyone. Massage huts and restaurants are not allowed right on the beach, so most can be found adjacent to it.

All motorized water sports are prohibited on all beaches in Khao Lak. So there is no jet skiing, banana boating or paragliding – here you can still find absolute peace on the beaches, except for a few fishing boats. You won't be bothered by beach vendors either – but you will usually find food options nearby.

Please note that in early 2018 **smoking was banned** on 24 beaches in 15 provinces. These include Patong Beach on Phuket, Khao Lak Beach and Phra Aer Beach in Krabi. Smoking on the beach is still allowed in designated areas, which usually offer benches and ashtrays. Vapes or electronic cigarettes or shishas are not an alternative as they are banned throughout Thailand.

Lam Kaen / Khao Lak Village

The village named Khao Lak or Lam Kaen is located **on the southern side of the Hill Lak**, over which highway 4 curves. Excursions to the Similan or Surin Islands start from **Tap Lamu Pier** – or to the offshore **Khao Na Yak** peninsula, where you can snorkel and find secluded beaches. The pier is next to the **Naval Base**, the military area of the

Thai Navy. There is a public **golf course** and a **sea turtle sanctuary** on their premises. Most foreign visitors look for hotels further north that are by the sea and only see this place on excursions.

Poseidon Beach

Poseidon Beach is located at the end of a small, paved road that branches off to the left of the Highway 4 in front of the hill Lak and the town here. There are a few parking spaces for motorbikes and cars (often full, which shows the popularity of this beach). Next to it are the Poseidon Bungalows and the new Kalima Resort. The beach and the infrastructure here is almost as it used to be – typically Thai. Simple, but everything is there. 3 restaurants, massage huts, toilets, beach chairs and umbrellas, all on the beautiful sandy beach, which is lined with picturesque round rocks. A small, white lighthouse is visible in the sea some distance away.

Khao Lak South

The small town right in front of the Lak hill offers several hotels, restaurants, shops, and tour providers. The selection is smaller than further north, but with more local flair. Nearby you can visit elephants, go **bamboo rafting**, visit **Ton Pling Waterfall** or relax on the beach.

Khao Lak South Beach / Lam Kaen Beach

The associated beach with golden sand is 2 km long, nestled in the **Lam Ru National Park** with the Khao Lak River on the right and flat rocks on the left. It is called Khao Lak South Beach or Lam Kaen Beach. In parts it has very pretty round rock formations. However, it is almost completely taken over by the large hotels here – and is hardly worth a visit from outside.

Small Sandy Beach

The lonely, small, sandy beach is located in the middle of the Lam Ru National Park at the foot of the Lak hill. It is only accessible via a short but steep hiking trail from the top of the main road. Infrastructure is available: small shop, toilet block, swing, picnic area.

La On

The village of **Bang La On** is often (falsely) simply called Khao Lak and is the centre of the Khao Lak region. It is, except for Bang Niang, also the most touristic place with the most **shops and restaurants** (and tailors, art galleries, diving centres). The large Nang Thong supermarket specifically caters to the western tourist's taste. La On attracts visitors who like to have many choices but still prefer a more relaxed experience.

Sunset Beach

About 1.5 km long stretch of beach with sand in front of an impressive jungle landscape on the slope of the hill. Quieter than the sections of beach further north, some hotels are located directly on the slope (sloping away from the road). e.g. the Sunset Resort.

Laguna Beach

That's what the small, rocky stretch of beach in front of the Laguna Hotel is called. From here the land behind the beach is getting flat.

Nang Thong Beach

The most famous beach belonging to La On is approx. 2.5 km long and divided by **long rocks** overgrown with mussels, the rocks protruding up to 45 m into the Andaman Sea. The iconic **little white lighthouse** stands on these rocks – you can walk to it at low tide. The **rock formation Nang Thong** (Golden Woman) gave the beach its name. You cannot swim here during monsoon season because of the waves. The darker sand spots (partly black) look striking. They are remains of the tin deposits that were mined in the area. In the north, the beach is bordered by the Bang Niang River, which you can wade through at low tide.

Bang Niang

Bang Niang, located 2-3 km north of Bang La On, has the **most restaurants, bars, shops and an active nightlife** with discos and a cabaret. If you want lots of options within walking distance and like things to be busier, this is the place for you. Thais do their daily shopping on the "**Fresh Market**" in the morning and go out to the **Night Market** in the evening. The **Chong Fa Waterfall** is in the hills behind the village.

Bang Niang is suitable for people who like to have everything within easy walking distance and enjoy a bit (or more) of hustle and bustle. It's not so suitable for those seeking peace and quiet or for people who (like us) are traveling by car. Bang Niang is very densely built, has narrow streets with a (therefore) unusual one-way system, and limited parking.

Bang Niang Beach

The fine sandy and golden-brown beach is divided into an 800 m long southern and about 700 m long northern part, which is separated from Khuek Khak Beach by a picturesque **lagoon**. The beach here is largely rock-free. Unfortunately, the sand gets washed away more and more every wet season. This makes fastening measures such as **walls and sandbags** necessary. Sometimes these are not very attractive. The most beautiful part of the beach is at the lagoon in the north.

Khuk Khak

The village 2-3 km north of Bang Niang is the **administrative headquarters** of the area and there are small **shops, a post office, a police station and a petrol station**. The area is mostly residential, but has a few restaurants, luxury hotels and Rainbow Waterfall (**Sai Rung**). Those seeking peace and quiet and who would like a little more upscale accommodation choose the hotels here on the beach, and still find dining and shopping opportunities outside of the accommodation in the area.

Khuk Khak Beach

The sandy beach is gently sloping, without rocks, about 8 km long and divided by two rivers. On the south, it borders the headland of Coral Cape (Laem Pakarang). It is not overcrowded and – since it is flat far into the sea – very child-friendly.

Memories Beach

The extensive sandy beach with fine sand lies just south below the headland of Pakarang Cape on a bay. The beach is a paradise for **surfers** all year round (but especially from May to October) and has **surf shops, a skatepark** and a **restaurant.** You can swim here or just lie on the beach on one of the rental sun loungers. Because of the waves, the beach here is not so suitable for children or poor swimmers.

Coral Beach

You should wear bathing shoes here because of the **pieces of coral** in the sand and because there are stingrays here. At low tide an extensive coral slab peeks out of the sea.

Laem Pakarang (Coral Cape)

Some restaurants, bars and resorts and (some say) the most beautiful beaches of Khao Lak – this is Cape Pakarang, the **headland** in the north.

Coconut Beach and White Sand Beach

The Thais call the bay Ao Thong. The beach has white and fine sand with bigger pieces of coral. Natural vegetation provides shade, and you can swim in front of the gently sloping beach. There are a few small restaurants and massage stations and loungers to rent. Even in the rainy season you can swim here occasionally since the beach area is somewhat protected by the peninsula.

Pak Weep Beach

Interesting rock formations resembling lying menhirs can be found on this beach. It is excellent for swimming. The beach can only be reached via an unpaved, somewhat bumpy path. The TUI Mai Khao Lak Hotel is located here, otherwise it is a lonely, pretty beach with some infrastructure such as 2 good restaurants.

Bang Sak

In the northernmost part of Khao Lak you find hotels and restaurants and little more. If you are just looking for some peace away from tourist crowds, this is the place for you.

Bangsak Beach

Over a length of 5km you can find very different beach structures here. Fine, light sand, a large part is very natural. A few small restaurants and shops cater to the needs of local and foreign visitors.

Small Sandy Beach

Nang Thong Beach

Bang Niang Beach

Memories Beach

White Sand Beach

Khuek Khak Beach

Happy Beach and Restaurant

At the upper end of Bangsak Beach lies this beach with a simple restaurant where you can eat good and cheap Thai food with your feet in the sand. Toilets, showers, loungers and tour operator are available. Special: you can see free-roaming pigs on the beach here. The beach has dazzlingly light sand, and the sea is shallow. No rocks or large pieces of coral here. Next to the Le Meridien and Graceland Hotel. The path to the beach continues to the left (unpaved) of the Meridien. DG 8.80315, 98.25838 / GMS N 8°48'11.3", E 98°15'30.168"

Hat Bang Lut / Long Beach

The northernmost bay of Khao Lak is the longest at 6 km and extends to Ban Nam Khem off the island of Ko Kho Khao. It is left absolutely natural and has fine, light sand. If you go for a walk on the beach with swimming stops, you should take enough water with you, as there is no beach bar or restaurant here.

Other beaches near Khao Lak for excursions

Sunset Beach, Hapla Beach on Ko Kho Khao

The long golden beaches are the main attraction of the island. Sunset Beach in the very north is very popular and has a restaurant. Crossing is possible by car on a ferry or by longtail boat.

Ko Pah

The smallest island off Khao Lak, right in front of Ko Kho Khao consists only of fine, white sand (beach). A stately dune that invites you to rest, especially at low tide. A quiet place to relax and maybe snorkel, although visibility can vary greatly. You can only visit it by longtail boat. There is no shade and no infrastructure whatsoever.

Khao Na Yak

The long peninsula off Khao Lak, which stretches from Thai Mueang to the Tap Lamu Pier, is Khao Lak's house reef. It is very natural (as it is difficult to reach), with a clear sea, miles of deserted sandy beach, lined with brilliant blue water on one side and dense pine trees on the other. Swimming is possible in some places. Snorkeling and diving from the beach is not really possible, but there are a few nice spots for it right in front of it.

Beaches on the Similan and Surin Islands

They are only accessible via official excursions, as they are part of a national park. However, snorkelling is here sometimes possible right from the beach. The beaches are often very light, almost white, and contrast beautifully with the turquoise-blue water.

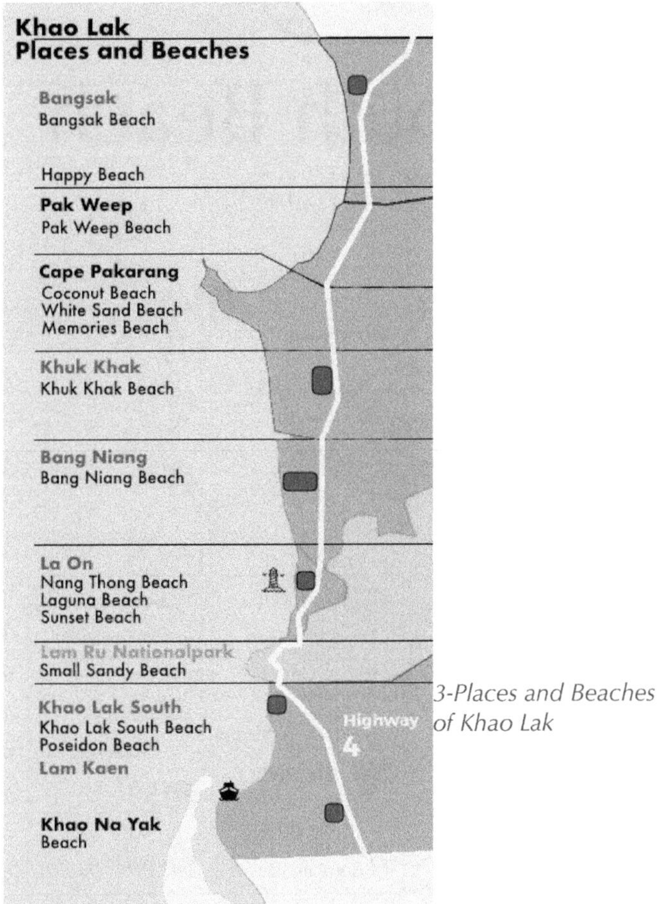

3-Places and Beaches of Khao Lak

South Beach

N

(Hügel) nach Khao Lak

nach Phuket

Hotel:

1 The Anda Mani
2 Briza Resort
3 Emerald Beach
4 Merlin Resort
5 Eden Beach
6 Poseidon Bungalow

Restaurant:

7 Tip Top Restaurant
8 E-sarn Restaurant
9 Rasoi Restaurant
10 Ruanthai
11 Nana on the Beach

Bar/Pub:

12 Jojo Bar
13 Elephant Bar & Thaiboxing
14 Absolute Bar

Diverses:

Elephant Sanctuary (eh. Asia Safari)
Ton Pling

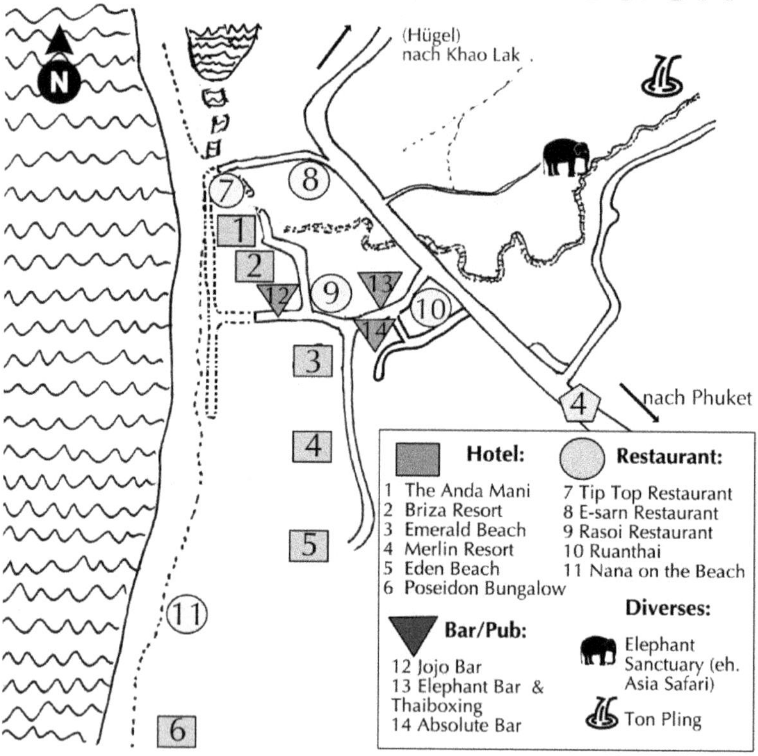

4 Map of Khao Lak South Beach

Bang
La On
Bang Niang
Nang Thong Beach
Laguna Beach
500 m
Sunset Beach
Highway
4
Phuket
N
Hotel:
1 KhaoLak Bayfront
2 Moracea
3 Laguna Resort
4 Nang Thong Beach
5 Suwan Palm Resort
6 Centara Seaview
7 Ocean Breeze
8 The Sands
9 X10
10 La Own Resort
11 Monkey Dive Hostel
Restaurant:
12 Sun Star Siam
13 Qcumber
14 La Piccolo Maria
15 P'Ann
16 Peter Pan / Orchid
17 Spinach / Jasmine
18 Happy Snapper 2
19 Phu View
Bar/Pub:
20 Walkers Inn
21 Monkey Bar
Diverses:
Leuchtturm
Nang Thong Supermarkt
Praxis Dr. Chusak
Dental Clinic
Sea Dragon Dive Center
Andaman Optic
Alive Market Lighthouse Bar

5-Map of La On

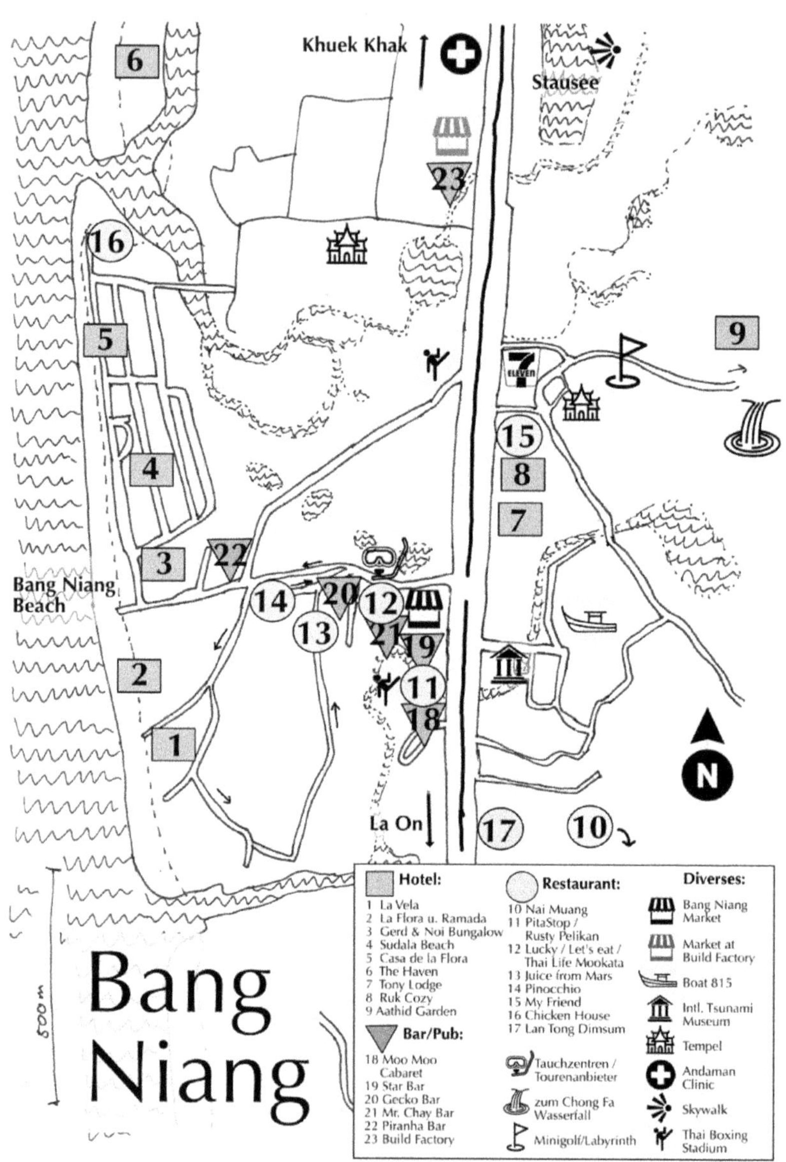

6-Map of Bang Niang

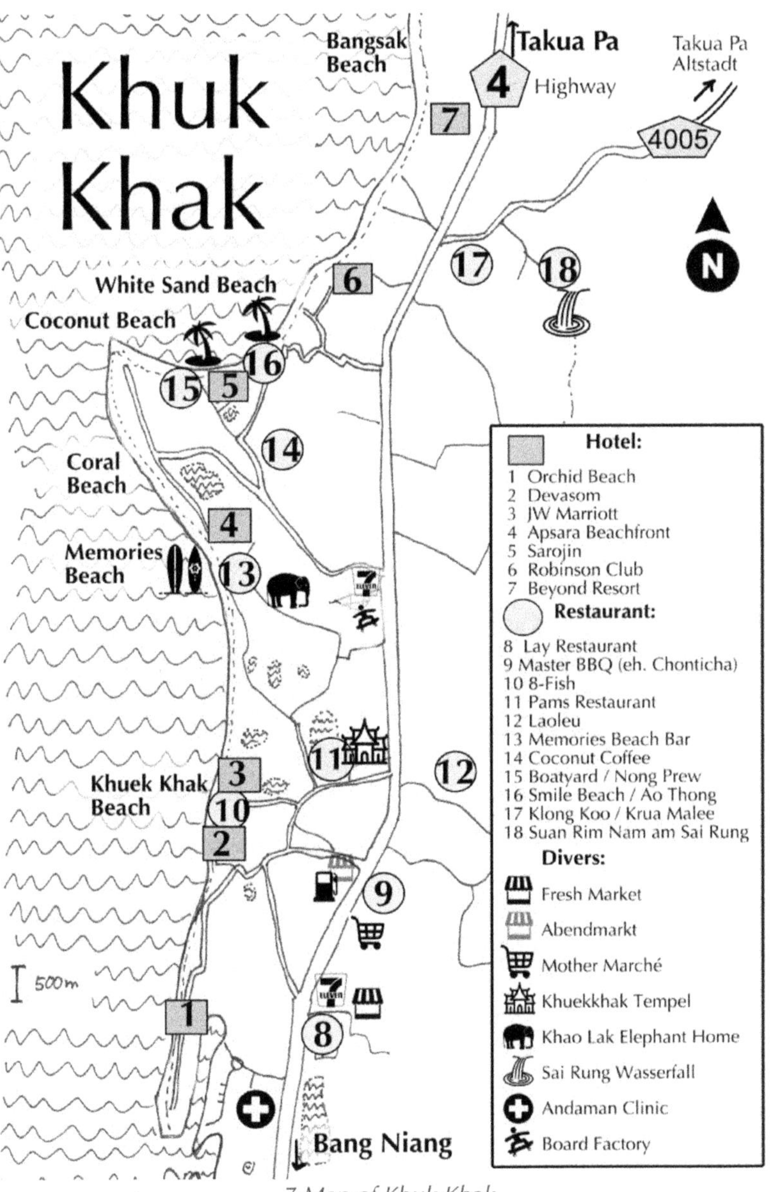

7-Map of Khuk Khak

Hotel Impressions Khao Lak

ACCOMMODATION, EATING, DRINKING AND SHOPPING IN KHAO LAK

Hotels and Accommodation

Hotels and accommodation in Khao Lak are plenty and there is something for every budget: from backpacker hostels to luxury hotels. In general, they still focus less on mass tourism here than down in Phuket, but of course you can also get super-cheap deals or just stay all-inclusive where you never (have to) leave the hotel area – which would be your loss, with all the good and cheap food here. It is up to your personal preferences and budget which accommodation you choose – and where in Khao Lak.

When choosing a hotel, you should consider what you want or need for your vacation. Khao Lak has numerous hotels spread across a more than 20-km-long coastline. The surrounding infrastructure (restaurants, shops, taxi stands, attractions, etc.) depends heavily on the chosen location – and to avoid unpleasant surprises, it's best to check it out beforehand. The easiest and most up-to-date way to do this is with the Google Maps map linked above. Without internet access, our local maps provide an overview:

Some general information: **Most of the real luxury resorts** and large hotels can be found in the northern part (Khuek Khak, Bangsak). These include the JW Marriott, Sarojin and Beyond Resort. Around these hotels, infrastructure with smaller restaurants and shops has developed. **Smaller excellent hotels** can be found along the whole coast. **More affordable accommodation** is closer to Highway 4. Apart from that, the room rates are the highest in Bang La On, cheaper in Bang Niang and the cheapest in Khuk Khak. However, keep in mind, that if your accommodation is way down in the south or far in the north, that (cheap accommodation) is diminished by the transport costs to attractions.

If you want nightlife and many restaurants, I recommend the area around Bang Niang. If you like it more relaxed and want to stay close to restaurants and shops and will be mainly on foot, then choose La On. If you like it quiet and idyllic choose Khuk Khak or Bangsak. The beaches are nice, wherever you stay in Khao Lak.

Use Google Maps to check the location of the hotel and see what food options or shops are available within walking distance or how far it is to the beach. Be careful: Highway 4 represents a barrier that is often not easy to cross!

Pro Tip: Do not choose all-inclusive or full board. There is plenty of good food available all over Khao Lak and it would be a waste!
This also applies to more remote hotels, unless you expect high alcohol consumption every day and do not want to look at anything apart from the hotel, pool and possibly the beach.

Examples of accommodation and location in Khao Lak:

Khao Lak Beach (beach south of hill Lak)

Widely spaced hotels on the beach, some bars, restaurants and shops, most on the side road of the 4 leading to the beach.

- Khao Lak Merlin Resorts (kid friendly)
- Eden Beach Resort (African style)
- Poseidon Bungalows (budget)
- Khao Lak Emerald Beach Resort & Spa
- Kalima Resort (eh. Khaolima)
- The Anda Mani (adults only)

Bang La On (beach and village)

Hotels mostly on the beach or near the beach. Restaurants, bars, shops – most of them on Highway 4, but also on the streets leading to the beach. A lot is within walking distance.

- Sentido (ex Tui Blue, ex Sensimar) now not adults only anymore
- Moracea (5*)
- Khaolak Bay Front Resort
- Khao Lak Laguna Resort (kid friendly, avoid the road side)
- Rakkawan Residence (budget at the Highway)
- Kokotel (3*, at the beach, surfer hotspot)
- Nang Thong Beach Resort (bungalows, at the beach)
- The Sands Khao Lak (5* kid friendly, big)
- X10 (5* kid friendly)
- Monkey Dive Hostel (budget)
- Jerung Hotel (budget)

Bang Niang (beach and night life)

Restaurants, bars, shops – most of them on the main road connecting the night market at Highway 4 and the beach. The beach here isn't the best, but there's plenty to eat, drink and shop within walking distance from most hotels.

- •Ramada Khao Lak Resort
- •La Vela (modern, 4-5*)
- •La Flora Resort & Spa Khao Lak (4*)
- •Chongfah Beach Resort (5*)
- •Gerd and Noi Resort (close to the beach, budget)
- •Casa de La Flora (5*)
- •Aathid Garden (budget, inland)
- •The Haven (isolated, on a headland)
- •Orchid beach (isolated)
- •Ruk Cozy Khao Lak (on the 4, budget)
- •Tony Lodge (on the 4)
- •Riverside guesthouse (budget)

Khuk Khak and Bangsak (North: Beach und Solitude)

Mainly individually located hotels, somewhat remote but with an infrastructure of restaurants, bars, shops and taxi ranks close by.

- •JW Marriott Khao Lak Resort and Spa (5*luxury with the longest pool in Thailand, kid friendly)
- •The Andamania Resort (budget, on the beach)
- •Suthawan Resort (budget, between highway and beach)
- •Apsara Beachfront Resort and Villa (5*)
- •Coconut homes (bungalows, inland close to white sand beach)
- •Kantary Beach Hotel (5*, adults only)
- •The Sarojin (5*luxury)
- •Robinson Club (children friendly)
- •Khao Lak Mountain View Bungalows (in the hills)
- •Beyond Resort Khao Lak (adults only)
- •Bangsak Village (adults only)

Food in Khao Lak / Restaurants

There are many restaurants in Khao Lak (over 200!), from small local joints to luxury restaurants with continental food (there even is a McDonalds, if you should need that) with countless recommendations on the internet. One travel site even wrote that they have received as many recommendations just for Khao Lak as for the rest of Thailand. Why? The food is good in just about any restaurant, but what stands out in Khao Lak is the wonderful friendly service, which ensures that customers return. You often get to be friends with the staff.

That was not different with us – although we have initially tried many restaurants, we ended up with Jin. At the time, she was working in the Phulay Bar and Restaurant, at the very southern end of Bang La On (before the hill). Not only does she cook fantastically, but she treated our little boy so great. In 2013 she opened her own restaurant, The Sky Restaurant was located between La On and Bang Niang, on the road leading to the X10 Hotel. It was our favourite restaurant—until it was forced to close in 2021 due to a combination of a lack of tourists due to COVID and a greedy landlord. Today, a restaurant is back there, unfortunately without Jin, with whom we still keep in touch. If she opens another restaurant somewhere else, we will definitely go and enjoy her cooking.

Visitors to Khao Lak will find plenty of good restaurants, bars, cafes and food stalls everywhere. In this guide we can only bring a selection, but there is much more to discover for yourself. It's fun here, as you eat well almost anywhere and find something for every budget. In fact, we haven't found a single truly bad restaurant yet – and we eat at a different place every day. Personally, we prefer restaurants that still offer authentic Thai cuisine: well-seasoned, not overly touristy.

A few restaurants have two menus and pricing systems: one for locals and one for tourists. This may be inconvenient, but perhaps understandable given the wage disparity. Just be wary if a restaurant doesn't offer a menu at all and doesn't give you any indication of the prices.

Restaurants in Khao Lak Village (south of the hill):

Ruanthai Kitchen

Good food: Thai, Fresh Seafood, Hot Pan, European. Low prices and extras like free fruit and a cold towel at the end. Guests praise the authentic, friendly atmosphere. Located on the main road, near the main path to the beach.

Rasoi Restaurant

Delicious food at reasonable prices. Thai and Indian cuisine and a large cocktail menu. Friendly service. Located on the main path to the sea opposite the Emerald Resort.

Nana on the beach

A classic Thai restaurant with plastic chairs right on Khao Lak South Beach. Thai dishes, fruit shakes and cocktails with your feet in the sand and sunset views in the evening. Beachfront, next to the Eden Hotel on Khao Lak South Beach.

Mr. Ju Khaolak Zero Kilometer

The restaurant, which had to close during the coronavirus pandemic, is back after a four-year hiatus. You can watch the chef and team cooking and see how everything is freshly prepared and beautifully presented. Located at Highway 4, beach side, before the hill.

Tip top restaurant

The last restaurant before going up the hill. Also located on 4 Main Street, it offers freshly cooked Thai food at reasonable prices and in slightly larger portions. At full capacity, there may be waiting times.

Other restaurants to try: *Komols Corner 7, Isan Seafood, Rer Dung Seafood, Mali Restaurant, Isarn Beachside*

Restaurants in Bang La On:

Sun Star Siam

The small Thai restaurant in La On offers tasty and fresh Thai food at an almost unbeatable price-performance ratio. You sit elevated above the main street on an open veranda. It's one of those restaurants that tends to get overlooked alongside its more conspicuous neighbours, but visitors keep coming back. Free WIFI. +66 81 476 0500. 11am-9pm. Opposite Laguna Resort on Main Road 4 just before going up the hill.

Gold Elephant

The restaurant in La On opposite the Laguna Resort regularly gets good reviews - and it's easy to see why: It's a bit more expensive, but you get cloth napkins, uniform tables and decorations (instead of the usual somewhat thrown-together things from plastic), a cold towel to welcome you and the occasional "show cooking" where they flambé some things in public. The food is Thai and some western dishes, such as burgers. In terms of quality, I found the food here to be a bit watered down for tourists: not so well seasoned and a bit bland.

Qcumber

The Qcumber Salads & Fruit Shakes is a small, cozy restaurant that offers (in addition to the classic Thai cuisine) salads and wraps – something you don't often find elsewhere. Fresh, healthy dishes not only for vegetarians and vegans. The atmosphere is reminiscent of alternative cafes in Europe, the service is friendly. They offer cooking courses. 💻 facebook.com/QcumberSaladBar 🏝 La On at Main Street 4, landside since 2024, at the southern end (before Lak Hill).

Khaolak Restaurant Thai Food

Located on a side street, unassuming, with a generic name, but serving absolutely authentic Thai food at reasonable prices! And... as we learned, our friend Jin supplies the curry pastes for the restaurant. Unfortunately, she no longer has her own restaurant (and no longer works as a cook), but the demand for her food was so high that they offered it here. The restaurant has been around for a long time and is an institution for the locals.

P'Ann

Authentic Thai restaurant in the middle of La On (opposite Nang Thong Supermarket). Very unassuming from the outside and simply furnished – but many Thai guests. Extensive menu, well cooked and fair portions at reasonable prices.

Orchid

Serving authentic Thai cuisine such as shrimps with tamarind, grilled chicken with green mango salad, sweet and sour pork, all at reasonable prices. 🏝 La On, located at the northern end of Highway 4, on the land side.

Jasmine Thai restaurant

The restaurant on the main road in La On towards Bang Niang impresses with good quality food (both Thai and European) and attentive service in a pleasant ambiance. At the back you have a view of the greenery towards the sea. Prices are a little higher, but within reason. 💻 jasminekhaolak.business.site

Spinach restaurant

Wide range of food and cocktails, good value for money. From Thai food, seafood to pizza, everything is available and well prepared. The pizza has a thin, crispy crust, the green curry is spicy, but also edible for tourists. Like many, the Restaurant is located at Highway 4, but you sit quietly and comfortably on the veranda in the back in a jungle setting. Live music many nights with a pretty good guitar player. 🏝 La On, on the main road north of Nang Thong Supermarket, seaside. 💻 m.facebook.com/Spinachrest

Pizzeria La Piccola Maria

Long established restaurant, the first Italian trattoria in Khao Lak. 2016 it moved to a new place on the Highway 4 in La On. They serve the best (wood oven) pizza in Khao Lak and Italian specialties (also gluten-free). La On, about 50 m north of the Nang Thong supermarket.

PeterPan Pizza Pasta Steak

Italian restaurant at the highway. If you've had enough Thai food and really want something different, you can get pizza (from the wood-fired oven), homemade pasta and steak (imported from Australia) as well as classic starters such as bruschetta and tomatoes with mozzarella or Caesar salad and Italian ice cream for dessert. The prices (especially for the meat) are higher than the average restaurant here, but still reasonable. The food was good, but the house wine came from a tetra pack, but it was OK (and certainly never corked). Other wines weren't available? Free WLAN and you can pay by card here.

Lah Own Restaurant

The beach restaurant belonging to the small La On Resort is also accessible to non-residents. It offers fine and affordable Thai food and cocktails. A great alternative to the (expensive) X10 hotel restaurant and easily accessible via the beach.

Phu View Restaurant

A restaurant with a view and the highest located in Khao Lak. In the evening a reservation is recommended. The way up is a bit difficult – and not possible with all vehicles. There are only 2 parking spaces. You can order a shuttle from the restaurant, which is free. The shuttle also takes people that stand at the entrance to the main road. You eat overlooking Khao Lak, the sea and possibly the sunset. Something for a romantic meeting. The food is Thai and cheap. ✆+66 89 872 2089

In the hills behind Bang La On. The driveway branches off Highway 4 about 350 m north of Nang Thong Supermarket. The restaurant is signed there.

DG: 8.6495, 98.25474 / GMS N 8° 38'58.2", E 98°15'17.063"

Other restaurant recommendations in La On: *Jais Restaurant, Madam Thai Food, Bussaba Thai, The View Restaurant*

Restaurants in Bang Niang:

Nai Muang

The Nai Muang Restaurant is located on a side street between La On and Bang Niang and is therefore away from the tourist crowds. It is exotic for several reasons: the decoration made of metal and old equipment and the vintage furniture is reminiscent of the times when tin was still mined in Phang Nga. The facade is made of corrugated iron. Inside, authentic Southern Thai food is offered without compromises to the tourist taste. The quality has earned the restaurant several entries in the Michelin Guide of Thailand. Seafood, lotus soup and Thai iced tea are recommended.
💻 facebook.com/Naimuang.Khaolak

Sanji Kitchen Khao Lak

Fantastic food, super-fresh sushi with fish from the Andaman Sea (here!), all prepared right before your eyes, with explanations of the fish, spices, and story behind each dish. Prices are definitely on the higher end, but worth it for what you get! Sanji Kitchen offers Japanese food (like sushi) prepared by an excellent chef with a passion for cooking and a focus on local ingredients. Chef Pon is Japanese, married to a Thai woman, and has a traditional culinary background. He has worked as a chef in hotels in Bangkok and Khao Lak (such as the Marriott) and now has his own (small) restaurant. Reservations are highly recommended due to limited seating. Parking is available between Bang Niang and La O on Highway 4, near the pedestrian crossing. 💻facebook.com/profile.php?id=61583264729821 ✆+66 81 053 5358

Beyond the Root

The place for vegetarian/vegan food in Khao Lak. Good and fresh products – they just need a little more time to prepare (especially when there are a lot of guests), but it's worth it. Extensive menu with Asian dishes such as curries, soups and spring rolls, but also salads and vegan burgers. Pleasant atmosphere and nice owners. Something for non-vegans too. On Highway 4 between La On and Bang Niang, hill side.

Tuk Tik Restaurant

One of the many restaurants on a side street in Bang Niang catering to the guests of the large hotels here. The restaurant is somewhat unassuming, but very clean and nicely decorated. The drinks (cocktails) were okay, the food was very good. They have an extensive menu, and they do serve Thai-spicy dishes upon request. Free Wi-Fi (which our son loves). They offer taxi to the airport for 1300 Baht (2026).

Thai Life Restaurant & Mookata

Swiss chef restaurant serving good quality European and Thai food in a nice setting. It is said that the "Thai Hot Pot" (Mookata) popular in Khao Lak was originally invented here. Other restaurants copied the concept, but the original is still unsurpassed. The restaurant has a guest house and bungalows nearby. The Thai hot pot consists of a metal table grill, in the middle of which on the dome the meat and shrimp are grilled and in the edge the vegetables and mushrooms cook in the chicken broth. When you order, you tick what you want on a piece of paper. A "set" for 1 person consists of a vegetable platter and a meat or fish platter. You can have pork, beef, poultry, bacon, shrimp or fish. facebook.com/mookatakhaolak

On the Bang Niang-Sea main road, near Bang Niang Market.

Let's eat

Restaurant with Hungarian chef and European menu. Besides pizza, schnitzel, burgers, they also have goulash and vegetarian langos. Apparently, this is one of the few restaurants here that has real cheese! Big portions and decent prices. If you want a change from Thai food and still want a good atmosphere, this is the place for you. In Bang Niang, on the road leading from the market to the beach, on the southern side.

Lucky Restaurant

The restaurant serves Thai and Scandinavian dishes, the owner couple is Swedish / Thai. The wide menu is adapted to European palates. They offer draft beer (Chang) in ice-cold mugs to colourful mixed visitors. In Bang Niang, on the road leading from the market to the beach, on the south side, close to the Let's eat.

facebook.com/Lucky-Restaurant-SeaThai-European-food-292717934081497

Noi Bar and Restaurant

A small, classic restaurant in Bang Niang, a little off the road to the beach (behind Pinocchio) and opposite the new "Local Market" here. Fine Thai food, cold drinks and very attentive and friendly owners (even if the waitresses don't speak English very well). Pool table and large screen, music or live music from the restaurants of the local market next door.

Chicken House Restaurant, Bar and Massage

A restaurant right on the best part of the beach in Bang Niang, in the very north, on the lagoon. You can eat with your feet in the sand or on grass under a tented roof and on plastic chairs. It has cheap, typical Thai food served by dedicated women. They rent loungers and there are massage places.

Pita Stop

Since 2021, Mike and his wife have been serving pitas, falafel, gyros, Greek salad, fried onion rings and more (also vegetarian) freshly made. Small pub with Swiss owner. You sit away from the traffic noise in a cooled room. 🕒 12.00 to midnight. just next to Bang Niang Market at 4 Main Street. Beside the *Meeting Point Bar*. 💻 facebook.com/PitaStopKhaolak

Wonderland Bar & Restaurant:

Lovingly furnished restaurant with committed staff, varied food and good cocktails. They organize trips and courses such as cooking classes or pottery. In the main link road in Bang Niang.
💻 facebook.com/WonderlandKhaolak

My Friend Restaurant

Very good Thai food by Juea, the owner, who is considered the best cook in the village of Bang Niang. From Bang Niang on the main road towards Build Factory, about 300 m on the right

Juumpo Family Recipe Restaurant

The food at this restaurant managed to pleasantly surprise our Thai friend Jin. It offers very well-cooked and seasoned classic local Thai dishes different from the usual dishes here. "Like it used to be". We can recommend it. It's no wonder the restaurant has been featured in the Thai Michelin Guide for the past few years. Located on Highway 4, at the Hotel Gahn, north of the traffic lights near Bang Niang, towards Khuk Khak. 💻 facebook.com/Juumpo

Blue Sky Restaurant - Blauwe Hemel

Restaurant halfway on the road to Chong Fa waterfall. Quiet, modern construction on the hill overlooking the green surroundings. It serves Thai and international food: Crocodile Steak or Macaroni are also available. Good stop for a lunch if you visit the waterfall.
DG 8.67998, 98.26873 /GMS N 8°40'47.928", E 98°16'7.428"

Qin Ai Restaurant

Newly opened Chinese restaurant for lunch and dinner, specializing in hot pot. You sit down, choose one or two of the eight soups, and the food to cook in them arrives directly in front of you on a conveyor belt (vegetables, meat, fish, mushrooms, dumplings, etc.). You can choose from various dipping sauces, and fruit and ice cream are also dispensed. You have 90 minutes to eat for only 285 baht. Currently mainly locals are served.
On Main Road 4 between Bang Niang and the reservoir on the land side. Next to Relax Time.

Restaurants in Khuk Khak:

Master BBQ buffet (formerly Chonticha BBQ)

They offer a good hot pot. The food is cheap (all you can eat), you can put it together yourself and then cook it in the hot pot. The hot pot (here made of metal) is placed at the table over coals, the soup is cooking in the rim and the meat and seafood can be grilled in the raised middle. The preparation of the soup and the meat takes some time, which you should bring with you here. Compared to pre-Covid, the restaurant has shrunk quite a bit: It no longer has a walk-in fridge, you get a piece of paper to tick and choose the things you want to eat. Khuk Khak, about 300m south of the gas station on Highway 4. DG 8.69109, 98.25392 / GMS N 8°41'27.924", E98°15' 14.111"

Ojoei Sushi & Izakaya

Sushi and Japanese food such as ramen and gyoza. Very fresh, first-class ingredients. Japanese decor. Often fully booked, so service may take a little longer. Ordering and paying via mobile phone is possible—at least for Thais. Prices are a bit higher but reflect the quality. On Main Road 4, land side, just before the turnoff to Khuk Khak Temple and JW Marriott. facebook.com/ojoei.sushi

Pam's Khao Lak

Pam's restaurant philosophy is: Cook the food like you're cooking for your best friend. Enjoy fresh food and drinks in a cultivated and cosy garden atmosphere. Seafood, cocktails, fresh fruit shakes, coffee, ice cream and homemade desserts. Private compartment in the restaurant for group reservations and they adjust menu and service accordingly. Take away and delivery service. Cooking classes. Taxi service. Reservations recommended on 085 211 8725 (Whatsapp or Facebook Messenger), especially after 6.30 pm Located on the road to the Marriott, behind the Khuk Khak Temple, approximately 2 km outside the "centre" of Khao Lak.
facebook.com/Pams.Thailand

Phens Restaurant

Located right next to the JW Marriott and accessible from the hotel via the beach, the restaurant is heavily dependent on the large hotel next door. It's not a beach restaurant (it's set back about 100 meters) and offers a simple, affordable, yet fine alternative to the expensive hotel restaurants. The atmosphere is friendly and informal, and the food (Thai and child-friendly) was good. Massage tables are available next to the restaurant.

Laoleu Restaurant:

Beautifully made, typical Thai restaurant in a pretty location on the small river. A wooden bridge leads to the rustic restaurant with a terrace and a view. Fine Thai food (can be spicy) and specialties like local mussels, salad with lotus, soft-shell crabs. Not easy to find – but worth the trip. Khuek Khak Hinterland at Rawai Muay Thai Stadium. DG 8.69953, 98.26428 / GMS N 8°41'58.308",O 98°15'51.407" facebook.com/Chanakanmay999

Mist Valley Camping Khuk Khak.

Small restaurant inland of Khuk Khak. You eat on a platform in the (artificial) lake. Beware of mosquitoes at dusk. Very, very reasonable prices for classic Thai food: papaya salad, Tom Kha Gai soup, crispy fried squid, plus drinks. We were the only guests, but it was impeccable nonetheless. The restaurant belongs to the campsite, which, in addition to the campsites, has simple bungalows by the lake (with or without air conditioning) and free breakfast. They offer ATV jungle adventures with a stop at a waterfall and a viewpoint. 30 minutes for 1200 Baht (driver) 600 Baht (passenger). 1 hour: 1500 Baht (driver), 800 Baht (passenger). Only a narrow road leads here, but it is well signposted. DG 8.69965, 98.27529 / GMS N 8°41'58.74", E 98° 16' 31.043" Contact mistkhaolak@gmail.com +66 98 595 3510
facebook.com/profile.php?id=61582929914893

Kuarommai Khao Lak

This typical Thai restaurant serves predominantly Thai customers and, when we visited in 2025, didn't yet have an English menu. Instead, they had pictures of their dishes on an iPad. In addition to classics like curries and soups, they also offer more exotic dishes like horseshoe crabs. The food is fresh and the restaurant is simple but very clean. In Khuk Khak located on Main Road 4, land side, between the Board Factory and the turnoff to Memories Beach.

Memories Beach Bar

More than a simple beach bar: Restaurant, Bungalows and activities like Volleyball, Skating, lessons in Thai boxing, Thai cooking courses as well as surfing equipment and lessons. Traditional Thai food and Bar favourites such as salads, burgers, pasta and grilled fish and meat are served. If your hotel does not offer "private dinners" on the beach, you can book this here. Set menus from 2800 baht per couple, including cocktails, appetizer, main course, dessert (fruit plate), bottle of red or white wine, sky lantern. Contact: +66 93 578 5846, memoriesbar-khaolak.com
In the north of Khuk Khak Beach, just before reaching the Pakarang Cape. Turn off Highway 4 in direction of the beach: 200 meters after the petrol

station for about 2.5 km. Or park at the Apsara Hotel and walk to the left over the bridge. DG: 8.71976/ 98.23473, GMS: N 8°43'11.136"/ E 98°14'5.027"

Klong Koo Restaurant

A small local restaurant in an interesting location: You sit in the middle of the forest, in the creek with your feet in the water. Good for lunch – not so much for dinner, as mosquitoes appear with the dusk. Don't forget your mosquito repellent! 🕒 11 am until 5 or 6 pm – they close early in the evening because of the mosquitoes. In the north of Khao Lak on the way to Sai Rung Waterfall. Contact: ✆+66 87 883 3247 DG: 8.74765, 98.26759 / GMS: N 8°44'51.54", E 98°16'3.323"

MaMa Mr. Lek Restaurant

Located on Pakweeb Beach. The road to the beach and restaurant is unpaved but can be done by car or motorbike. Next to it is the TUI Hotel. The restaurant is behind a small river, over which a simple wooden bridge leads to the sandy beach. It has massage huts, tours (friendly tours), free WiFi, free beach chairs when using the restaurant. Everything you need for a day at the beach – and not crowded. The restaurant was fine, they also have fruit mojitos, which are bigger (and cheaper) than in the restaurants in Bang Niang. You can see the sunset, but it's a bit "around the corner" here, a small headland with trees and rocks in between.

Kate's Kitchen @ Bangsak

This restaurant is located directly on the tranquil Bangsak beach and offers breathtaking sunset views over the ocean in the evenings and delicious food during the day. Run by a dedicated Englishman and chef Kate herself, you can also book a private dinner on the beach (more affordable than at the hotels) – complete with all the trimmings, including decorations and a canopy. Cooking classes with Kate are available upon request. Recommended: the 4 Curry Signature Menu, which introduces two people to four typical Thai curries. Spice level is adjustable (and they can even serve it Thai hot upon request. Seriously!). Good drinks. Average prices. Located directly on Bangsak Beach. Note: There's another restaurant called Kate's Kitchen just south of the hill in South Beach. ✆Whatsapp +66 83 1808129 💻 facebook.com/profile.php?id=61565710937849

Eat like the locals

Food Stalls

Thailand's cuisine is not only represented with numerous restaurants in different categories and price ranges, but also in countless mobile food stalls. You can find them even in the smallest places, as many Thai people eat out. They are in side streets, in front of temples, bus stops and tourist attractions as well as on markets. The quality of these mini-kitchens is rarely inferior to the big ones. Especially if you see many locals buying food or eating there, you can be sure that the food is delicious. Customers are not just the average citizen, but also bank employees, policemen and the wealthy eat there or take the food out with them. Menus are often missing and occasionally there are no chairs or tables. To choose your food (and you can often try it before making your final choice) you just point on it. The choice ranges from stalls cooking dishes (curries and rice dishes) to some grilling various skewers to those that only offer sweets such as pancakes, coconut milk rice balls, fruit, ice cream etc. If you want to know if something is spicy, ask "pät mai?", "Mai pät" is not spicy, with "pät pät" caution is advised. Most stalls are very clean, but they are certainly not up to our western hygiene standard. Hence it is good that meat, fish and vegetables are boiled or roasted in the food stalls – and in Thailand, critical things like raw salad is almost unknown. If in doubt, better refrain from drinks with ice in them (occasionally served in plastic bags) and buy a bottle or a can. We have already eaten in various food stalls – without any negative effects. Most of the food is simple, but really good and tasty. The portions may not be huge, but super cheap.

Markets: Night markets and Sunday Markets

On all markets, especially the night market in Bang Niang there are many food stalls (as usual in Thailand) – something for the more adventurous to try. If you don't want to try fried insects or crispy pork skin, treat yourself to something more traditional, like satay skewers or a stir-fry.

Thai, local, very affordable

Here are some very affordable (but still very good) places to eat in Khao Lak:

Mun Pochana (South Beach), *P'Ann* (La On), *Khaolak Thaifood Restaurant* (La On), *Krua Pi Bao, Mae Pa* (between La On and Bang Niang), *Krua Luang Ten* (Khuek Khak)... and many more.

Look out for plastic chairs, mismatched (but clean) decor, lots of Thais eating there, possibly an open kitchen, and a Thai cook who speaks little or no English. The menu is often simple, perhaps not even translated.

Non-Thai Alternatives

Tired of Thai food? Need a change? Homesick – need some comfort food? Don't worry, we won't judge... With over 200 restaurants, Khao Lak also offers a good selection of alternatives (although most also serve Thai food).

German: SchniPoSa etc. *Tiffys & Florian Restaurant* (La On), *Souls Café* (La On), Let's eat (Bang Niang), *Thai Life Restaurant Mookata* (Bang Niang), *Sunset Boulevard* (Bang Niang). *Sontaya german food* (Bang Niang)
English Pub: *Walkers Inn* (La On), *Juice from Mars* (Bang Niang), *Moose's Pub* (Bang Niang)
Steak: *Woods Bar* (La On), *Golden Elephant* (La On), *Sunset Boulevard Khao Lak* (Bang Niang), *Joe's Steak House* (Bang Niang), *Motown on Fire Steakhouse* (Pak Weep)
Burger: *Khao Lak Cuisine* (South Beach), *Walkers Inn* (La On), *Patty's Khao Lak* (La On), *Souls Cafe* (La On), *Give me five* (Bang Niang), *Khao Lak Burgers* (Bang Niang), *Sunset Boulevard* (Bang Niang), *Lucky Restaurant* (Bang Niang)
Mediterran and Pasta/Pizza: *Sorrento Italian Restaurant* (South Beach), *Medici Pizza & Thai seafood* (South Beach), *Al Dente Italian Bistro* (La On), *La Piccola Maria Pizzeria & Ristorante* (La On), *Peter Pan Restaurant* (La On), *Pizzeria Ristorante Bella Italia* (La On), *Little Italy* (La On), *Little Marghe* (Bang Niang), *Pinocchio Pizzeria* (Bang Niang), *Mario Pizzeria* (Bang Niang), *Amici Italien Bistro* (Bang Niang), *Ben's Restaurant* (Bang Niang),
Greek: *Mykonos Greek & Mediteranean Restaurant* (Bang Niang), *Pita Stop* (Bang Niang)
Turkish: *Cappadocia Turkish Restaurant* (La On)
Mexikan: *Red Chilli Restaurant* (La On), *Taco Time* (zw. La On und Bang Niang), *Rusty Pelican* (Bang Niang: geschlossen?), *Centrico Mexican Restaurant* (Bang Niang).
Japan: (Sushi) *Sushi Mai* (South Beach), *Sanji Kitchen* (zwischen Bang Niang und La On), *Khaolak Sushi & Izakaya* (Bang Ninag), Ojoei Sushi & Izakaya (Khuk Khak)
Indian: *Mali Restaurant, Rasoi Restaurant* (South Beach), *Flavours of India Restaurant* (Bang Niang), *Taj Mahal Khaolak* (Bang Niang), *Taste of India* (Bangsak)
Burmese: Burmese Corner (Bang Niang)

Coffee, Cake (and Breakfast)

There are quite a few places where one can get good coffee and cake in Khao Lak or breakfast, if it is not included in the hotel:

In Nang Thong / Ban La On:

Delicacy Khaolak

Cute, stylish cafe with fresh flowers, which they also sell. A treat for Instagrammers. They serve homemade pastries as well as breakfast and brunch cafe. Open until the evening. Near the McDonald's, across the street.

Kinaree Bakery Souvenir

One of the few places in La On for a delicious breakfast, coffee, and other food. They make the best cappuccino in Khao Lak. Newly renovated, friendly staff. Open from 8:30 am to 9:30 pm On Main Road 4, across from the Nangthong Supermarket.

The Eight Room Café

The well-known Mata Café continues to exist in "The Eight Room by Mata Café". Delicious cheesecake and ice cream, plus specialty coffees and shakes. Modern wooden house on the outside, cute decor on the inside. Garden to sit in behind the house. Popular with Thais, despite slightly higher prices. 10am-7pm. La On, on Main Road 4 quite north but before the entrance to The Sands Hotel on the seaside. facebook.com/TheEighthRoom Tel +66 80 875 8411

Vallhalla Villas & Teahouse

New, modern furnished café. Located on the hill with a fantastic view of the sea and Nangthong Beach through large arched windows. The menu includes more tea than coffee, plus snacks and drinks. Prices are more expensive. 9am-6.30pm. Attention: no parking spaces! valhallakholak.com

Duo Coffee

Coffee specialties and sweets in a dollhouse-kitschy atmosphere in Ban La On at the main road, facebook.com/pages/Duo-Cafe-Khaolak/128427524004721

In Bang Niang:

The Bistro

Homemade bread, baguettes, sandwiches, yogurt with fresh fruit, smoothies, muesli, homemade meatloaf. If you're in the mood for a European breakfast this is the right place for you (the owners are a Swiss-Thai couple). Open 8 am to 3 pm Located in the heart of Bang Niang on the street from the market to the sea.

Juice from Mars

After closing the well-known Mars Bar, English owner Mars (Marcel) has opened in a new place offering coffee, healthy fresh juices, smoothies, and sandwiches made with home-made bread and home-smoked meat or salmon. 🕒 Daily 10am-6pm.
Bang Niang, at the crossroads of one-way back to main road 4.
facebook.com/Juice-From-Mars-1377710149023920

Jack & Cherry Bar and Café

From breakfast (from 9:30 am) to evening drinks. Friendly owners, delicious and affordable cocktails (fruit mojitos!) and snacks. Right next to Bang Niang Market on Main Road 4 (towards Khuk Khak).

Lan Tong 333 Dim Sum

A different kind of breakfast: Asian. Dim Sum are small Chinese dishes with fish, poultry, vegetarian or sweet. The dishes are arranged in small raffia bowls and are cooked in hot steam. Open only in the morning. Inexpensive, fine selection of fresh dim sum and soup. The selected dim sum is steamed and brought to the table. There is also iced tea – or drinks from the mobile shop. Bang Niang town entrance on the 4 towards La On. 300m south of the police boat.

In Khuk Khak:

Oceanpana Bakery Cafe:

Located in the heart of Khuk Khak on the road to Devasom and Andamania Hotel. Chic French-Swiss inspired cafe with fine drinks and baked goods. Take away or eat in: inside and in the garden.
facebook.com/OceanpanaBakeryCafe

Coconut Homes & Café

Those with accommodation in Khuk Khak in the north of Khao Lak will find close to the Coconut Beach a small, clean resort with the resort's own (public) café with homemade cakes, snacks and good coffee specialities. The place is somewhat off the beaten track but very good for a rest stop on an excursion. Owner Franky lives here since before the Tsunami and has rebuilt the resort with an emergency platform and further away from the beach.
DG: 8.72826/ 98.24221, GMS: N 8°43'41.736"/ E 98° 14' 31.956"

Other notable "coffee stops" outside of Khao Lak

Hug Kapong Coffee – cute coffee house at Kapong.
Dredger Café: Coffee on top of Bangmara Hill at Takua Pa with a view.

Burong Café Takua Pa – newly opened pet café with parrots.
360 Degree Coffee – Andaman Viewpoint Sky Crane: Food, Drink, Views and Mini Water Park towards Phuket
Tree Cups Phang Nga Coffee – a coffee on a tree down at Phang Nga.

Private Dinner at the beach

This is romance pure. Because of the location of Khao Lak at the west coast you have many places to eat with a view of the sunset – mainly those located on the beach. But if you want something very special, check out if your hotel offers private dinners on the beach. There is little more romantic than a fine meal at sunset, with rustling waves and your feet in the sand. And it is often less pricey than you may expect. It is about as much as a meal in a good restaurant at home – without all these extras you have here.
These hotels offer private dinners – on request also for non-resident guests: *JW Marriott, La Vela, The Sands,* (and more).
Dinner at the beach (slightly cheaper than in the hotels) can also be had in the *Memories Bar and Restaurant* at Memories Beach.

Candle dinner at the waterfall in the rainforest:

At the *Sarojin,* hotel guests have the option of booking a private candlelight dinner by the waterfall. All in all, quite expensive – but certainly a unique experience.
Much cheaper and available for everyone is the dinner from 6 pm in the middle of the jungle by the waterfall. This is possible with prior booking at *Suan Rim Naam,* the small restaurant right by the Sai Rung Waterfall. ✆+66 89 971 5630. The restaurant is otherwise only open from 9 am to 5 pm

Sunset Dinner Cruise

Cruise on the ocean in front of Khao Lak with sunset dinner. Available as a group (up to 15 people) or on a private boat. Aloha Khaolak also offers snorkeling trips during the day.
Contact via Whatsapp ✆+6681 737 5413 +6683 508 5981
💻 facebook.com/profile.php?id=100047635757109

Thai cooking class

Learn to cook Thai dishes yourself in Khao Lak. There are show-cooking or cooking demonstrations of typical Thai dishes, such as Pad Thai, Papaya Salad, Tom Kha Gai and various curries on some excursions. Many hotels and restaurants offer cooking classes, and the prepared meals are eaten together afterwards.

If you want something more personal and maybe learn more about cooking (and living) in Thailand, for example where to get the ingredients and what to look for in the ingredients, book a private course here:

Pa Kin Na Ka Thai cooking class (Pakinnaka) near the Chong Fah waterfall). Price: 2000 baht per person, from 2 persons. Morning or afternoon courses. Including round trip from hotel, market tour, cooking course for three dishes, food and drink. ✆+66 88 760 0767 💻 Khaolakcookingclass.com

Pui Cooking: Price: 1500 baht per person including hotel pickup, market excursion, three dishes and drinks. Morning and afternoon. Contact: 💻 puicooking.com/, ✆+66 86 281 5103

Khaolak Thai Cooking Class by Ann, 💻 annkhaolak.wordpress.com ✆+66 87 908 0289

Ning in Khao Lak Cooking Class: Ning runs a successful video channel and offers cooking classes. 💻 facebook.com/people/Ning-in-Khao-Lak/100068285378071

Pam's Restaurant & Cooking Class: Pam runs a very nice restaurant, and also teaches others to cook. 💻 facebook.com/Pams.Thailand

Suchanyas Cooking Class Khaolak one person 1700 Baht, groups 1500 Baht per person. 💻 sites.google.com/view/suchanyas-kochkurs . Whatsapp +66 651616353

Suchanyas Kochkurs Khaolak speaks german, english, single persons 1700 Baht, Grgroops 1500 Baht per person. ✆+66 651616353

💻 facebook.com/profile.php?id=61571336795395 / sites.google.com/view/suchanyas-kochkurs

Qcumber Restaurant, Chef Ploy ✆ +66 85 218 8808

💻 facebook.com/QcumberSaladBar,

Kate's Kitchen Restaurant @Bangsak Beach, Kate ✆ +66 83 1808129

💻 facebook.com/profile.php?id=61565710937849

Ann Khaolak Thai Cooking Class ✆ +66 87 908 0389

💻 facebook.com/profile.php?id=100057699180173

Walkers Inn, Chef Ju ✆ +66 86 821 7668 💻 facebook.com/walkersinn

Beyond the root Restaurant - Vegane cooking ccourses ✆ +66 83 248 6216

💻 facebook.com/profile.php?id=100069028073416

Thai Cooking Class by Nuch, Elephant Bar ✆ +66 633 059 8330

💻 facebook.com/profile.php?id=61566873841118

Foodie Culture Tours

These Tours for food lovers are a different way of exploring the area around Khao Lak. They combine the opportunity to get in touch with local people and get to know Thai specialities. For example the tour: *Local food tasting at hidden Takua Pa* for 1590 baht per person. You start at the hotel from 3 pm, drive on Takua Pa and get to know the food until the evening – from production to tasting, from finger food to street food, curries, soups, seafood etc. Takua Pa is known for its Chinese residents, which is also reflected in the food. Tours can be adapted to special diets (gluten free, allergies).
Contact: 💻foodieculturetours.com ✆+66 88 760 0767

Mealdropper

Food delivery is also available in Khao Lak. Mealdropper is a delivery service that allows you to order via app (for iOS and Android) or website: 💻 mealdropper.com
Certainly not my first choice for food, given the number of restaurants with friendly staff, but it's an option in emergencies, such as when you're sick and can't leave your hotel. A number of local restaurants have since joined.

Cannabis and CBD

The cannabis market in Thailand is currently undergoing a major restructuring (as of 2026) following its decriminalization in 2022. In effect, many of the freedoms previously enjoyed by cannabis users are being reversed. Remaining cannabis businesses will have to meet stricter licensing requirements or close down. The market is moving back towards a purely medical use with fewer retailers, who will be subject to strict controls. Cannabis will only be permitted to be sold in these (authorized) establishments: medical facilities, pharmacies, herbal shops, and traditional medicine clinics. These establishments must have a certified professional on-site and adhere to high standards regarding storage, odour control, and hygiene. According to the Thai government, patients with legitimate medical needs will continue to have access. However, recreational cannabis use will again be prohibited and punishable by law. Public smoking will also be banned. As a reminder, smoking regular cigarettes in public places is also prohibited.

Laoleu Restaurant

Klong Koo

Private Dinner

Phu View Restaurant

Nai Muang Restaurant

Pams Restaurant

Nightlife in Khao Lak

Khao Lak has not earned its reputation as a family destination unjustly. Those looking for excitement and party life can find more of this further south in Phuket (namely Patong) or on Pattaya. But even here you can find friendly bars and small clubs with live music that are open after 11 pm and serve alcohol and snacks – Especially in high season. In most bars you can get (good) food as well as cocktails and drinks.

Bars and Pubs

It is striking that most of the **bars and pubs** are situated on the road inland. The reason for this is that all the buildings located on the beach were destroyed in the 2004 tsunami and the owners were therefore reluctant to build there again. That has changed since then, so that there are beach bars again.

Bars in Khao Lak south of the Hill

Jo Jo Bar

Of the bars here, this is probably the most stylish. They have a huge range of drinks. The super friendly host Bishnu is also happy to give tips on what to do. Khao Lak Village on the road to Emerald Beach Resort.

Black Jack Sports Bar

Bar and restaurant with 4 screens, lots of cocktails for 100 baht, very friendly team. Khao Lak Village, Near 4

Tiger Bar

A typical Thai bar in the heart of Lam Kaen/Khao Lak Village. Rock music plays, a few stray dogs hang around. Happy hour runs until 8:30 pm when you get a free small Chang Beer with your large Chang and a shot with your cocktail. They don't serve food here but you can eat next door. They also offer cheap laundry service.

More bars in South Village: *Absolute Bar, Why Not Bar, Khaolak Bar & Restaurant*

Nightlife in Bang La On / Nang Thong

Walker's Inn

A real English pub with English owner. They regularly show live sports broadcasts (AFL, NRL, World Cup). For dining they serve European food like fish and chips, roast beef and of course Thai food. Free WIFI. Because of Covid they had to "downsize" a bit and can now be found 100m further south of the original location (and without rooms to rent). They offer a full English breakfast from 8 am in the morning. La On, off Highway 4, across from the Laguna Beach Hotel

Monkey Bar

Monkey Bar with reggae music. Opening times vary. On Highway 4, inland side slightly north of the centre and the Nang Thong supermarket. The striking facade cannot be overlooked.

Woods Bar and Bistro

The bar behind Nang Thong Beach offers cocktails and food: Thai, Burgers, Kobe and Waygu steaks(?!), free billiards, screens for watching football, a movie screen, occasional live music and fire shows. On the road at Nang Thong Beach behind the mini-lighthouse, next to the Alive Market.

The Snapper 2

The former Happy Snapper Bar in Khao Lak is now a full-fledged restaurant in a new location. There is a Roof terrace for cocktails directly under the stars, or you can sit comfortably in the pretty gardens. The food is Thai with individual Western dishes (burgers, steak) and very well done – the cocktail (and mocktail) list is detailed and excellently executed. Live music from around 7.30 pm is well worth listening to. Bass legend and host Pitak also offers live music – jazz, blues, pop, rock and metal (upon request). The Snapper is located on a side street between La On and Bang Niang in the hill direction... it's hard to get there without a taxi or motorbike – which is a shame, hosts Pitak and Aeh would deserve more visitors with what they have to offer! thesnapper.net

More Bars in La On, all at Highway 4: *Dream Bar, Chang Bar, Sakai Bar* (Billard, Tischfußball, Sport schauen), *Green Mamba Bar, Forest Bar, Acoustic Bar* (Livemusik), *Khao Lak Beer Garden.*

Nightlife in Bang Niang

Gecko Bar

Open from 7 pm in the high season, from 9 pm in the low season. Closing time is when the party is over. Very good late-night bar, led by the Thai couple Black and Lin. Billiards, table football, WiFi.
In the middle of Bang Niang.

Mr. Chay Bar

Also at the Bang Niang Market. On the south side under a Tamarind tree. Open on market days from 2 pm until 2 am. Mr. Chay speaks German and English.

Rusty Pelican

The Mexican restaurant calls itself "world famous." Open from 12 noon -10 pm. Mexican food: nachos, fajitas, frozen margaritas and ice-cold beer. Located on Main Street 4, opposite the entrance to the Tsunami Memorial. rustypelican.business.site

Stjarn Bar - Starbar Khao Lak

Biker bar with a female boss. Chilled atmosphere, free pool table. Location: Opposite Police Boat 813. Between Moo Moo Cabaret and Bang Niang Market.

Sunset Boulevard Khao Lak (Sunset Biker Bar)

New bar and restaurant, German-Thai owners. Very good burgers and draft beer. They also serve tacos and Thai food. Sometimes live music. Definitely more than just a biker bar. facebook.com/p/Sunset-Boulevard-Khao-Lak-100089825831356

Moose's Pub

A Nordic pub and European sports bar in the heart of Bang Niang. 15 different beers, cocktails and burgers. Opening hours are from 4 pm until late (weekdays) or later (weekends). They sometimes open earlier for sporting events so you can watch them there.

Piranha Bar

Long established popular bar and hangout in Bang Niang. At the end of the meal you get a nightcap herbal schnapps. Place to watch Bundesliga and other soccer games. Owner Pak is very dedicated and helps with trips. piranha-bar.com

Other bars in Bang Niang: *Songs Bar, Toilets Bar (*the only one without 80s music or reggae*), Thai Bar Restaurant & Weed Shop (*live music*), Red Eye Bar (*billiards, TV*), Fat Shark Bar (*billiards, table football*), Lan La Bar, Buffalo Bar*

Khao Lak Local Market

The square in Bang Niang has changed significantly since its opening in 2023. It now has fewer food stalls and no longer has the market atmosphere; it's simply a square surrounded by new, modern restaurants with live music. In the middle of Bang Niang, a little off the main road to the sea.

Kokulo Beach Club

This club/bar is part of the La Vela hotel in Bang Niang and appeals to a younger, mostly foreign clientele, offering classic cocktails and food, modern decor, lively music, and frequent themed events (Tiki, Afro, Women), buffets, and fire shows. Access is also open to non-La Vela guests, cash only. Located on the beach in front of La Vela Hotel. Access via Bang Niang or on foot (or by ferry during the day) across the river from La On. .facebook.com/kokulobeachclub

Moo Moo Cabaret Show

Moo Moo is Khao Lak's answer to Phuket's well-known Simon Cabaret and puts on colourful and noisy ladyboy/ drag queen shows with performances every night. Starting at 8.45pm during the high season (from 15th September to mid-April), duration approx. 1 hour. Apparently also suitable for younger people. Entry for 300 baht – this includes a free drink. After the show you can take photos with the performers (costs!). facebook.com/MooMooCabaret
Bang Niang on Highway 4, seaside. just south of Bang Niang Market before the bridge.

Nightlife in Khuk Khak and further north

Build Factory

Hip indoor and outdoor nightclub. Modern building and furnishings, live music and viewing on big screens during sporting events. Both Thais and foreigners relax in the club. Entrance fee 300-400 baht per person. On Highway 4, in the northern part of Bang Niang, opposite the water reservoir.

Restaurants serving cocktails and where you can hang out can be found on all the beaches from Khuk Khak all the way up to Ban Nam Khem.

8Fish Khao Lak Bistro and Surf

More of a restaurant than a bar, but a place for sunset and after drinks right on the beautiful beach. Open until 8 pm They rent beach loungers. On Khuek Khak Beach, to the left of the *JW Marriott*.
facebook.com/8fishkhaolak

Happy Beach and Restaurant

Simple restaurant and bar at the top of Bangsak Beach. Good Thai food with your feet in the sand. Special: you can meet and photograph free-roaming pigs and occasionally horses here on the beach. Northernmost part of Bangsak Beach next to *Le Meridien* and *Graceland Hotel*. DG 8.80315, 98.25838 / GMS N 8°48'11.3", E 98°15'30.168"

Fire shows

Fire shows on the beach take place especially in high season. They are organized by hotels and restaurants. You should research or inquire online shortly beforehand. A fire show is not a display of fireworks, instead the artists put on a spectacular and, in the truest sense of the word, hot show at night with flammable liquids, powders and other objects and to music. Memories Bar (daily, weather permitting)
Mr. Bao Family Restaurant at Pakweep Beach, *La Vela – Kokulo Beach Club* Bartender Fire Show several times a week. *Pullman Khao Lak* Beach Club. *X10 Beach Bar*, Saturdays. *Karkinos Beach Club and Restaurant* in front of *Apsara Kalima Resort*. *Meridien Hotel*

Thai boxing – Muay Thai

Thai boxing is a popular sport in Thailand and participants train long and hard for it. Some stadiums in very touristy areas (I'm looking at you: Patong) present mock fights to the audience, but others take it very seriously. Khao Lak is increasingly becoming a mecca for Muay Thai fans. There are now 3 boxing stadiums in Khao Lak for the Thai national sport. The advertising is done by driving up and down the street in Khao Lak with (loud) loudspeakers and posters: "Tonight, and Tonight only ...!" All fights start at 9 am Booking is not necessary, you can buy tickets at the door and generally have a good view of the fights from everywhere.
Monday: *The One Bar* in Bang Niang
Tuesday: *Khao Lak Stadium*
Thursday: *Beyond Stadium*
Friday: *Khao Lak Stadium*.

Khao Lak Boxing Stadium

Fights take place on Fridays and occasionally Tuesdays, after 9 pm. Ticket prices depend on seating – there are stalls for drinks and food. Bang Niang, new about 1 km north of Bang Niang Market – on the back road. facebook.com/kholakboxingstadiummuaythai

Beyond Boxing Stadium Khao Lak

The boxing stadium is right next to Bang Niang Market (towards La On) and is clearly visible from the Highway 4. Tickets cost 1200-1500 baht. A beer costs 80 baht. facebook.com/profile.php?id=61555748502105

The One Bar & Muay Thai Gym

Located on the main road in Bang Niang to the sea, close to Bang Niang market (towards La On on the 4). Fine cocktails and watching Muay Thai lessons – real fights on Monday evenings.

Elephant Bar

South of the hill you can also find Thai boxing in **the Elephant Bar**: bar, billiards, watching sports and Thai boxing show every Sunday from 8.30 pm Free entry (drinks payable). They also offer training sessions in Thai boxing. On the road to the Emerald and Merlin hotels.

Shopping in Khao Lak

Markets

Markets play a major role in Thai life: this is the place where you shop for food or go eating. Therefore, the markets in and around Khao Lak are not exclusively a tourist thing. If you really want to get to know a place in Thailand, you should visit the market.

The Bang Niang Night Market

The well-known night market in Bang Niang takes place on Monday, Wednesday and Saturday afternoons – the biggest market is on Saturday. There are food stalls right at the entrance, after which the market divides into three main paths with a mix of shops offering different things – as a night market it has mainly souvenirs (handicrafts, silk, soaps, clothes...). Further back you will find what you need for everyday life: fruit, vegetables, meat, fish, spices. The

food stalls sell all kinds of snacks: chicken wings, sticky rice, pad thai, meat skewers and more. Particularly courageous people try the fried beetles and larvae. Next to the market there are small restaurants and bars where you can sit and watch the market life. Bang Niang Night Market caters very much to foreign tourists, and prices for clothes and food are higher than on other markets. In addition, last year there were complaints from visitors who had been tried to cheat by charging more money than stated on the menu ... or there was no menu at all. Luckily these are isolated cases.
You can't miss the market – it's by the traffic lights in Bang Niang and actually has a pedestrian crossing where the police keep order during market hours.

Ruam Jai, daily evening market in Khuk Khak.

The Night Market is located behind the PTT petrol station – access via the petrol station or from the Highway 4 about 50 m further up. Open daily from around 2 pm to around 10 pm At the entrance there are food stalls with cooked food, further back stalls with basic foodstuffs. In between there are a few stalls with clothes or kitchen utensils. The market is covered, the atmosphere is more festive than that of morning markets – music plays and people negotiate, talk and laugh. It has only been around since 2019 and it has become a permanent local institution.

The Land Mark Night Market (in Bang Niang)

A brand new market located directly to the left of the Bang Niang Market, near the Boxing Stadium. The new market is clean and features modern, permanent stalls selling food, souvenirs, and clothing. String lights and colourful lamps create a festive atmosphere. Currently, it mainly attracts Thai visitors who also eat there – which can be considered a recommendation in terms of food and prices. Opening hours weren't listed anywhere in February 2026, but it appears to be open daily. It's somewhat surprising that it opened right next to the established Bang Niang Market but it might be a good (and nearby) alternative to the somewhat overcrowded main market. To get there, simply walk along the main road and turn in after the small river (behind the Moo Moo).

Bang Niang Nightmarket

Fresh market Khuk Khak

Takua Pa Sunday Market

Seasonal Market at Thai Muenag

Souvenirs

Takola Market / Takola Village (Bang Niang)

Another new market near Bang Niang Market, opened on February 14, 2026. It's very small and seems to focus mainly on handcrafted items and souvenirs from local artists/vendors. It also has food stalls, live music, and seating. Opening hours are Monday, Wednesday, and Saturday from 4 PM to 10 PM. It's likely to be busiest during peak season. Location: Near and behind the Starbucks in Bang Niang – just at the entrance to the main road leading to the beach, to the right of Bang Niang Market.

Build Market (in Khuek Khak)

The night market next to the Build Factory nightclub is currently (2026) closed again. Temporarily?

Alive Market (in La On)

The small evening market in La On by the sea, which only opened in 2024, has unfortunately closed down.

The Khuk Khak Fresh Market

About 3 km north of Bang Niang, at the bus station (slightly set back from Main Road 4), is an extensive fresh produce market that is open daily from early morning until around noon. Here the locals (and the restaurant operators) stock up on fresh vegetables, fruit, fish and meat. Visitors can buy fine and fresh fruits and watch the locals trade.

Takua Pa Sunday Market

On Sunday there is a market well worth seeing in the old town of Takua Pa. The Sunday Market, or Takua Pa Walking Street Market can be visited on tourist tours or by oneself. More info in the chapter on Takua Pa.

Fresh Market at the Takua Pa Bus Station

You'll mainly see this market when you stop here on a tour or when you change buses at the bus station here. It is a classic local market selling only food. The smell of fish might be a little overwhelming. Behind the market is a skate park with graffiti by the well-known Thai street artist Alex Face.

Sunday Market in Kapong

The Market in th village of Kapong takes place early in the morning, often picturesquely still in the fog.

Saturday Market by the River in Takua Pa

The Takua Pa River Market is located in the new part of town, south of the Highway 4 by the river.

General Goods

For most things to buy go to the *7-Eleven supermarkets.* There are quite a few of them in Khao Lak and the surrounding area. Western products can be found in the *Nang Thong supermarket.* It is located on the corner of Road Nr. 4 (the main street) and the road that leads to the Nang Thong beach. You will also find a wide range of wines there. Of note is the *Mother Marché* in Khuk Khak, a supermarket of considerable size and variety. The *Tesco Lotus fresh* that is in Khuk Khak near the PTT gas station is nothing special.

Alcohol

Alcoholic beverages are not easily found in stores in Thailand and there are some restrictions, so you cannot always purchase alcoholic beverages. (Although that is not followed equally strict everywhere). Alcohol can be bought between 11 am to 2 pm and from 5 pm to midnight. You may not be able to buy alcohol anywhere on election days or religious holidays. In restaurants and hotels you can get everything to drink. Wine is relatively expensive.

A good selection of wine and a few spirits can be found at *Nang Thong Supermarket* and the *Mother Marché.*

The House of Wine just behind Bang Niang Market has the best wine and whiskey selection in Khao Lak. The owner is happy to advise you. You can not only buy, but also sit and drink. 🕒 8am-9pm

Mao Mao Craft Beer Camp in La On below Phu View. Thai craft beer for beer lovers. Beer garden (and Pakinnaka cooking class) by internationally renowned chef Wannabee. The only place in the region with award-winning craft beers, which won World Beer Awards in 2016 and 2019. 💻 foodieculturetours.com/mao-mao-craft-beer-camp

Blue Zone at Bang Niang Market is a bar for beer and craft beer lovers. Open during market hours.

Clothes

T-shirts, bathing suits, trousers and more can be found in the many souvenir shops in Bang La On and on the markets (e.g. Bang Niang Market). You can have more elegant clothes in good quality made **by a tailor** –this is comparably cheap, but don't forget to bargain! There are no outlet stores or department stores in Khao Lak, they are only in the big shopping malls on Phuket.

Electronics

Electronic brands generally are not cheaper than in Europe or the US –unless they are counterfeit and then caution is advised since counterfeits are forbidden to be imported into your home country. Khao Lak is not a good place to buy a camera, smartphone or tablet. Equipment for underwater photography is sometimes found in the dive centres and shops. SIM cards, batteries etc. can be found in the 7-Eleven. In the larger mini markets, there are also cheap phones and simple cameras.

Eyeglasses, contact lenses

There are some opticians in Khao Lak, especially in Bang La On. So, anyone who has broken his glasses, needs contact lenses or new sunglasses (even with prescription glasses) is in the right place here. The opticians mainly get their goods from Bangkok, so it may take a few (4-5) days, but they have a good selection and good quality. They are often much cheaper than the opticians at home. A prescription from your ophthalmologist is advisable, but the Thai opticians can also test your eyes.
Andaman Optics at Bang La On is often recommended.
NP Optical Shop in Bang Niang. *Pro Optic* in Bang Niang.

Souvenirs

Souvenirs of all kinds can be found everywhere in Khao Lak, especially in the shops in Bang La On, on the market of Bang Niang, in some bars or restaurants, on street stalls. Typical of the region are:

Paper

Products with Sa Paper, hand-made, often coloured and with visible fibre. Sa Paper is used in lamps and painted paper umbrellas, but also in books, picture frames, fans and artificial flowers.

Shadow play figures

Shadow play, called Nang Talung, is specific to southern Thailand and uses flat figures with moving parts. They are not made of paper, but of cow or buffalo skin. In some markets you can still see performances, even if they are not so common anymore. Smaller versions of the figures or pictures of fish, elephants or landscape scenes with amazing details cut from paper can be found in some souvenir shops or markets.

Thai silk

Wonderful scarves or ties, colourful patterned fabrics, handbags, bedspreads, pillows. With pillows you better only take the pillowcases to save not only space: the finished (often triangular) cushions contain natural fibres ... and occasionally insects that you do not want to import.

Leather Goods

Leather goods from all kinds of animals including snakes, frogs, lizards, crocodiles, cows and even chickens can be found in many markets processed into shoes, belts, purses, bags etc. Please note that the import of crocodile or snake leather is prohibited in many countries.

Coconut products

Wind chimes, bowls, salad servers, monkey statues and of course coconut oil.

Thai Spa and Wellness Products

Essential oils, massage and body oils, herbal packs and compresses, scrubs and masks, carved soaps –wonderfully fine works of art that look like real flowers. Stone mortars and pestles.

Thai food and alcohol

While it is impractical (and sometimes forbidden) to take fresh fruit or even fresh meat or fish home with you, this does not apply to packed products such as snacks, dried durian, coconut candy, Thai Curry Mixes, spices.
Western alcohol is quite expensive in Thailand because of taxes, but local products can also be as delicious and are reasonably priced. Sang Som Whiskey, Magic Alambic Rum (Ko Samui, Singha or Chang Beer are usually good to take with you –but not in your hand luggage…)

Cashews

The popular nut snack is expensive to produce. The nut grows protected by a hard shell at the end of a fleshy red fruit. The entire nuts are dried in the sun for three days, because the rubbery shell is very acidic and causes skin burning on contact. The roasting ovens are therefore maintained by someone covered from head to toe, except for a narrow slit in the eyes. Once the nuts have cooled, the coal is scraped off. Each nut must then be cracked open by hand in a device able to get through the hard shell.

If you keep your eyes open, you can also discover the nuts on the trees around Khao Lak. They are grown, harvested and processed in the area. There is a *cashew nut factory* on Main Street 4 in Bang Muang, north of Khao Lak which can be visited. "Factory" is saying a bit too much –but after all, cashews from the north are processed in the green building and the land beyond.

Elephants

Of course, not the living ones and not their ivory, but since elephants are the symbol of Thailand, you can commemorate your visit with small memorabilia with an elephant on it.

Paintings

Another, rather different souvenir is a painting by a local artist. Besides buying one of the exhibited pictures you can also have one painted after your idea or template. The paintings on canvas are delivered without a frame and can be taken home rolled up (as carry-on luggage) or sent by post.

Nasin Art by talented artist Atchara Nuntong, At the moment without a gallery, she offers her paintings at the Bang Niang market or here: 💻 facebook.com/Nasin-Art-Gallery-Khao-Lak-1551872855043006

In's Galley behind the Bang Niang market by artist Inplaeng Fansai, who moved from Krabi to Khao Lak in 2012. In the evenings, the studio front serves as a mojito bar. 💻 facebook.com/Ingallerykhaolak

Batik

Batik is a traditional way to decorate and dye clothing by drawing or printing patterns with liquid wax and dyeing the areas in between. The technique originated in Java, Indonesia, but has also gained popularity in southern Thailand. At *Batik Home* in Khao Lak, you can learn this craft and create your own batik scarves with owner Art. A creative and relaxing experience, also ideal for children and rainy days. The workshop takes at least 2-3 hours. Prices vary depending on the size and number of scarves. Register directly with Art via WhatsApp. Workshops are usually at 10:00 AM – he sometimes also accepts walk-ins. Art sells his scarves at markets, such as the Sunday market in Takua Pa. ✆+66 82 817 2290 At the very tip of Cape Pakarang

Antiques

There cannot be as many antiques as there are offered in Thailand's antique shops. Experts at the National Museum estimate that nine out of ten pieces offered are counterfeits, but often so excellently done that even local traders fall for them. Antique counterfeiting has developed into a small industry, especially in the north of Thailand. Authentic antiques are rare and then it should be remembered that every antique that is exported needs an export permit from the Department of Fine Arts. Buddha statues (no matter in which size and how old) may not be exported at all.

Jewellery, gold, silver, gems, pearls

There is a lot of cheap jewellery made of natural materials. Caution is advised with products from shells, horn or leather (as possibly from protected animals). Pretty silver jewellery comes from the north of Thailand. The *Gems Gallery* is often promoted on trips to Phuket. They are professionals – but with corresponding prices. If you are not a specialist, be cautious as there are many forgeries, even with pearls: although natural pearls come from Phuket, some of them are artificial: made of glued pearl dust.
Khaolak Gems & Silver: Jewellery store with a large selection and expert advice. 💻 facebook.com/khaolakgemandsilver

At the Tailor

In Khao Lak there are many tailors. In 2019 there were around 30, even if Covid might have reduced that number. Some of them have started with a tactic that has been in use in Patong or Bangkok for a few years: they are waiting on the road in front of the shop and talk to everyone in hope that somebody enters. I do not like that particularly, but on the other side, going to a tailor is something you should do once when in Thailand. Therefore, I compiled **a small guide for it**:
Even if the tailors like to have you in their shop to convince you, it is better to come somewhat prepared, to have a plan of what you want or how much you want to spend. There are several options: You can have changed favourite clothes that no longer fit. You can have your favourite dress, trousers or shirt recreated from a different fabric (or length, etc.). Take it with you to show. Or you can have made something completely new. Templates can be obtained from magazines; they have a lot of visual material in the shop.
Choose from the (many) cloth samples in the store. If the tailor does not have the desired one in stock, they can often get it from other stores. – Obviously these "many" tailor shops often have the same owners. Experience says that it is good idea to listen to the recommendations for the cloth. Not every material is suitable for any type of clothing. I was always satisfied with the recommended cloth

– even in terms of durability. After selecting the piece of clothing and material you are measured.
The price is a not an easy topic. I can only recommend negotiating. The first price I was normally told was on the same level as a similar purchase in Switzerland – and that is (too) high for Thailand, even if the dress is tailored. Negotiate and ask for a quantity discount (if you can order 3 of the same shirts) then you should get a fair price.
Agree on everything in writing and make an appointment in a few days (at least 2), after which you go back to the tailor for the fitting. The clothes are still held together temporarily during the fitting and the tailor notes the changes that are to be made with his chalk. You make the next appointment (again in 2 days or so) when you may hopefully try the finished product. If something does not fit right or needs to be changed, you must come back again. Usually, it fits. You pay (mostly by credit card) and take your custom-made clothes home.
Please note: there are various customs regulations for the import of products from a different country: maybe you have to pay VAT. (If you do not, at least customs won't confiscate your clothes as they do with fake brand clothes).
A few words about the fabric used: You are often offered high-quality fabrics: cashmere, wool, silk, etc. However, it has reportedly happened that a different fabric was used than advertised: polyester or other synthetic fibers. To be sure which type of fabric was used, you can check the roll of fabric you would choose to see whether it is natural or synthetic. This is done, for example, by burning. You pull a few threads from the fabric (easy to do at the cut points of the fabric rolls) and then light them. Natural fabrics and fibers such as wool or silk burn away slowly, while synthetic products burn away quickly and emit a blue flame, like oil or gas. If you don't trust the tailor, repeat this process when trying on the first cut.
Tailors: *RK Tailor, Monty the Tailor, Mark One Tailor, The Best Tailor, Mr. Tailor, Khaolak Tailor House* ... and many more.

Tattoos and Bamboo Tattoo

Tattoos are regarded by many people as a souvenir, especially those with traditional motifs and methods. In Thailand, there is the traditional **Sak Yant** (or Yantra) **tattoo**, where old geometric patterns are applied with Buddhist prayers. This was originally practiced by Buddhist monks on warriors who sought protection and strength in battle. The location and pattern of the tattoo was determined by the tattoo artist. These tattoos are brought into the skin with a long sharp metal tip or bamboo. This needle is dipped in ink and repeatedly pricked into the skin and flesh. In Khao Lak, there are some tattoo studios that also tattoo with bamboo (but without accompanying prayers), but modern equipment is more common – and the choice of motifs is up to the customer. A bamboo tattoo hurts as much as a classic tattoo but injures the skin less and scarcely scars. After having had a bamboo tattoo done, you don't have to wait as long to get back into the water (pool or sea) as after a normal tattoo. Since a tattoo is an open wound, you have to wait two weeks because of the considerable risk of infection. With a bamboo tattoo the waiting time is only 2 days if it is protected with olive oil or Vaseline.

Tattoo-Studios
In La On: *Namo Tattoo, Rong Bamboo Tattoo, Top's Tattoo*
In Bang Niang. *CT Bamboo Tattoo, Noom Tattoo, Jack Tattoo, Maori Tattoo and Bar, Thai Smile Tattoo* (and many more).

TO DO AND SEE

Diving, Snorkelling and the Islands

Long before Khao Lak was a known tourist destination, it was an insider tip for divers and snorkelers. The now known beautiful dive sites are situated off the coast: the nine **Similan Islands, Ko Tachai** (45 km north), **Richelieu Rock** (85 km north), the **Surin Islands** and **wrecks** like the Boonsung, Premchai and Sea Chart. **Trips and diving courses** can be booked at many places in Khao Lak. The range goes from half-day excursions to multi-day trips where you stay on the dive boat.

Diving is a wonderful sport and it can be very rewarding to pick it up. To be able to experience the underwater world so close (and for so long) is wonderful – so it is worth learning it where you have access to such great dive sites. When choosing a diving centre or diving course, make sure that they are PADI or SSI qualified. To really learn it, you have to invest some days and learn the theory correctly as well as going out to dive. Anyone who is uncertain can try a (one-

day) **introductory course** – after which you go diving at the Similan Islands down to a depth of 12 meters.
The prices are not cheap; however, you must bear in mind that the courses include material (snorkel, fins, mask, suit, bottle, vest), the study materials and guided excursions to the dive sites: 1 day is about 6000 baht. Open Water courses including a local half-day course and a 1-day tour to the Similan cost about 15,000 baht.
Children from the age of 8 can do an introductory course in the pool (to 2 m depth), the Bubble Maker. They are accompanied and instructed by parents and an experienced instructor. Price: about 1500 baht. Minimum age for Junior Diving courses is 10-12 years.

Snorkelling at Khao Lak

Although Khao Lak is an excellent starting point for diving and snorkelling trips (especially to the offshore islands such as Surin and Similan), the sea right in front of Khao Lak itself is not too good for it. The water is very shallow and the sand is whirled up by the waves which are mostly not broken by a coral reef offshore. Therefore, the visibility is not the best. This is not only so in the rainy season, in which the sea is particularly turbulent. Snorkelling from the beach is generally rather un-spectacular, but if you know where to find them, there are still some very nice places for snorkelling close by:

Snorkelling excursions to the peninsula of Khao Na Yak

Since the tsunami, the corals have recovered and grown. Parrot fish, lionfish, moray eels, cuttlefish, giant clams can be found in the mini-garden-like table corals in the 2 to 4 m deep water. You can discover the underwater world from a longtail boat. A snorkelling excursion with the operator includes the equipment, a simple lunch on the secluded beach and non-alcoholic drinks. The excursions start in the morning, after 3 pm you are back at the hotel. They only take place from November to around the end of March. When the waves are stronger, it is better to postpone it, as the view is very cloudy due to the churned-up sand. Prices range from 1800-2800 baht per person depending on tour operator, day of the week and number of people. The tours are also offered as private tours, in which case the longtail boat is not shared with other tourists.
Take a t-shirt with you and put it on in the water as sun protection! Or use coral-friendly sunscreen.

Tours are offered by:

5Star Motorbikes: 💻 khaolak.de/en/schnorcheln
Discovery Travel Khao Lak: 💻discoverykhaolak.com
Khaolak Guru: 💻khaolakguru.net
Seadragon Dive Center: 💻 seadragondivecenter.com
And other diving centres – see their websites. Attention: Some equipment must be rented separately.
Or you can ask at your local restaurant in Khao Lak, because for sure someone knows someone who has a boat (and gear), like Pak from the *Piranha Bar*.

Khaolak Underwater Museum

About 4 km in front of the Nang Thong Beach is a diving spot where various things have been sunk in about 15 m deep water and there are corals that form a habitat for various sea creatures. It has a military jeep, motorbike and a ship. Exciting for beginners to intermediate divers.

Here is a (incomplete) **list of providers of diving and snorkelling excursions and diving courses in Khao Lak:**
Sea Dragon Dive Center 💻 seadragondivecenter.com
IQ Dive 💻 iq-dive.com
Khao Lak Explorer 💻 khaolakexplorer.com
Sea Bees Diving 💻 sea-bees.com/diving-khao-lak
Wetzone Divers 💻 wetzonedivers.com
Andaman Snorkel Discovery 💻 andamansnorkeldiscovery.com
LOMA Diving Adventure: 💻 loma-diving.com
Go 2 Similan 💻 go2similan.com
Khao Lak Explorer Diving Center: 💻 khaolakexplorer.com
Pirate Divers: 💻 piratediversinternational.com
Monkey Dive Hostel: günstiges Hostel und Tauchzentrum in La On. 💻 monkeydivekhaolak.com
Flippers Dive Khao Lak 💻 flippers-dive.com
Andaman Scuba Diving 💻 andamanscuba.com
Big Blue Diving Khao Lak 💻 bigbluedivingkhaolak.com
Raya Divers 💻 rayadivers.com

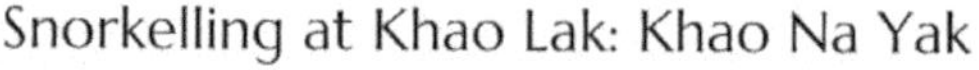
Snorkelling at Khao Lak: Khao Na Yak

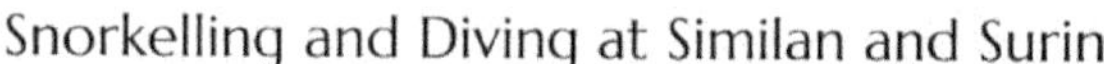
Snorkelling and Diving at Similan and Surin

Similan Islands

The **Similan Island Marine National Park** is located about 70 km off the coast from Khao Lak. It includes 140 km2 and 9 islands, but only 2 of them are accessible for tourists: Islands No. 4 and 8. On these islands there is some infrastructure like toilets and a restaurant, and they are the destination of many day-trip tourists.

The course of **a day trip to snorkel / for sightseeing** is as follows:
You are picked up at the hotel at the lobby (time: early in the morning, depending on how many other hotels are to be approached, between 7 am to 9 am). You will be taken to the pier – mostly to **Thap Lamu** (in the south), occasionally to **Bang Muang** (in the north), depending on the tour organizer and the tide. At the port you will be equipped with snorkel, mask and flippers (everything in your size and also for children). Before the boat ride there is a short introduction about the islands you are about to visit and the diving / snorkelling sites. You can take a pill against seasickness offered for free (active ingredient: dimenhydrinate 50mg). I highly recommend it if you are prone to seasickness: the **speedboat** ride can be very bumpy if the wind picks up.
On the boat you must wear a lifejacket. There are better seats and worse: in the front part of the boat you may have a nice view but are in the blazing sun. You cannot talk much because of the engine noise, but there are free drinks and occasionally you can already see flying fish. After an hour you arrive at the island with beautiful round rock formations and turquoise waters with lots of colourful fish and coral.
You now **snorkel** at a site by the island. If you are lucky, you see turtles (some of the tours feed them bananas so they return here) and certainly you can see corals and lots of colourful fish. A disposable underwater camera or waterproof case is worth bringing here. The water is warm, usually around 30 degrees Celsius and the visibility mostly good – unless there is a lot of wind. After snorkelling (each stop is about 30 - 45 minutes and you have 2 or 3 of them on a trip) you head for the "main island" with its white beach. Every excursion boat moors at that place, so it is quite busy and you have to watch out while in the water.
The island has a viewpoint: **Sail Rock**, which is relatively easily accessible. Just a short climb that you can do barefoot – but because this is literally a "hot thing" on the sun-baked rocks, it is better to take trekking sandals with you (waterproof if possible). Lunch is on the

island along with the other tourists. There is a (quite decent) buffet and after that you have the possibility to take a rest before you have to find your speedboat to head for another snorkelling stop.
During the transfers you always get fruit and drinks on board. Everything is taken care of. Back at the pier you return your snorkel gear (and pay for lost material), are allocated to a minibus and return to the hotel.
Equipment needed: sunscreen (high-factored and water-resistant and coral friendly), bath towels, swimming gear (already wear it, so you do not have to change), T-shirt and pants at will, (water-resistant) trekking sandals, camera (possibly with waterproof shell).

Important: The National Park and the islands are closed from 1st May to about 31st October!

To protect the ecosystem, **new regulations** were also enforced in 2018: Only 3325 visitors a day are allowed to visit the Similans for beach visits and snorkelling. Staying on one of the islands in Ko Similan National Park is no longer allowed. Disposable plastics are prohibited. The number of divers at the dive spots in Similan National Park has been limited to 525 divers a day.

Surin Islands

Even further north are the Surin Islands, which belong to the best diving sites in Thailand (with the Similan Islands) with an incredible underwater world and which are also within easy reach from Khao Lak. It is possible to stay overnight on the islands, but the places in bungalows or tents are very limited. Alternatively, there are day trips or, even better, live-aboards (overnight stays on the dive boat), which are worthwhile despite the lack of comfort.
There is no regular ferry service, neither on Similan nor on Surin – but you can get there and back with the tour providers.

Snorkelling Day Trip:

Pick up from the hotel is around 7 am. You are driven to the pier and taken by Speed Boat to the Surin Islands. Snorkelling at Maeyai Bay at Chong Kard. Lunch is on the island of Chong Kard. Visit the Moken village (sea nomads on an isolated island). Snorkelling on Ao Tao and

Pak Kard. Relax on the beach, then you are driven back to the pier and transferred to the hotel. Back about 6 pm.

Ko Pah

This is the smallest island off Khao Lak, just in front of Ko Kho Khao. It is also called "the unseen island" because it is hard to find. It only consists of sand (read: beach). A stately dune and quiet place that invites you to relax at low tide. and maybe snorkel (visibility can vary greatly). You can visit via longtail boat, an overnight stay is not possible. Bookable for example at the *Memories Beach Bar* or *Khaolak Wonderland Tours and Café.*
💻 m.facebook.com/KhaolakWonderlandTours

For all these trips to the islands west of the coast of Khao Lak and the diving / snorkelling sites it is worthwhile to have a **look at the weather before booking.** Wind (or a storm) does not only make the crossing rougher, but also affects the visibility in the water. Also, you have to expect changes in the trip.

Waterfalls

The Khao Lak area is rich in rivers and waterfalls, most of them of manageable size. The falls and the pools below are not only a tourist attraction but also a destination for locals (on weekends and holidays). During weekdays some waterfalls can be seen being used for personal hygiene and laundry.

Sai Rung / Pak Weep Waterfall (Rainbow Waterfall)

Sai Rung is the best accessible waterfall of Khao Lak. The road turns off Highway 4 just north of Bang Niang at km 71 approximately 500 meters behind the entrance to the Robinson Club (former Le Meridien), across the street at the height of km 72. Now take the small concrete road and follow the sign "Rainbow Waterfall" (for 1 to 2 km) and then turn right. After another 1.6 km you reach the parking lot at the end of the road. Parking is 20 baht per Car, 10 baht per bike. After only a short (5 minute) walk you are there. The 60 m waterfall has a broad step at 20 meters from the bottom, which lets the water cascade down quite impressively. It is almost always possible to take a cool bath here because the waterfall has always

water and there is still water in the lower pool even at the end of the high season (April). This makes the waterfall a popular Sunday destination for many Thai families.
DG 8.74143, 98.27988 / GMS N 8° 44′ 29.148″, E 98° 16′ 47.568″

Ton Chong Fa Waterfall

Ton Chong Fa Waterfall has water all year round, so you can have a cooling shower or bath in the knee- to waist-deep waterholes. Bathing is still possible in the prevailing water in the large water hole of the second cascade even at the end of the high season in April.
You access the 5-step Ton Chong Fah waterfall by the small road that branches off Highway 4 at kilometre 62.7. Follow the road to the sign for the "Chong Fah Waterfall" and then turn right. After another 5 km you come to a barrier: the entrance to Lamru National Park, where the waterfall is located. After paying entry (adults 200 baht, Children 100 baht) you can proceed to the car park.
DG 8.65626, 98.28714 / GMS N 8° 39′ 22.536″, E 98° 17′ 13.703″
After a strenuous walk (but at least through a shady forest) of about 15-20 minutes you get to the first cascade of the 200 m waterfall. If you want to go further up, keep right. There is a small path signposted near the waterhole. It is worthwhile in any case, because at the top fifth stage, the water drops down more than 20 m and with a little luck you can observe rare swallowtails or other pretty butterflies, insects, and birds. The waterfall is pretty – but this is the only place in Khao Lak where we have picked up leeches. As they often sit in the bushes you not necessarily need to be in the water to pick one up. They are pretty gross, but not dangerous. Actually, they are a sign for a natural, unpolluted environment. To remove the leeches, either wait until they are full and drop off by themselves (after about 20 minutes) or scrape them off close to the skin.

Ton Pling Waterfall

A waterfall just south of Khao Lak at the foot of Mount Lak and part of the Lamru National Park – but you do not have to pay an entrance fee here. Single-level, but divided into three parts, with a large stone in the water just in front. In older pictures you may still see a wooden bridge over the basin under the waterfall. Today only the remains of the concrete pillars are visible. Apart from some tours, local children also come here to bathe and the mothers to wash clothes. It is an easy

to reach destination for families. The short and steep way goes off at km 55 from the Highway 4 to a parking lot very close to the fall.
DG 8.61556, 98.24542 / GMS N 8° 36′ 56.016″, E 98° 14′ 43.511″

Bor Hin Waterfall

The northernmost waterfall that can still be counted to Khao Lak is also called Bo Hin. In the rainy season (or after rain) it is certainly worth a visit. In the dry season however, only the part on the right has water and the dry rocks on the left are a bit unspectacular.
At the sign to the Bangsak Bungalows take the road into the hills from Highway 4. The paved road through older palm plantations takes you directly to the parking lot next to the waterfall.
DG 8.7744, 98.2799 / GMS N 8° 46′ 27.84″, E 98° 16′ 47.639″

Lampi Waterfall

It is a nice 3-stage waterfall, best visited in the morning or late evening. The pool under the waterfall is deep enough to have a swim. The locals come here for bathing and washing their clothes in the cascades. The waterfall is a popular stop after several tours. About 30 minutes south of Khao Lak, the street branches off Main Road 4. The walk from the parking lot to the waterfall is short (about 5-minutes). If you cross the (somewhat dilapidated) bridge to the left, you'll quickly reach the second stage of the falls, where you can swim as well. There are restrooms and a shower/changing room at the falls. There's a park entrance fee: 100 baht per person, 30 per vehicle. DG 8.46443, 98.28009 / GMS N 8° 27′ 51.948″, E 98° 16′ 48.324″

Ton Prai Waterfall

Only a little further south than Lampi is this 3-stage waterfall, which can be reached after a tiring (but only 650 m long) ascending walk through the jungle. The path is well posted, but leads over roots, a bamboo bridge, stones and in some places concrete. The waterfall is often quiet and not so crowded. Sometimes, a full parking lot may be misleading as the lot is also used by a nearby campsite. The road 1030 from Highway 4 goes off 30 km south of Khao Lak. Follow the road that gets more and more narrow and thickly wooded for 6 km. At the visitor centre you must pay an entrance fee (100-200 baht) for the Khao Lampi Hat Thai Mueang Ntl Park.
DG 8.43654, 98.30888 / GMS N 8°26′11.544″, E 98°18′31.968″

Other waterfalls:

(Descriptions in the associated chapters)
At Kapong:
Lam Ru Waterfall. It belongs to the Lam Ru National Park, but is about 35km away as the crow flies near Kapong.
In the North:
Tam Nang Waterfall in Sri Phang Nga National Park. A real insider tip.
In Khao Sok:
Mae Yai Waterfall,
Wing Hin Waterfall,
Sip Et Chan Waterfall,
Ton Kloi Waterfall
Except for the first case, all of them are in the national park and can only be reached on longer hikes.

In the south:
Ton Sung - Phu Pha Sawan Waterfall
At Phang Nga:
Sa Nang Manora Forest Park
Raman Waterfall Forest Park,
Namtok Song Phraek in Ton Pariwat Sanctuary
Tao Thong Waterfall (shallow, with suspension bridge)
On Phuket:
the **Bang Pae Waterfall** in the north at the Gibbon Project
the **Ton Sai**.

Temples and Religion

There is no official state religion in Thailand and they have freedom of religion, but 95% of the population belongs to the Theravada Buddhism – the king even by law. Buddhism in Thailand has a strong undercurrent of Hinduism and a Thai-Chinese part practices diverse Chinese folk religions including Taoism. In the south of Thailand, a part of the population (mostly Malays) are Muslims and make up about 5% of the total population. Only about 1% are Christians.

Buddhist monks can be seen walking through the streets, particularly in the morning. They usually have a bowl with them, in which they receive food donations. Women cannot be monks (or nuns) in Theravada Buddhism, but many men have spent some time as a novice in a monastery as boys – formerly the only way to reach a

Wat Khuek Khak

Wat Samnak Song Daeng

Geisterhaus

Wat Phanat Nikhom

(higher) education. Today, there is an education system run by the state, but the schools often still cooperate with the temples and monks.

The temples are open to visit for everyone (also tourists), but you should behave respectfully:

- Wear decent clothes: miniskirts or shorts and tops with spaghetti straps are not okay, neither is going shirtless for men.
- Take off your shoes before entering the temple. In the temples there are often shoe racks, but you can also simply place your shoes on the floor in front of the entrance.
- Do not step on the doorstep as the house ghost lives there and stepping on its head brings misfortune.
- Do not touch or climb the Buddha figures. In addition, as already signposted at the airport, buy neither Buddha statues nor images.
- Take pictures respectfully – without flashlight and ask people in advance whether they agree.

However, the Thais are very easy going and forgiving regarding the behaviour of the tourists ... and the atmosphere in the temples is often anything but subdued.

Temples and Shrines in Khao Lak

Wat Khomniyaket – Khuk Khak Temple

The temple is located close to the Highway 4 right at the entrance of the JW Marriott. To see it, you drive through the eye-catching gate further into the area. It is a very beautiful, newly renovated, classic and large Thai temple with animal figures around it, which hint at the animistic part of religion, which is tolerated here.
DG 8.70564, 98.2543 /GMS N 8° 42′ 20.304″, E 98°15′15.48″

Wat Pattikaram

Also located off the Highway 4, the large, classical temple is clearly visible from the road. South of the hill at the Ton Prai waterfall.

Wat Phanat Nikhom

A small, but pretty temple in white-and-gold near the police boat in Bang Niang (on the same side, a bit further back in the direction of Khuk Khak). In the evening it has a light show.

Wat Phadung, Tham Phothi Wat

Also in Bang Niang, in the direction of the beach, there is a temple complex with a large seated white Buddha whose silver "crown" seems to hover above its head.

Wat Tao Gong

Small Chinese Temple in Khuk Khak. From the 4 you drive under a gate onto the side street where it is hidden behind a driveway. It is a small Taoist shrine built by Chinese migrants from Hai Nan Island and dedicated to Bun Tao Gong: a god and protector of fishermen. A visit to Chinese New Year and the Vegetarian Festival is particularly interesting. DG 8.69914, 98.25202 / GMS N 8°41'56.904", E 98°15'7.272"

Other temples in the surroundings:

(Descriptions in the individual chapters)

South of Khao Lak at Thai Mueang:
Wat Tha Sai – very pretty wooden temple right on the beach
Leng San Keng Shrine – Chinese temple in Thai Mueang
At Kapong:
Wat Pak Mok with stucco figures and a Chinese fat Buddha
Wat Inthaphum
In Phang Nga –
Wat Suwan Kuha – well-known cave temple with reclining Buddha
Wat Thamtapan – the Dragon Mouth and Hell Images Temple
Wat Bang Riang – Temple with 3 styles on the hills.
Wat Bang Thong – huge new temple with almost 70 m high golden central tower
Dragon Cave Temple – cave temple with a view
In Takua Pa:
Wat Khongkha Phimuk – gold-plated all around and with mirror mosaic on the inside
Big Buddha of Takua Pa – **Ban Dok Daen monastery** complex between Khao Lak and Old Takua Pa.
2 **Chinese temples**: both at the old town of Takua Pa.
At Khao Sok:
Wat Tham Phanthurat the Monkey Temple
On Phuket:
Wat Chalong – one of the largest and most famous complexes.

3 Temple Tour

Many tour operators offer 3-Temple tours, with different temples. They almost always include *Wat Suwan Kuha* with the big Buddha in the cave and frequently *Bang Riang* on the hill. This is a full day tour, including transfers, temple entrance fees and lunch / beverages and some information on religion in Thailand. Pick up from the hotel is in the morning and you are driven to the temples (by van), where you can learn something about the religion and history. In between the temples, there is a nice lunch in a Thai restaurant. In the evening you will be brought back. Because the temples are somewhat far away and apart (especially Wat Bang Riang) this tour includes a lot of driving, which is why it is not ideal for children. But you can also do a tour by yourself and put it together differently and with closer temples.

Ghost houses

Numerous houses in Thailand have these little houses or shrines in front of them – mostly on stilts or a pedestal. The size varies from shoebox size to the size of a small single-family home. These are ghost houses, the shrines for the nature spirits in Thailand. They are the remnants of the old animistic faith, which is tolerated by Buddhism. Once a house is built at a site, these are erected to appease the ghosts living there. They are also found next to accident-prone roads. The spirits receive sacrifices in the form of food and drink and the style of the houses is often more attractive than the main building – so that the spirits do no move there.

The 2004 Tsunami

Khao Lak was one of the regions hit hardest by the tsunami which occurred after the earthquake in the Indian Ocean in December of 2004. Much of the infrastructure on the coast was destroyed. The local economy was also severely affected. At that time many resorts were under construction and were destroyed by the tsunami. That and the loss of over 4000 human lives (compared to 300 victims in Phuket) was a huge setback to the rising tourism economy. However, Khao Lak has recovered. The resorts as well as the local infrastructure have been rebuilt and the population independent from tourism is again on a level as before the tsunami.

Today you are no longer able to see any of the devastation, neither in the landscape nor the buildings, but there are places where the consequences of the tsunami are commemorated.

Navy Boat 813

A lasting memory of the tsunami provides the Navy Boat 813, which was washed ashore by the wave and is still there – now as a monument. The boat was anchored off the coast and had the task to protect a member of the royal family, the grandson of the king, who was jet skiing in front of Khao Lak. The power of the tsunami has torn the almost 25-meter-long boat loose and carried it over 1 km inland. The grandson was killed, his mother, Princess Ubolratana was ashore and had to take refuge with others in the upper floors of the La Flora resort, where they survived. The large Navy boat is still in the same place where it was stranded – almost 2 km inland from the sea. It was left there as a memorial – and over the years the area has been developed. Earlier the boat lay on its side, almost lonely in a wide, green field; today it has been stabilized and the field paved. Plaques commemorate the incident. Along with the newly constructed concrete structures next to it, it is known as the **Tsunami Memorial Phangnga**.

Some souvenir vendors have set up huts where they aim to attract tourists with "Free Information Here" signs and a few photos on the walls.

Inland, somewhat off Highway 4, opposite the Bang Niang market. Meanwhile, it is no longer as clearly visible from the street because new houses were built there.

DG 8.66649, 98.25469 / GMS N 8°39'59.364", E 98°15'16.883"

International Tsunami Museum

The International Tsunami Museum is near the memorial (since 2018 directly next to it). It offers for 300 baht entrance small, barren rooms with photos and videos running continuously with information about tsunamis in general and the 2004 tsunami but less about the impact on Khao Lak and the surrounding area. That is because the museum was opened with international help with the aim of educating people. Some of these films you may have seen on YouTube before. They are accounts and recordings of eyewitnesses, which impressively show the power this wave had – and that it is not, as often imagined, a meter-high tidal wave, but an unstoppable force.

The reason it is so dangerous is that it takes a lot of debris with it, crushing everything and destroying more than water alone would. There used to be a second tsunami museum here, the *Tsunami Memorial Museum*. It was located directly on the access road to boat 813. In it, the focus was on life in Khao Lak before and after the tsunami. Unfortunately, it had to be closed during the Covid period.

Tsunami Memorial in the Navy Centre

Located next to the Sea Turtle Conservation Centre on the Phang Nga Naval Base are the remains of another military boat and victim of the tsunami of 2004. The Coastal Reconnaissance Boat T 215 was off the coast at the La Flora Resort when the tsunami came. It was damaged and capsized. A person was killed. The whole structure was demolished – only the body of the boat remains, so it looks much less representative than the Navy Boat 813 in Bang Niang.
The Naval Base (with a public golf course) is located a few minutes south of Khao Lak and the Lak Hill – on the way to Tab Lamu Pier.
Today, the boat T 215 also stays where it came to a rest, surrounded by a small pool and an information board – it is the tsunami memorial of the Naval Base. DG: 8.58113, 98.234 / GMS: N 8° 34′ 52.068″, E 98° 14′ 2.29″

Tsunami Memorial in Baan Nam Khem

A site particularly affected by the Tsunami was the fishing village of Baan Nam Khem, north of the beaches of Khao Lak. It is now the site of Baan Nam Khem Tsunami Memorial Park, just west of the piers to Ko Kho Khao. The park on the beach is well maintained. The memorial consists of two longer walls that face each other. One is concrete and shaped like a big wave; the opposite wall is covered with tiles, some with photos, others with fresh flowers. A wall full of names of people who ceased to exist, but who have not been forgotten. At the headland near the pier to the island of Ko Kho Khao. DG 8.85919, 98.26523 / GMS N 8° 51′ 33.084″, E 98° 15′ 54.828″

Ban Nam Khem Tsunami Museum

Newly opened Museum in February 2022. A touching video introduces the topic: the effects that the 2004 tsunami had on Khao Lak. There is information about protection against future tsunamis and what the children learn about it here at school. They have lots of recovered memorabilia, 2 fishing boats are moored in the courtyard

Navy Boat 813

Tsunami Memorial Ban Nam Khem

Ban Nam Khem Tsunami Museum

and there is a good view of the area from the roof. 🕒 From Wednesday to Sunday 8.30am-4.30pm. Admission is free - donations are appreciated. 🚗 Near the Tsunami Memorial but inland. Follow the signs. DG 8.6067645, 98.2617416 / GMS N 8°36'24.352", E 98°15' 42.269"

Tsunami warning system

A warning system was set up because of the 2004 tsunami. It faced a test in April 2012 and successfully passed it: after an earthquake off Sumatra it issued a warning about 2 hours before the (small) wave – enough time for everyone to reach higher ground. Signs indicating the evacuation routes can be seen in many places on the coast today, even if some of them are pretty faded by now. They point to elevated ground where you should retire to in the event of a tsunami warning. Islands such as Ko Kho Khao, which have no significant elevation built "Tsunami Shelter", multi-storey buildings made of strong concrete.

Elephants

Asian elephants are endangered. There are only about 2000 (still an optimistic estimate) of the approximately 200'000 wild elephants in Siam left. The animals, which were used as working animals for moving loads and in wars for centuries (the power of the ruler was measured by the number of elephants he owned) are now replaced by machines. The Forest Protection Act of 1989 in Thailand left thousands of elephants and mahouts unemployed. The owners then tried to earn money from the tourists with the animals. An elephant consumes about 200 kilos of food a day and he must be moved, fed and entertained. Many mahouts do that well and take good care of their animals. But of course, there are exceptions.

Nevertheless, today attractions with elephants are viewed controversially. You should remember that despite all the years of working for the humans, they are still wild animals, even if most are now raised in captivity and are not kept in a near-natural environment. They cannot range free at night, they are trained with various, sometimes quite cruel methods. Therefore, occasionally unsuitable animals could be found as tourist attractions. Male elephants in the rutting season react aggressively. Accidents during elephant rides were therefore not that uncommon. On the other hand, there is hardly anything left for the animals to do – and you can't simply release a house or working elephant into the wild. In addition, the areas in which the elephants can safely stay and look after themselves are becoming fewer and fewer. In the south, only the Khlong-Saeng - Khao Sok forest complex has wild elephants.

If you (still) want to go elephant riding, you should take a look at how the elephants are treated. In case of bad treatment, I would do without a ride. Here are some signs of mistreatment to look for:

- Does the elephant have scars or wounds at the joints, on the head or buttocks? These can be from the mahouts' equipment, which they control their elephants with. However, it is also possible that the elephants have been scratching on trees.
- Is there any powder (white or purple) at these locations? – powder is often used for wound care.
- Does the elephant constantly shake his head, or does he have other behavioural problems?
- How is the condition of the farm? Do the elephants have enough space? When and where do the elephant rides take place? For example, it is also a torment for the elephants if they must walk in the blazing sun without shade at lunchtime.

– Having said all that, we have gone elephant riding several times in earlier years and have seen different providers. Only once we have not felt "comfortable": that was at the Khao Sok Park, with one of the largest suppliers then. There we had a large (male?) Elephant and a mahout with a long rod with a sharp hook, who was getting visibly nervous when Junior came too close to the elephant during the subsequent feeding. A few weeks later a tourist couple got injured in the same park because two elephants started fighting with each other. Today we don't ride anymore. There are numerous elephant camps that promote more animal-friendly activities with and around elephants – and as more people choose not to ride, more of that will be offered.

Other activities with elephants:

Go bathing with the elephants: There are different providers in Khao Lak – I recommend checking beforehand what it's like, otherwise you may end up with the elephant in a rather murky pool.

Interaction with elephants: watching, feeding and possibly washing. We discovered this a few years ago and have preferred it to riding ever since.

Some camps also offer **Mahout programs** for one or more days (adults only) or **making paper from elephant dung**.

Here are a few **eco-friendly tour operators for elephant contacts:**
Khao Lak Elephant Home – Elephant feeding and bathing, mahout program (adults only). Near Memories Beach. 💻 khaolakelephanthome.com
Khao Lak Elephant Sanctuary – new provider near Sai Rung Waterfall. Elephant viewing and information, full-day mahout program, combinable with other activities. Winner of the Responsible Thailand Award 2024-25 in Responsible Animal Welfare. Since 2025, feeding is no longer offered, only observation. 💻 khaolak-elephantsanctuary.com
Khao Lak Elephant Conservation near Pakarang – small elephant centre near Khao Lak. Owned by a family that has kept elephants for six generations (over 160 years). They are part of the Phang Nga Elephant Park, Khaosok Elephant Conservation, and Phuket Elephant Conservation. Small groups, ethical interactions (feeding, walking alongside, observing). They support the Southern Thailand Elephant Foundation and its animal hospital 💻 khaolak-elephantsanctuary.com
Phang Nga Elephant Park – about 20 minutes from Khao Lak on the way to Phang Nga, offers ethical elephant tours and elephant interaction. 💻 Phangngaelephantpark.com
Elephant Hills – near Khao Sok: 2- to 4-day tours including information and elephant feeding. Accommodation in the rainforest and on Cheow Lan Lake in luxury tents. Highly recommended, but not inexpensive. 💻 elephant-hills.com
Phuket Elephant Sanctuary – Just look and maybe feed. Park in the heart of Phuket. 💻 phuketelephantsanctuary.org

Hot Springs

♨ Thailand has 114 hot springs, most of them not commercially used, neither for energy production nor in baths. There are also hot springs around Khao Lak, thanks to the activity of the Australo-Indian plate, which slides under the Eurasian plate (far) off the coast. Mostly north of Khao Lak in Ranong, or south in Krabi some hotels offer the hot springs as a tourist attraction. The springs here in the south of Thailand hardly smell of sulphur – in contrast to those in the north, but they are just as hot: You can even cook eggs in them.

Rommanee Hot Springs

Hot springs with good infrastructure and kept clean. There is a wardrobe building and four different pools with different temperatures, the hottest so hot that you can get burned at the water inlet. 🕒 8:00 am to 7:30 pm. Also used by Thai families who want to do something for their health together. Admission is 50 baht for adults, children are free. 💻 rommaneehotspring.com (thai only).
About 40 km north of Khao Lak before the Khao Sok National Park. DG 8.82665, 98.43297 / GMS N 8° 49′ 35.76″, E 98° 25′ 58.691″

Ban Bo Dan Hot Springs

Publicly accessible hot springs with infrastructure on hotel premises. Day visitors are possible. 💻 thehotspringbeach.com
They are located south of Khao Lak, about 10 km below Thai Muang. DG: 8.30735, 98.27383 / GMS: N 8°18′26.46″ O 98°16′25.788″

Kapong Hot Springs

The hot springs, called Plai Phu by locals, are located inland just outside of the Lam Ru National Park near Kapong. They have their source in a small river and are almost completely undeveloped – apart from a few stones in the river that have been piled up to form bathing hollows. There is now a stall by the parking lot where you can buy drinks – and eggs together with a basket to cook in the springs. DG: 8.66979 98.47132 / GMS N 8° 49' 11.244" E 98° 28' 16.752"

Viewpoints

Behind the flat west coast of Thailand with the wonderful sunsets over the sea lies hilly country. The coastal areas consist of sandy beaches or mangrove forests. Imposing limestone cliffs rise below at Phang Nga and above in Khao Sok. To see something of the country, we recommend visiting one or more viewpoints.

Andaman Viewpoint and Coconut Viewpoint

Two viewpoints next to each other just north of Khao Lak (not to be confused with the 360° viewpoint with a similar name close to the Sarasin Bridge). Easy to reach by scooter or car. Parking space and drinks available. You have a view of the sea from a slightly elevated position. Beautiful and lonely during the day, but a bit unspectacular – maybe something for the sunset. Just before Bangsak Village, head north on the non-beach side. The entrance is signposted.
DG 8.76819, 98.2734 / GMS N 8° 46′ 5.484", E 98° 16′ 24.239"

Khao Khai Nouy

Viewpoint with wonderful views especially early in the morning when the hills are covered in light morning mist.
The viewpoint is only about 30 minutes south of Khao Lak. The road goes up from the upper part of the 4240 road triangle. With a normal car the journey can be extremely difficult. More information in the chapter "the undiscovered south".
DG 8.55965, 98.29488 / GMS N 8°33′34.74", E 98°17′41.568"

Phu Ta Cho Viewpoint

Also called Phutajor. Located inland and very "off the beaten track", overlooking the hilly wide land. From the 860 m high summit you have a view of the "sea of fog" in the morning, which attracts mainly northern Thai visitors. The viewpoint is located near Kapong, about an hour's drive from Khao Lak. More information in the chapter Kapong. DG 8.68694, 98.5224 / GMS N 8°41′12.984", E 98°31′20.64"

Khao Sok Viewpoint

Located just off the main road, the viewpoint is on the way to Khao Sok National Park, about an hour's drive north of Khao Lak. Unfortunately transport or taxis don't regularly stop here. But it's worth it, as it's one of the few places in the park where you have an overview of the hilly landscape – without hanging cables in front of it. DG: 8.88534, 98.50 255 / GMS N 8°53′7.224", E 98°30′9.179"

Samet Nangshe Viewpoint and Ao Toh Li Viewpoint

Offering a wonderful view of Phang Nga Bay. It is just over an hour's drive south of Khao Lak and is described along with the nearby Ao Toh Li in the Phang Nga chapter. The view over the sea and the

islands during sunrise is spectacular, so there are now tours (taking off early) there or you can just spend the night up there. The glass floor path built right next to it is now finished (2024).
DG: 8.23999, 98.44634 / GMS: N 8°14'23.964", E 98°26'46.824"

Khao Nang Hong View Point

The panorama road between Phang Nga and Krabi is one of the most beautiful in the area (although very, very winding), the viewpoint is nothing more than a short stop on the way (for example to Wat Bang Riang). There is a small parking lot, we didn't see a restaurant. There is a path up the hill to the viewpoint, which was not passable when we visited. DS 8.53515, 98.5593 / GMS N 8°32'6.54", O 98°33'33.479"

Thai Massage

Thai massages are world famous and hardly any hotel opens in Khao Lak today that does not have "Spa" in its name.

Traditional Thai massage has a history spanning over 2,500 years. Practitioners believe that a multitude of invisible energy lines run through the body. The masseur uses their hands, elbows, feet, heels, and knees to apply pressure along these lines and release blockages, allowing energy to flow freely. Many Thais believe in the positive effects of these massages on health and their use in treating illnesses. After a session, one should feel both relaxed and energized. Although spas (wellness centres) were only introduced to Thailand in the 1990s, it is now one of the world's most popular spa destinations. In addition to traditional Thai massage, a variety of international treatments are offered, including aromatherapy, Swedish massage, and more
You cannot only get the massages at the hotel spa, but also **on the beach**. The advantage is a very low price (starting from 300 Baht). Disadvantages: the quality is very dependent on the person that does the massage. Even in the shade it can get very hot on the beach. For your own protection, have a look at the pad you lie on and possibly lay your own towel on it. On the beach you are massaged through the bathing suit, which can be an obstacle.

Another possibility are **massage parlours**, which can also be found in Khao Lak. The massages there are a step (or maybe more, depending on the place) above the beach, they can get as good as a really good hotel spa massage. In Phuket / Patong we have often visited the Let's Relax, a place I highly recommend. I have also never been proposed to have a "happy ending" there ... which sometimes still can occur, depending on the site. (Though less in Khao Lak, I believe).

Massage parlours in Khao Lak (selection)

Bangniang: *Bangniang Slimming and Massage, Parsap Massage,* 💻 facebook.com/parsapp,

Bussaba Thai Massage 💻thaimassagekhaolak.com,

La On: *Casi Thai Massage, Ying Thai Massage, Coconut Massage* 💻coconut-massage-khao-lak.business.site, *Namfon Massage* 💻namfon-massage-khao-lak.business.site

Khuek Khak: *Didi Massage*

La Vita Sana Khao Lak – A new, modern and large wellness oasis in Khao Lak near Bang Niang. There is a Restaurant and cafe included. Prices are rather higher, but typical for a modern spa.

💻 lavitasanakhaolak.com

Here is **a description of a spa visit** (*Quan Spa at JW Marriott*):

You start at the reception with a cold towel (it is hot outside) and a refreshing green tea drink. Then you proceed into the spa area. There is a private room with an anteroom, where you can change: undress to your underwear (take off the bra), maybe use the hygienically packed uni-size net underpants and put on the provided bathrobe and slippers. Before starting the massage, you get a footbath and a foot scrub, and the person massaging you will also explain what the procedure and ask for your preferences.

Then you lie on the massage table (in massage parlours, you are often massaged while on the floor on a mat), first on the stomach, then on the back. Thai massages are usually done through clothes or a towel and without oil, but there are of course fusion massages, or you can choose an aromatherapy or Swedish massage. The body parts that are not massaged are always covered, so you do not get cold. The rooms are air-conditioned. During the massage, you look at a pretty flower arrangement on the floor, listen to soothing music and just enjoy it. I regularly manage to doze off for a while, but for my wife the massage is usually too ... energ(et)ic. Upon completion and clothing again, you finish with a sweet-sharp ginger tea.

Bamboo rafting

Minigolf

ATV

Kayaking

Turtle heaven

Ton Pling Waterfall

CLOSE BY

Khao Lak Lam Ru National Park

Lam Ru National Park is 125 km2 in size, ranging from the sea in the west to the hilly hinterland in the east. It is named after its two highest elevations: Lak and Lam Ru. On the way to Khao Lak you cross a small part of it when you drive over the hill. Entrance to the park costs 100 baht for adults, 50 baht for children 5-14 years. The ticket can be used for 72 hours – also at other park entrances.

Chong Fa Waterfall in Khao Lak is located in the western part of the park. **Lam Ru** and **Hin Lad waterfall** at Kapong are in the eastern end of the park. The **hot springs of Kapong** are located just outside the National Park.

The **park headquarters** are located about 50 meters off Highway 4, towards the sea. The road there is signposted and goes off on the top of the hill. There is a restaurant overlooking the sea. 🕒 8 am to 6 pm Accommodation and camping in the national park are limited. Bungalows are only available with prior booking and payment; tents are subject to availability upon arrival. 💻 thainationalparks.com/khao-lak-lam-ru-national-park DG 8.62685, 98.23904/ GMS N 8°37'36.66", E 98°14'20.544"

Small Sandy Beach

The short, 1.5 km long **Hat Lek Nature Trail** along the cape starts at the headquarters. It takes about an hour and offers viewpoints over the coast and sea and ends at a beautiful, secluded beach: the Small Sandy Beach. Be sure to bring enough water with you and use sturdy shoes – even if the path here is not that demanding.
There is a shorter route to Small Sandy Beach: it starts just above "Small Sandy Beach" from Main Road 4 about 1.2 km from HQ (posted). The route goes down about 400 m through the forest. There is now a small shop, where you can buy soft drinks at the beach.

The Lam Ru nationalpark has several other trails, for example the **Namtok Ton Fa Nature Trail**, which is 5 km long. However, you will need a guide (a park ranger) if you want to do this or one of the other trails. You can get a guide at the headquarter.

Khao Lak Minigolf

This is something to do with the family if you want a change from the beach. The course is surrounded by green plants and tropical landscapes. The trees give shade, there is an "ancient temple" and the minigolf course is well maintained. Use mosquito repellent! You get a small bottle of water and a cold towel for free. Prices: 450 baht for adults, 350 baht for children. At the road to the Chong Fah Waterfall, in Bang Niang. DG 8.67177, 98.2574 / GMS N 8°40'18.372", E 98°15'26.64"

Khao Lak Labyrinth and Mirror Maze

The labyrinth was built in 2017 right next to the mini golf course. Entrance to the maze alone is 150 baht per person. The entrance fee for the combination maze / miniature golf is 500 baht per person. Children over 120 cm pay the adult price. The facility is well maintained, the hedges are over-man high. As attractions, there are several little gardens in the labyrinth, a signpost pointing towards all sorts of big cities in the world and an oversized bench. The labyrinth, however, is quite small. Good for about 5-10 minutes, 15 minutes if you sit down to rest. From the high bench you have an overview of the labyrinth ... but not on the rest of the landscape. I can only recommend the maze in combination with the mini-golf course – and to buy it as a combined package right at the beginning. The latest addition, which opened in 2025, is a mirror maze.

The Park Khao Lak

A fully equipped small public park on the beach between the X10/La On and the La Vela. You can get there either via a small access road from the Highway 4 or by walking across the beach. The park has walking paths under trees, a small seating arena, a sea turtle monument, toilets (also for the disabled), parking spaces (also for the disabled), small empty buildings that were perhaps intended for massage or restaurants. However, the *Chumpoo restaurant* here has preferred to stay just outside – probably at the original location by the parking lot. It offers typical inexpensive Thai food, with massage areas and lounger rentals.

There's something strange about the park, it is new, maintained and somehow abandoned. There were few visitors even in high season – and most of them go directly to the beautiful sandy beach with a few rocks in front of it. Thanks to the restaurants present, this is an easy-to-reach, yet lonely beach with excellent infrastructure – making it perfect for visitors on a budget who are looking for something uncrowded.

You can walk north from the X10 or south from Bang Niang to the park – along the beach. A small stream runs between The Park and Bang Niang, or rather the La Vela Hotel (with the Kokulo Beach Club). At low tide, it's about knee-deep, but at high tide, the water reaches up to your hips and represents an obstacle for beach walkers. However, a resourceful entrepreneur has taken advantage of this and offers ferry rides for 20 baht per person. The stream effectively forms the border between the towns of La On and Bang Niang.
Information about the current and future tides in Khao Lak can be found here: 💻 de.tideschart.com/Thailand/Phang-Nga/Ban-Khao-Lak

Khaolak Skywalk

A somewhat curious new attraction that (in 2024) doesn't even have an official name: A glass-bottomed walkway out onto the reservoir. The facility is new, very modern, with plenty of parking, a ramp, animal figures (turtle and dolphin) and toilet blocks (where the water did not work). The approximately 10 m long glass floor path leads out on the eastern side of the lake – so you have a great view of the reservoir, but unfortunately little else. The lake is pretty, a popular spot for a morning or evening jog and recreational activities such as aerobics and yoga. : By the lake opposite Build Factory in Bang Niang. Free access and parking. DG 8.67917, 98.25429 GMS N 8° 41' 22.624", O 98° 1' 4.794"

Golf

Golf came to Thailand over 100 years ago under the reign of King Rama V. Once only played by the nobility and other members of the high society, golf has grown in popularity in Thailand over the last 10 years and is now played by Thais and visitors alike. The popularity is also due to the comparatively low costs for membership in golf clubs and low course fees. You do not need a green card to play golf in Thailand, but caddies are mandatory. They cost 200 baht per round plus a tip of the same amount. Dress code is golf clothes: a shirt with a collar and shorts. Swimming shorts are not allowed. Golf shoes – if you cannot rent them, you can often buy them cheaply.

Tublamu Royal Navy Golf at Khao Lak

18 holes, 6825 yards, par 72. The golf course on the grounds of the Royal Thai Navy has been open to the public since 2002. It is located near the sandy beach of Son Ngam in Ao Khao Lak – this is the original bay of Khao Lak, south of the hill. The golf course offers pretty views of the bay and the green hills inland. It was destroyed by the tsunami in 2004 but has been completely rebuilt and is well maintained. 🕒 Daily from 6.30 am to 6 pm. 💻 tublamunavygolfcourse.net ⛵ Naval Base and Golf Course are located a few minutes south of Khao Lak, in front of Lak Hill – on the way to Tab Lamu Pier. DG: 8.58475, 98.24708 / GMS: N 8°35'5.1", E 98°14'49.487"

Kirinara Golf

9-hole golf course near Khao Lak at Takua Pa on Pakweep Road. The name Kirinara means mountain and river, which describes the surroundings quite well – if you remember that Thai mountains are mere hills. You can play as a member or guest and rent the equipment. Even as a non-member you can have a drink in the café with terrace and view. 💻 kirinara.com
DG: 8.80293, 98.34565 / GMS N 8°48'10.548", E 98°20'44.34"

Ratchaprapha Dam Golf Course

Close to Khao Sok National Park, adjacent to Cheow Lan Lake and the causeway, this golf course offers a beautiful location amidst the green landscape of Khao Sok National Park, with an excellent layout. The place is rather demanding and something for sportier natures. ⛵ Just below the dam at Cheow Lan Lake. DG: 8.96139, 98.80689/ GMS: N 8°57'41.004", E 98°48'24.803"

Aquella Golf & Country Club

Golf course, clubhouse and restaurant near Thai Mueang. Very well-maintained course, beautiful clubhouse. High-quality caddies and golf carts with GPS. A rather expensive ride-along fee if you're not playing and equipment rental (if needed) will also be charged separately. 💻 aquellagolf.com

Katathong Golf & Resort

New golf course amidst the green hills of the fantastic landscape of Phang Nga. You can hear and see various waterfalls while playing. There was historically a tin mine in the area and the clubhouse was built in the Sino-Portuguese style and contains memorabilia from this time. 💻 katathong.com.
⛵ Next to 4090, the upper road that leads from Khao Lak to Phang Nga.
DG: 8.55993, 98.48155 / GMS: N 8°33'35.748", E 98°28'53.579"

Tennis

There are no public sports facilities, but these hotels / resorts have tennis courts and let you play as day visitors:

Khao Lak Village: *Merlin Resort.*
Nang Thong / La On: *Centara Seaview Resort*
Bang Niang: *La Flora*
Khuk Khak: *J.W.Marriott,*
Pakarang: *Takolaburi Cultural Resort & Spa*
Bangsak: *Sentido Graceland, Mai Holiday, Robinson Khao Lak, Avani*

Bamboo Rafting

This is something to do as a romantic getaway or as a family (also with smaller children). The river on which you float down has a gentle current and hardly any rapids. You can glide comfortably (as the guide steers you) through the lush forest, half-sitting in the water on the rustic bamboo raft, and see plants, perhaps snakes, monitor lizards, birds and butterflies. The trip takes between 40 minutes and one hour, covering about 3 km. From January to March the water may be low. Normally, two people fit on a bamboo raft; but at low water, only one person can go, without extra charge.

Price: Children aged 4-7 pay 400 baht, adults 600 baht.
Bamboo rafting is often included in excursions, but you can also book it individually or visit on your own.
Equipment: Swimming gear, waterproof bag, waterproof phone case, mosquito repellent, towel. You can leave your valuables in a lockable compartment at the station.

Bamboo rafting at Khao Lak

On the Lam Ru Yai River, south of Lak Hill and just south of Khao Lak Village, inland. There are various providers.
DG 8.6064724, 98.2715001/ GMS N 8° 36' 23.301", E 98° 16' 17.4"

Komol's Corner Bamboo Rafting

They have an onsite restaurant where you can eat (and wait, if necessary). They offer half-day or full-day trips combined with bamboo rafting. 💻 komolcorner.com facebook.com/KomolCorner ✆ +66 95 410 1988 (Whatsapp)

Sutingroup Bamboo Rafting

Right next to Komol's Corner on the same river. Have some snacks and a drink while you wait. ✆+66 96 653 9696 💻 .facebook.com/sutingroupbamboorafting

Lungrong Bamboo Rafting
A cheaper provider further up the river with mixed reviews regarding safety.
✆ +66 97 990 2607

Other places to go bamboo rafting:
Bamboo Rafting in Khao Sok on the Sok River.

Bicycle tours

You can see much more of the surroundings by bike than from a car or bus, and in Khao Lak / Bang Niang more bike paths are being created to ensure safe cycling. On the other hand, cycling is rather strenuous in Thailand, especially in the hot season, even though the area around Khao Lak is mostly flat. That may be one of the reasons why you mainly see tourists on bicycles ... and those more of the sporty and equipped type. You can rent bicycles in many places – sometimes even in the hotels. If you are unsure what to visit despite the guidebook, you can book one of the guided bike tours that take you to interesting points (waterfalls, villages, manufacturing plants, temples). Some of the tours are combined with kayaking or swimming in the river. Or ... try it yourself (Just keep away from having to use or cross Highway No. 4 too much).

Tour providers for bicycle tours and other environmentally friendly tours: *Green Biking Club*, excursions in German and English.
💻 greenbikingclub.com

Ideas for bike trips:

Short tour in Khao Lak:
Start in Bang Niang – Tsunami Memorial – small temple – Ton Chong Fa Waterfall – Back to Khao Lak and market (Fresh Market in the morning) – Cross Highway 4 to the Wat Phadung Temple with the Big White Buddha Statue – relax on Bang Niang Beach – have a drink in the Thai Beach Bar – head back to the start.

North of Khao Lak:
Khao Lak – north to Sai Rung Waterfall – stop at Klong Koo Restaurant in the river – spend time at the Memories Beach by the sea – have a drink in the Memories Beach Bar (or go up to the White Sand Beach and have a coffee at the Coconut Cafe) – back to Khao Lak on the small roads between Beach and Highway 4.

Takua Pa Old town
Khao Lak – Khuk Khak – continue on the new beautiful road 4147 – Big Buddha – Takua Pa Old Town (Sunday market) – return.

Takua Pa culture trip
Arrange transport to the "Little Amazon" – Takua Pa Fresh Market – Iron Bridge – Wat Khogkha Phimuk (with the golden chedi), have ice cream or try Taosor Cake in one of the coffee shops/bakeries – Takua Pa Old Town – return via scenic road 4147 on Khao Lak

Ko Kho Khao day trip
Khao Lak – Tsunami Memorial Ban Nam Khen (about 23 km on flat road, but Highway 4 has heavy traffic– maybe organize transport to get there?) – Pier – Ko Kho Khao – ride to the north of the island and back with side trips and stops on the beaches – Pier – Khao Lak

Khao Lak's south
Arrange for transport over the hill – Ton Pling Waterfall – to the backcountry for bamboo rafting and ATV – to the sea: Tap Lamu Pier – Sea Turtle Conservation Centre – back.

Phang Nga
The area around Phang Nga offers scenic routes and tours that can be combined with kayaking in Phang Nga Bay and visiting various caves, temples and waterfalls. Providers as t-globe offer such a "triathlon" as a day trip including transfer and equipment.

ATV or Quad Biking

ATVs, or quads, are four-wheeled, all-terrain motorcycles that can be driven independently after a simple introduction. They take you over bumpy forest paths, sometimes through small streams and up hills. They are not permitted on roads in Thailand. Excursions can be booked through tour operators, or you can arrange it yourself. Prices start at around 500 baht for 15 minutes to 2,500 baht for 1.5 hours. Passengers (children) travel cheaper. Officially, you are allowed to drive yourself from around the age of 15. A fun outdoor adventure!

Khaolak Andaman ATV Bamboo Rafting

On the river where the bamboo rafting takes place, there is a quad biking operator that also offers camping, bamboo rafting and night safaris. 💻 facebook.com/khaolakmyfriendbamboo kiengkhuresort@gmail.com

Kiangkhaolak ATV

Quad biking at Khao Lak Village south of the hill. The provider also offers accommodation. Varied terrain, way off the main road 4. Contact 💻 facebook.com/kiangkhaolakresort ✆+66 76 595 389.
DG 8.60676, 98.26174 / GMS N 8°36'24.352", E 98°15'42.269"

Amazon ATV

A pair of siblings offering ATV tours in Khao Lak. Aum speaks (some) English, his sister JJ speaks German. New vehicles, customized tours available. They are located in Bang Niang. Contact via WhatsApp +66 86 682 2432

Garden House ATV

The successor to ATV Sairung has newer and more vehicles, but is still located in the same spot: on the road to Sairung Waterfall. Excursions to the rubber tree plantations, forest, river and waterfall are available. Contact 66 81 367 4394, Jinamon16@gmail.com
💻 facebook.com/profile.php?id=61550552828407

Khao Lak Waterside

This place was advertised online as a beach club – it isn't. It's located on the river where the bamboo raft rides take place. They have a restaurant and waterfront areas with (cheap plastic) water playground. They offer activities like ATV riding, tubing, bamboo rafting, and combinations with elephants or ziplining. They work in partnership with the Khao Lak Elephant Sanctuary near Sai Rung Waterfall. Open daily from 9 am to 5 pm. WhatsApp: +66 98 663 6194 💻 khaolakwaterside.com DG 8.60239, 98.26985 / GMS N 8°36'8.604", E 98°16'11.46"

Zipline / Rope Park

Since the end of 2025, there's a new zipline/rope park in Khao Lak. A new operator has taken over the facility at the location where the Flying Elephant used to be. Enjoy fantastic jungle scenery, beautiful views, and adventurous fun right near Khao Lak. The longest zipline is 200 meters long, and there are bridges, abseiling points, and spiral staircases. It's suitable for families with ages 4 to 80 (though there is a weight limit of 100-120 kg). At the top of Lak Hill between La On and South Beach, near the entrance to Lam Ru National Park. 💻 skyrockkhaolak.com

Horseriding

Khao Lak Horse Riding on Laem Khan Beach south of Lak Hill. They offer horse riding on the beach at sunset for beginners to experienced riders. The horses sometimes go swimming in the sea. Prices start at 700 baht per person and 30 minutes. Contact via Whatsapp ✆+66 94 950 3306
💻 facebook.com/Khaolakhorseriding

VT. Horse Riding Ranch at Takua Pa. Kontakt +66 93 578 6962
💻 facebook.com/pages/V.t.horse%20Riding%20Ranc/1600369516878094

The **Kirinara Golf Course Khao Lak** (near Takua Pa) has a horse stable and offers individual and package lessons for beginners. Trails in the hills around Takua Pa. 💻kirinara.reservation@gmail.com ✆+66 93 6144759

Thai Boxing Course

Muay Thai is Thailand's traditional martial art with roots dating back hundreds of years. In it kicks and punches are used with knees and elbows. Instead of just watching **the professional fights at the Thai Boxing Stadium** in Khao Lak, you can also take courses yourself. The course rooms are in the northern part of Khao Lak. Or you can book at the Memories Bar at Pakarang Cape. The courses are suitable for absolute beginners as well as for professionals. A typical session consists of warming up, stretching, shadow boxing, technical instruction, sparring, work on the bag and more.

Khao Lak Muay Thai and Muan Boran: Located in the heart of La On, training camp for all levels, group training for 300 baht or private lessons starting at 800 baht per hour. 💻 khaolakmuaythai.com

Rawai Muay Thai: Traditional training centre, with accommodation. 💻 rawaimuaythai.com

Empire Muay Thai: Muay Thai, Dance Fitness, Yoga, MMA, Boxing, Jiu Jitsu Beginner Courses. 💻 empire-muay-thai.com

Yoga in Khao Lak

Several hotels offer classes; some offer outdoor classes (on the beach); some offer private lessons.

Khao Lak Hot Yoga: Also offers private lessons at the guest's hotel. Almost up at the Tsunami Memorial in Ban Nam Khen. facebook.com/khaolakhotyoga
Khao Lak Palm Hill Yoga – La On, near Nangthong Supermarket. facebook.com/khaolakpalmhillyoga
Soul Friend & Spiritual Garden, yoga and meditation classes, sound healing courses, a bookshop specializing in spiritual literature and a café. An interesting mix, the shop is located in the northern part of La On, right next to Dr. Chusak's clinic. soulfriendworld.com

Surfing in Khao Lak

Khao Lak has earned a reputation as a chilled-out surf spot. There are some good places to surf in Khao Lak, namely Nang Thong Beach, **Bang Niang Beach**, where the river enters the sea and famous **Pakarang Beach** and the riff there. The waves are not very high in the dry season, more so in the low and rainy season **from April to November**, when the monsoon winds are blowing.
The waves may not be very high (1 to 3 metres), but long and consistent – well suited for beginners. In stronger winds or in the monsoon season, it gets more interesting for experienced surfers. There is always some place to surf with the reef breaks and beach breaks, different winds, and tides. **The best surfing** on the Andaman coast **is from April to November**, during the more violent winds of the monsoon season. It is advisable to surf then only if you have experience and to seek the advice of local experts because of the sudden rip currents occurring in the wet season.
Surfboard rentals and information about the best surfing spots can be found in many places, but the heart of the surf scene is at Memories Beach. facebook.com/khaolaksurftown

Pakarang Surf Shop

At Pakarang Beach is the *Pakarang Surf Shop*, which is part of the *Memories Beach Club*. You can rent surf boards, stand up paddle or body boards there (200 baht per hour, 500 baht per day) or take surfing lessons (starting from 1000 baht for an hour). Price Board rental 1 hour 200 baht, 2 hours 300 baht, day 500 baht, 1 week 3000 baht. pakarangsurfshop.com

Salt Surf Café

Combined café/board shop with Balinese surfboards and a surfing hotspot in Khao Lak. They offer surfing lessons for beginners to advanced surfers, including children. Located on Pakarang Beach, slightly north of Memories Beach, next to Apsara. 💻 saltsurf.club

The Board Factory / Rip Curl Shop

The Board Factory professionally produces boards for surfing, stand-up paddling and skateboarding directly in Khao Lak. Sunova Surfboards is a world-renowned brand. In their building you can not only buy the boards in the Rip Curl Shop, but also hang out at the skate park and admire the graffiti of the well-known artist Alex Face here. 💻 sunovasurfboards.com/en/the-board-factory Approx. 200 m after the turnoff to Memories Beach on the sea side.

Some hotels and resorts offer surfing lessons and board rentals. The *Kokotel Khao Lak Lighthouse* in La On has established itself as a surfing hotspot further south.

Skate parks in Khao Lak

If you want to surf (i.e. skate) on land, you can do so in a few places in Khao Lak. Interestingly, many of these spots have graffiti by Thailand's well-known artist Alex Face – who apparently often visits "this little surf village".

Bangsak Beach Skate Park by Garang: This was Phang Nga's first surf skating rink. Bright red surface decorated with coral patterns. The builder created this to his personal preference to simulate wave ramp surfing. Next to it is a stylish café: Garang Artisan Ice-Cream, which serves homemade ice cream with local flavours. Skate lessons and boards for hire.
Boeing Skate Park: Behind the bus station in Takua Pa. A small riverside park with a 20m wave track, the longest in the area. It has an Alex-Face graffiti with skating bunny girl Mardi.
The Board Factory: Approx. 200 m after the junction to Memories Beach on the sea side. Not only can you skate here, but you can also see how Sunova and Suns boards are made. The brand is world-renowned. Café and shop included. Alex Face Graffiti of a bathing Mardi. 💻 sunovasurfboards.com/en/the-board-factory
Memories Beach Bar Skate Park: Practice surfing the perfect concrete wave before hitting the real waves next door. Surf and skate lessons by local surfers.
Laybay Skate Park: New park at La Vela Hotel in Bang Niang. Surf and skate lessons. Close to the beach.

Fishing / sport fishing

There is a lot of water around Khao Lak (both salt and fresh water) and Thailand has much to offer in terms of fishing. The locals fish to earn a living and are often seen fishing: from the Sarasin Bridge, which is a popular spot, from piers and from fishing boats (small and large). Sport fishermen find some of the most difficult species in Thailand, including Exotic "monsters" such as Arapaima, the Giant Mekong Catfish and the big Alligator Gar. Thus, there are tour operators that specialize in fishing excursions in the sea and on lakes.

Fishing Khaolak: 💻 fishing-khaolak.com

Turtles

If you are lucky, you will find turtles in the wild, for example on a diving or snorkelling trip or a transfer with the long tail boat. If this is not the case, you can visit these beautiful animals in the research and breeding stations, of which there are two south of Khao Lak. In 2018 there was a small sensation when, for the first time in about 15 years, a sea turtle laid its eggs on the beach at Khao Lak near The Haven Hotel in Bang Niang. Over 100 turtles have successfully hatched. In the years that followed, the turtles came back! The breeding sites are secured and cordoned off, and if the clutch is located very clumsily, the eggs are collected and taken to the breeding stations.

Phang Nga Coastal Fisheries Research and Development Centre

The Phang Nga Coastal Fisheries Research and Development Centre (also known as **Turtle Heaven**) was founded in 1985. At first it was only a research station and the aim was to breed mussels and shrimps. In 2002 it was reconstructed into the present centre. The aim of the centre is to accommodate, breed and protect a wide range of marine life to. For this purpose, they research the area out in the sea and set the rules for fishing. They also look for ways to get the animals to breed (for commercial purposes).

Here you can have a look at various species of turtles (and fish, crabs, giant clams, starfish and more) in large saltwater tanks made of concrete. It appears a little rough but does the job and the animals that can be found here are special. In the centre are four species of turtles which are endangered today: Green turtle, Riddley turtle, Hawksbill turtle and Leatherback turtle. These are species that can be found in the Andaman Sea, especially around the Similan and Surin Islands. They are hatched and spend the first few months here until they are released when about 8 months old. By donating you can release a turtle on the beach yourself – if you are there at the right time, early March. There are also tanks for the sick and injured animals that they look after and keep there.

The Centre is found on the road along the Thai Muang beach, about 30 km south of Khao Lak. The take off for this road is in the village of Thai Muang on Highway 4 – you drive through the large metal gate (which is next to the Chinese gate) rather than follow the curve of the main road. DG 8.42029, 98.24212 / GMS N 8°25'13.044", E 98°14'31.631"

Sea Turtle Conservation Centre at Phang Nga Naval Base

At Thap Lamu on the **Naval Base** there is the **Royal Thai Navy's Third Fleet Sea Turtle Nursery**. Similar to Turtle Heaven, young sea turtles from different areas of the Andaman Sea are raised here. They are fed and kept until they are strong enough to take care of themselves and then released back to the sea.

The buildings with the tanks are freely accessible to tourists – but you should not touch the sea turtles. You can see several turtle species in different stages of development (mostly green turtles) and some larger specimens that are treated here because of injuries. There are no other sea creatures here like in Thai Muang, but the facility is well maintained, clean, has information boards and exhibits. To get onto the Navy grounds, you must go through the entrance control, where you leave your ID (1 per vehicle is enough and you can also get in as a private person without a group and Thai guide). At the Turtle Heaven, which is located by the sea, you pay 100 baht per person and receive a visitor's pass, which you then hand in when you leave the site.

The Naval Base and the golf course are located a few minutes south of Khao Lak, in front of Lak Hill – on the way to Tab Lamu Pier. DG: 8.58113, 98.23397 / GMS: N 8 ° 34'52.068", E 98 ° 14'2.291"

Right next to the Conservation Centre there is **the boat T 215,** also a tsunami wreck, but not quite as well preserved as the more famous police boat 813.

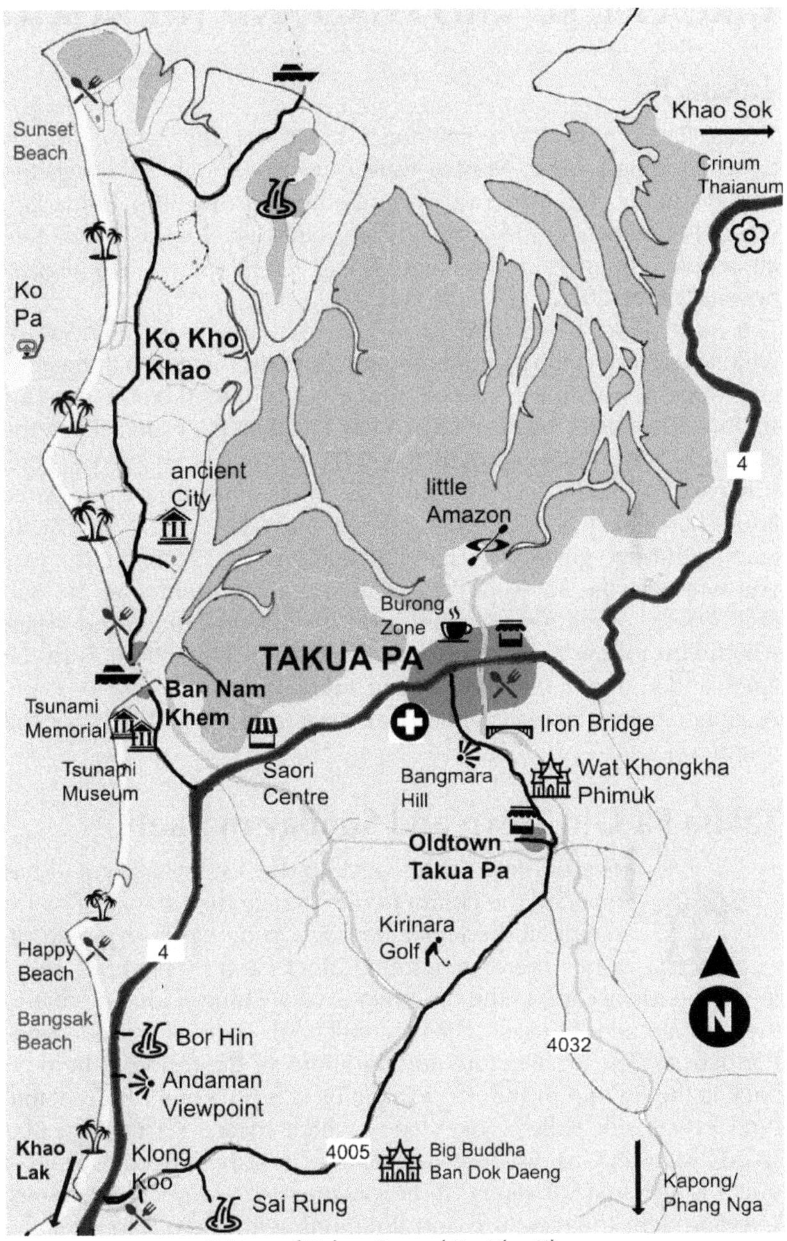

8-Map of Takua Pa and Ko Kho Khao

TAKUA PA, KO KHO KHAO AND THE NORTH

Takua Pa

Takua Pa is now the commercial centre of the region and is correspondingly busy. Most people drive comfortably through the new district (called Yan Yao) and miss the old town (Sri Takua Pa), which is somewhat hidden about 7km southeast. But this is the main attraction – apart from the large Takua Pa Hospital – the biggest hospital in the area.

The most direct route from Khao Lak to Takua Pa is Highway 4, which is well developed and busy and runs past the hospital, the new government buildings, school and the fresh market (at the bus station). The better way from Khao Lak to Takua Pa, especially to the old town, is **the Pakweep road**, the 4005. It is newer and very scenic. It is easy to handle, even by bike, as it has almost no steep parts. FromKhao Lak the 4005 goes off the main road 4 (at km 71.8), leading through green forests and plantations for 23 km. On the way you will pass the Sai Rung Waterfall and a big Buddha at the *Ban Dok Daeng monastery*. Continue on it until you reach the 4032, which you follow to the left (north) to the big T-junction. Turn left again and you're in the **Old town of Takua Pa**.

A songthaew or taxi from Khao Lak costs about 1500 baht for the round trip.

Takua Pa Old Town and Sunday market

The old town dates back to the 13th century and has retained the charm of old Thai culture. It is well worth seeing and compact enough to be easily explored on foot – there are about 2 blocks at a street about 300m long. The townscape in the old town is very Chinese looking due to the old arcade houses. The architectural style is called Sino-Portuguese. The architecture and traditions of the residents here go back to the tin mining industry. Takua Pa was built in 43 B.C., at that time it was still called Tok Kloa – which means Cardamom (the spice). After tin was discovered here, the city experienced its heyday under King Rama VII. Many Chinese came here to work in the mines. They brought their culture and traditions with them. House style, decorations, Chinese temples and altars, Chinese lanterns, mooncakes, the big vegetarian food festival "Jia Kew Ong Chai" in

September or October (according to the lunar calendar). Every second or third year in September, the city centre is flooded up to a meter high by the Takua Pa river. If you look closely, you will find the measuring sticks for the water depth on some buildings. The building fabric suffers from this, but the houses retain a certain morbid charm. With many wall paintings, Chinese house shrines and the work and dedication of the people living here, it is a real gem. It looks even more beautiful since the annoying overhead lines in front of the building fronts were finally removed at the end of 2022.

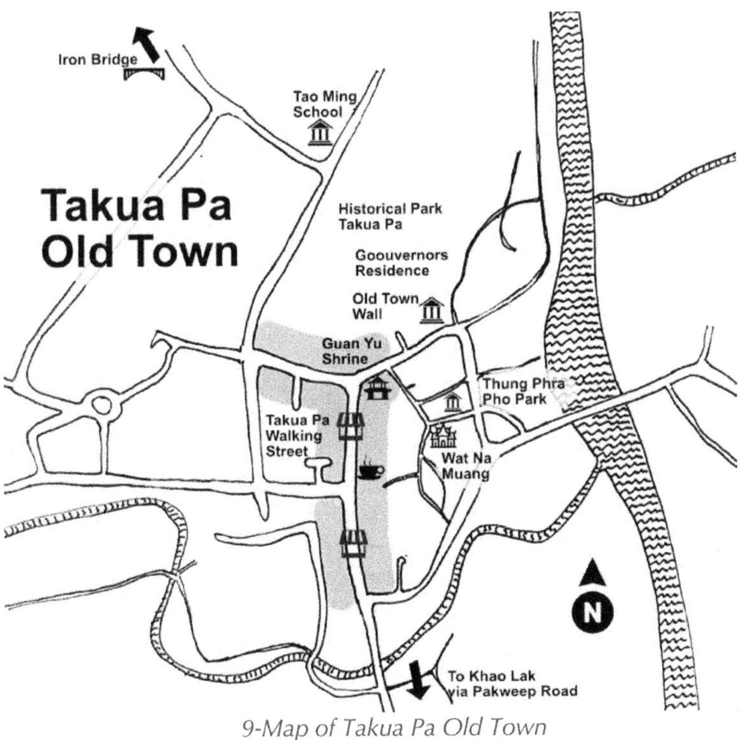

9-Map of Takua Pa Old Town

In the old town, at the end of the market street, there is a Chinese temple, the **Guan Yu Shrine** – if you are around during the Chinese New Year, you should pay it a visit. Another, newer Chinese temple can be found just outside the old town. Behind the old town, you can always find a parking space at **Thung Phra Pho Park**, the historical park of Takua Pa, and you can take a look at the mighty **engine of a tin mining ship** that years ago sifted through the sand for tin off the coast – one of the reasons why Khao Lak is said to have such fine sand. In a barn near the Thai temple **Wat Na Muang**, you will come across various old Buddha statues from the old temple that stood here, and on its pillars you will find the high water marks and dates of the floods of previous years. In the nearby **historical park** there are **remains of the old city wall** and the **old governor's residence**. The **old school building** of the **Tao Ming School** is also worth a look.

Takua Pa Sunday Market

A historic **street market** takes place in Old Takua Pa every Sunday afternoon. The Sunday Market is promoted as Takua Pa Walking Street and takes place from 3 pm to 8 pm. It is not limited to the high season anymore. Don't miss this, while you are in the area!
It is worth strolling through and tasting some unusual snacks, seeing how craftsmen carve soap or make batik or the intricate shadow figures. This is not a souvenir market though, there are more food stalls there.

Takua Pa Vegetarian Festival

Annual nine-day celebration beginning on the evening of the 9th lunar month of the Chinese calendar (in October or November). It celebrates the belief of the Chinese society that abstinence (from eating meat, chicken, seafood and dairy products) during the 9th lunar month helps to maintain health and mental strength while honoring the Taoist gods and ancestors. During the 9 days, participants in the festival wear only white. The festival consists of parades (often starting from **Guan Ou Shrine**) on the 1st and 9th days of the festival. Fireworks are used to drive away bad spirits. There is also fire walking and some have their bodies and cheeks pierced with sharp objects – but it is not quite as "graphic" as down in Phuket.

Boon Soong Iron Bridge – Khok Kanoon Iron Bridge

The old and narrow 200 m long iron bridge was built by the Boon Soong family for their tin miners in 1968 to cross the river Takua Pa to come to work. The bridge is made almost entirely of iron from old tin mining ships. It is privately owned but open to visitors (except the derelict factory on the other side, which is surrounded by a high fence). Today it is still frequently used by the local population (by

Chinese Temple

Wat Khongkha Phimuk

Old Town Takua Pa

Sundaymarket Takua Pa

Bangmara Hill, Dredger Café

Boon Soong Bridge

foot and by scooter) and is now also a tourist attraction. The crossing is somewhat adventurous, since the iron plates already have quite thin spots and holes, although it seems to have been renovated nine years ago, in 2557 according to Thai calendar. With a little luck you can watch water buffalo and herons from the bridge. Addendum 2025: trees (palm trees) were planted in the dry riverbed.
On the road between Old Town and New Takua Pa.
DG 8.85317, 98.35402 / GMS N 8°51'11.412", E 98°21'14.472"

Bangmara Hill and Dredger Café

The new viewing platform on Bangmara Hill directly opposite the Iron Bridge. It belongs to the Dredger Café – and is a somewhat curious mixture of a colourful plaster animal figure park, a coffee shop on several floors with a view, suspension bridges and many Instagram photo points. The most famous is the big white hand, but it also has a door to heaven and colourful frames. You can see the iron bridge from above and otherwise have a good view over the beautiful countryside. To get up, you pay 60 baht per person down at the road to climb the 200 or so steps (or a bit more if they drive you up). Part of the entrance fee is deducted when you buy drinks in the café above. The drinks are fine, the view is good. Some caution is required if you are traveling with small children: typically in Thailand there are no barriers and the like.

Wat Khongkha Phimuk

A temple with a lot of bling-bling! The Buddhist temple near Takua Pa captivates with its pomp and shiny exterior. In addition to the classic red-gold temple in Thai style, the Chedi next to it is completely gold plated on the outside and equipped with mirror mosaic on the ceiling and the interior walls. The builders apparently are from India, the Buddha images on the walls have a typical corny Indian style. Between Old Town and New Takua Pa.
DG 8.84074, 98.36307 / GMS N 8°50'26.664", E 98°21'47.051"

Saori Foundation Centre

This facility was established after the tsunami to provide a source of income for women who have lost their husbands. Everyone is welcome here from Monday to Saturday. You can watch the women at work and buy the finished products. They are not only pretty, but it also serves a good cause. The colourful range of woven fabrics and pretty designs includes T-shirts, caps, bags, pillows and toys. They also supply the local markets. The fabric is made on a handloom, each one is unique – there are no templates.

The Saori Centre is located north of Khao Lak and close to Takua Pa. From the main road 4, turn left shortly after leaving Ban Muang. Go through the official looking entrance, the Saori Workshop is on the left. DG 8.84783, 98.29471/ GMS N 8° 50' 52.188", O 98° 17' 40.955"

facebook.com/saorifortsunamithailand

Wat Samnak Song Daeng – Big Buddha of Takua Pa

The monastery and big buddha on the hill are located at the road 4005 between Khao Lak (Sai Rung Waterfall) and Takua Pa Old Town. It was built between 2018 and 2021 – even though they had to re-gild the Buddha statue in 2019 due to rain damage.

Very impressive are the large Naga stairs with the multi-headed snakes, the one on th left in gold, the one on the right in white mother of pearl. From the top you have a nice view of the hilly wooded hinterland. DG 8.75989, 98.3203 / GMS N 8°45'35.604", E 98°19'13.08"

Kwan Puk–Tree Tunnel

Touted as a viewpoint, this tree tunnel is located on the Road 401 between Takua Pa and Khao Sok. The road here runs under overhanging trees, the sight is especially interesting when they are in bloom or in the morning fog. DG 8.8047669, 98.380524 GMS N 8° 48' 17.161". E 98° 22' 49.886"

Takuapa Mangroves – „little Amazon"

They call the area "little Amazon" because the mangroves and watercourses are said to be reminiscent of the South American Amazon. From the pier here start guided kayak trips into the channels in the mangroves. You kayak through banyan trees and swamps. On the tour you can observe various birds and see reptiles such as snakes (on the trees), sometimes monitor lizards and frogs and – if you are lucky – monkeys. For being so close to a metropolitan area (Takua Pa), the area is surprisingly natural and biodiverse. Suitable for everyone, including the untrained and children, as you will have a guide doing the paddling.

The mangroves are a half-day excursion that can be booked with tour operators – sometimes combined with longer tours. Alternatively, you can simply take a taxi to take you there, or drive by yourself. 🕒 Daily from 8 am to 5 pm 💻 facebook.com/TK.Amazon

Eating and Drinking at Takuapa

Takua Pa has a diverse range of restaurants that mix Thai cuisine with Chinese and Western cuisine:

Khrua Nong (Khruanong) Restaurant

The acclaimed classic Thai restaurant has an extensive menu and affordable prices. It is run by couple Ae and Nok for 20 years and was mentioned in the Thai Michelin Guide for 3 years in a row. The most popular are the fried shrimp with shrimp paste and the crabmeat omelette. On Main Road 4 through Takua Pa near (opposite) the hospital.

Pun Thong Dim Sum

Original Chinese restaurant, extensive menu with small delicacies that are unusual for us. Slightly higher in price than the Thai average. Takua Pa, near 7-eleven between Main Street and Fresh Market.

The Fifth Steak & Restaurant

Restaurant with a mix of Thai and English (European) food. The "salted pork" Tom Yam is recommended. The steak is okay – but typical for Asia a little too well done. Off Road 4, about 400m east of Takua Pa Hospital.

Burong Zone Takua Pa

Pet cafe with parrots (ara and cockatoo) and other birds (lovebirds). No entry fee if you drink something. You can feed the birds under supervision and pay a food ration of 20 baht as entry to the aviary. Cafe 🕒 10am-9pm. The free-flight bird house is open 10am-6.30pm. Be careful with the jewellery, which the birds apparently like to steal – the signs are only in Thai and the Google translation is amusing ("Warning! Be careful with jewellery! The shop accepts no liability if your wife goes missing"), but the pictures are clear. The birds can make quite a lot of noise – and my wife found the smell in the sales room, where you sit and drink, a bit difficult to get used to. Takua Pa, in the main town, north of main road 4, by a small lake. DG 8.86969, 98.32949 / GMS N 8°52'10.884", O 98°19'46.164"
💻 facebook.com/profile.php?id=100083322455412

Saraan Icecream Homemade

Typical Thai ice cream parlour – with classic flavours that are perhaps a bit unfamiliar to us (lychee, durian) and toppings such as corn kernels, various fruits, blue rice. Served in a cute shop with seating in the garden. Popular with Thais. 🕒 11.30am-5.30pm.
Near the Iron Bridge in Takua Pa.
DG 8.8501034, 98.3489306 /GMS N 8° 51' 0.372", E 98° 20' 56.15"

Kopi Kuapa Café in Takua Pa Old Town

The café in the middle of the old town on the same street where the Sunday market takes place, serves delicious coffee and tea and is perfect for a relaxing break. It's located in a house that is over 100 years old and has an inner courtyard. Don't let the somewhat derelict front put you off. It can get crowded during the Sunday market. In addition to snacks and drinks, you can also enjoy some really fine dining here. They offer a limited number of dishes (on a menu without prices), but they are perfectly cooked, although the portions aren't huge. 💻 facebook.com/kopikuapacafe

Taosor Cake

Taosor cake is a popular dessert in Takua Pa. It is like the Chinese mooncake, but smaller. Mooncake is a Chinese pastry. They usually consist of baked, thin, fine puff pastry around a sweet, dense filling with several whole salted egg yolks in the centre, symbolizing the full moon. Less commonly, steamed or deep-fried mooncakes are also served. Traditional ones contain an imprint of the Chinese character for longevity or harmony, the name of the bakery and the filling as well as decorations such as moons, flowers, rabbits (symbolizing the moon). The production is complex, which is why they are considered a rare delicacy. You can try it on foodie tours, for example at the *Tuangarat bakery*, which makes and sells the popular pastry. A family business that makes them according to a 100-year-old recipe. Or at *Taosor JaeYee* – the shop is closer to the city centre and Mali Café or *Taosor Nantawan* (near the old town).

Ko Kho Khao

North of Khao Lak, almost at the level of Takua Pa, there is an island that is only a 10-minute boat ride from the mainland. On Ko Kho Khao you find the tourists (and families) who are looking for a beach destination in Thailand that is not too hard to reach but is still quiet. Ko Kho Khao is this for sure – the long golden beaches are its main attraction. They look like those further down south in Khao Lak. The water is not as clear or has the animal life that can be found at the Similan or Surin Islands, but you can swim there, walk along the beach and enjoy a romantic sunset. The island is about 16 km long and consists mainly of sandy beaches in the west, flat, grassy hills in the middle and mangroves and canals in the east. There are some hotels and infrastructure with taxis and restaurants. The busiest place is at the pier. In the far north on the island there is a larger (grass) field, which was used by the **Japanese** as an **airfield** during World War II.

Transport

The island is more a place to be than to visit, but you can take the **ferry or water taxi** to the island from **Baan Nam Kem Pier** near Bang Muang Village for little money.
Pier: DG 8.86554, 98.27409/ GMS N 8°51'55.944", E 98°16'26.724"

The price for the short crossing with one of the **small water taxis** is 20 baht per person plus 20 baht for a bicycle/motorbike. Smaller motorcycles cost 60 baht each way; larger motorcycles (150cc and above) must be transported by car ferry. The small water taxis run frequently during the day – you can always find one at the piers to take you across.

For car drivers, there are **two ferries** that operate almost year-round between 7:30 a.m. and 6:00 p.m. The two ferries wait at the piers and depart simultaneously. They often don't have an official timetable; during peak season, they run approximately every 30 minutes to 1.5 hours. In 2024, a timetable was posted: 8:30 a.m., 10:30 a.m., 12:30 p.m., 2:30 p.m., 4:30 p.m., 5:30 p.m. The schedule was displayed on the ferry itself – with a note that it was subject to change. Prices: approximately 200 baht for the car and 20 baht per person – you pay on the ferry. Bookings: +66 61 2088740 / +66 61 1732254.
Nothing works at night, as we found out there – and there is no doctor on the island.

Taxis are available at the pier on Ko Kho Khao and can take you to the resorts or beaches. One-way taxi fares (for up to 5 people): 150 Baht to close resorts, 300 Baht to most other resorts and Hapla Beach, 500 Baht to Sunset Beach and Hula Beach, or 1500 Baht around the

island. Prices are for up to 5 people; each additional person costs 50 Baht more. (Prices as of 2024)
The "Caution water buffalo tip over car" signs on the island are funny. There are plenty of water buffalo in the north... so it's better to keep your distance. We didn't see the deer that were also signposted. The island also has the largest tsunami evacuation route signs in all of Thailand. No wonder, as it is flat throughout. The routes then lead mainly to specially built tsunami shelters: taller house-like structures that are still well maintained today.

Restaurants on Ko Kho Khao

There are restaurants in and next to the resorts (all on the beach to the west), some can be found at the pier in the south and there are some in the north.

Harbour Restaurant Ko Kho Khao

The restaurant right on the pier. Good for waiting and having a drink if the ferry doesn't quite go when you would like... With a view of the harbour and the comings and goings of the water taxis at the pier, the car ferry and the fishing boats.

Narakorn Restaurant on Ko Kho Khao

It's open again in 2024 (even if Google says otherwise). Located in the north of the island right on a small lake with an adventurous suspension bridge you can get good food and drinks here and see the colourful birdlife: bee-eaters, kingfishers, cormorants, and white herons.

Sunset Beach Restaurant

The beach in the north of the island is yellow, sand throughout. There is some good infrastructure here such as loungers, a beach restaurant, showers, toilets – everything is clean and well maintained. There are swings and Instagram photo points on the beach itself. Very attentive employees who also help if you have a jellyfish accident. (Unfortunately, there were plenty of them when we visited there). It's also open in the evenings – but like everything on the island, it closes early. 🕒 Daily 9 am to 8 pm. Worthwhile as a destination by bike or scooter from Khao Lak. It takes just under 2 hours one way by bike). To the left of Sunset Beach, the bungalow complex (*Cousin Resort*) has been completed, so there is now accommodation here.

Sunee Restaurant

Alternatively, in the north and inland is this signature Thai restaurant, highly acclaimed by visitors for the fine dining. It is open until 11 pm in the evening.

Pirate Restaurant

A quaint bar and restaurant located in the middle of the island, serving Thai food and excellent burgers and pizzas. Prices may be a bit higher. Open from 3 pm.

Ban Thung Tuk Ancient City

Only the remains of an excavation site are visible of the historically important site. Artefacts were found on Ko Kho Khao, which were clearly not from the region but imported, which suggests that Thung Tuk (or Mueng Thong) was an important port and a centre for international trade between China and the Middle East in the 7th to 9th or 10th century. Thung Tuk was a transfer point from the large sea ships to smaller boats that were needed to cross the country via river. The artefacts that were found here include Chinese Tung ceramics and porcelain, Persian turquoise, glassware from the Middle East and the Mediterranean region and stone beads from the Middle East or India. Unfortunately, you won't see anything on Ko Kho Khao – what has not been sold can be found in in museums, such as the collection of the National Museum in Phuket. There might be more beneath the ground, but there is obviously no money for further excavation. The excavation site on Ko Kho Khao is easy to find: Take the one road from the port north. Keep to the right at the big junction soon afterwards and continue until you see a faded sign that leads to a small, paved road to the right. Follow this to the end of the path. Follow this until you are in front of two (unfortunately dilapidated) small buildings: the Archaeological Information Centre. Inside it has information boards that provide information about the site and the excavation. If there was any other exhibition material, it has unfortunately disappeared. There is also nothing left of the excavation in the area itself.

DG: 8.89427, 98.28113, GMS: N 8°53'39.372", E 98°16'52.068"

Ban Nam Khem Pier

Ko Kho Khao Pier

Mangroves

Tam Nang im Si Phang Nga Ntl Park

Biking on Ko Kho Khao

According to some, Ko Kho Khao is **one of the best bike destinations** in the Khao Lak area. A round trip on the island makes for a nice day trip with its miles of sleepy, traffic-free roads and paths, endless deserted beaches and shallow grassy plains. The hilly north-east zone has more challenging terrain with forested areas and gravel roads: perfect for discovering mountain bikers. Bring enough water with you along with a map or the smartphone.

In the north: towards Ranong

Tajood Canoe / Thajood

A (new) alternative to Little Amazon, far less known and visited. Tajood Canoe, northeast of Takua Pa offers guided kayak tours through the mangroves. You'll see crabs, monkeys, snakes, etc. Just go and ask. Northeast of Highway 4 in the mangroves. Coordinates: 8.89403, 98.36858 / GPS: N 8°53'38.508", E 98° 22' 6.887" Tel: +66 82 275 3527

Wat Bang Wan, Bangwan Temple

A small, elegant white temple on the way to Si Phang Nga Waterfall. It's new – we were lucky enough to be there during the temple's consecration, specifically the ceremony of the nine Nimit stones. These are round, consecrated, black stones that are buried at the perimeter of the temple grounds – and one is placed inside the temple itself. A lot of money is collected during such a temple festival. You can buy artificial flowers and gold leaf, decorate the stones with gold leaf, and thus do something for your karma. Located next to Highway 4 between Takua Pa and Ranong. At the entrance to the complex, you'll see a depiction of a Nimit stone, along with an oversized axe. DG 8.9709, 98.40058 / GMS N 8°58'15.24", E 98°24'2.088"

Crinum Thaianum Bang Wan Village

Known as the Thai Water Onion, the rare plant grows submerged in water, producing long leaves and lily-like white flowers. It only grows naturally in Phang Nga / Ranong in Thailand – but it is sold

worldwide as an aquarium plant. In the *Bang Wan Village* you can visit them and other rare plants in the area.
Between Takua Pa and Sri Phang Nga National Park.
DG 8.97346, 98.41145 / GMS N 8°58'24.456", E 98°24'41.22"
facebook.com/CrinumThaianumBangWanVillage

Tam Nang Waterfall in the Sri Phang Nga National Park

A real find: the waterfall in the Sri Phang Nga National Park, 30 minutes north of Khao Lak. Take Highway 4 through Takua Pa. Where it divides, you do not go to the right (to *Khao Sok* National Park) but proceed straight ahead in the direction of *Ranong*. About 40 km north of *Takua Pa* there is another National Park: Sri Phang Nga. It seems tourists have not yet discovered the park, although the most fantastic waterfall is there. The way to the National Park is well signed and goes off Highway 4 to the right. The road gets quite narrow when you proceed into the park, but do not let that put you off. There is an entrance fee (150 - 300 baht). At the main entrance there is a sign that the waterfall is located about 1.5 km further, but you can drive most of the way to it. Proceed until you reach a parking lot, then follow the well-signed footpath down to the river, where a lot of fish are waiting for you. Unfortunately it is not allowed to feed them anymore. After a walk of about 10 minutes up and down through the green jungle you get to the large Sri Tamnang waterfall, which is 63 meters high (according to the park site) and the largest in the area, including Phuket.
Amazingly, it is visited very sparsely, besides us there were only a few locals. We had the waterfall to ourselves for over an hour, until at about 12 o'clock a few more Thai visitors did show up. You can swim in the rock pool below the waterfall with the same big fish as in the river below. The waterfall is worth a visit, even if you must walk a bit more. DG 8.99635, 98.46823 / GMS N 8°59'46.86", E 98°28'5.628"

Kuraburi Pier

At the pier you can observe local life and activities of the fishermen. More fishing boats are anchored here than in Ban Nam Khem and Tap Lamu together. The popular pier for smaller boats is the starting point for tours to Surin and the Similan Islands, Koh Phra Thong, and Koh Ra with its secluded beaches. Several tour operators and an information centre, where you can book excursions, are located there. However, it's not crowded with tourists. Greenview Tour 💻greenviewtour.com

🚣 The pier is located approximately 70 km north of Khao Lak, reachable in 1.5 hours by car. DG 9.22676, 98.37507 /GMS N 9° 13′ 36.336″, E 98° 22′ 30.251″,

Thalay Wak Nuat Mungkon – the Dragons Back Dune

The new and still largely unknown attraction consists of a 3 km long natural sand dune in the sea, which is only accessible at low tide. The name means something like dragon back lake barrier. The natural dam curves in the sea for 3 km. The sand is extremely fine and soft to walk on. You can visit it from nearby *Kuraburi Pier* by boat, reaching the dune after a 20-minute boat ride. Watch the tide if you want to walk on it.

Ko Phra Thong

Phra Thong is a small island above Ko Kho Khao. The name "Golden Buddha Island" comes from a legend according to which a golden Buddha statue was stolen by pirates and buried somewhere on the island. It was never found. Today it is one of the last unspoilt coastal areas in Thailand with 15km of mostly uninhabited white sand beach. The interior of the island is reminiscent of an African savannah, the landside part has mangrove forest. Access is via Khuraburi and a longtail boat ride through the mangroves (1 hour, price abut 1700 Baht one way). There are a few resorts and bungalows on the northern part of the beach, the accommodations are simple and small, some without air conditioning, all-day electricity or hot water: *Moken Ecovillage Resort* (💻mokenecovillage.com) and *Baba Ecolodge*. Eco-tourism is a priority. Dining is available at the resort's restaurant, or at restaurants and bar outside. The island is the starting point for kayak tours in the mangroves and snorkelling and diving trips to the nearby Surin Islands and almost untouched coral areas.

More attractions in the north:

Ban Nam Khem Tsunami Memorial – by the sea near the pier to Ko Kho Khao.

Ban Nam Khem Tsunami Museum – the new museum.

Saori Center for Tsunami Victims – buy handmade souvenirs for a good cause.

Laem Son and Koh Kham National Park, 157 km north of Khao Lak. In the sea with 15 islands 6 km along the coast between Ranong and Phang Nga. A total of about 100 km of coastline. Highlights: mangroves, beaches, islands, snorkelling. Admission: adults 200 baht, children 100 baht.

Thung Nang Dam - a little islandwith secluded sandy beaches and only camping accomodation.

Tours to the north can be easily combined with a visit to the old town of Takua Pa or with attractions around Takua Pa such as Little Amazon, Boon Song Iron Bridge, etc.

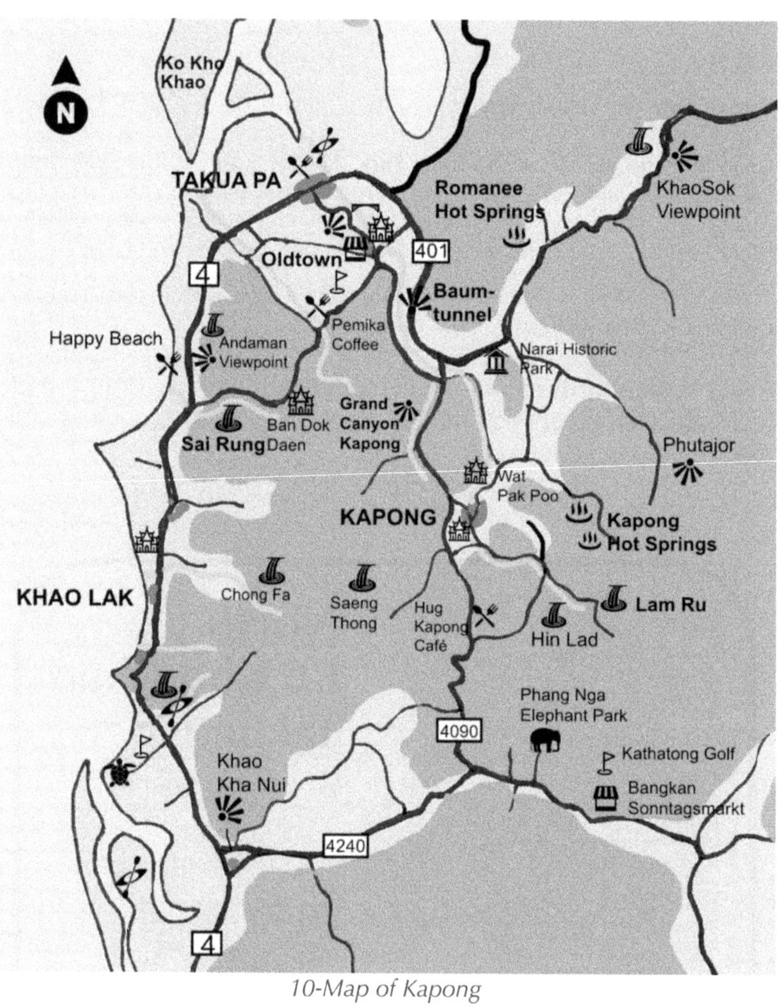

10-Map of Kapong

KAPONG

Kapong is the name of the district in the Phang Nga Province that is located inland behind Khao Lak. It was named after a natural canal, the Khlong Kapong, that runs through the area. Between Khao Lak and Kapong lies a range of hills that cannot be crossed. The whole area is very natural and unspoilt and few tourists find their way here. The attractions are advertised for Thai visitors – and are also worthwhile for tourists from abroad who want to see more of the original Thailand.

The village of Kapong

Kapong itself is a very original Thai village, nestled around the river/natural canal of the Kapong. In the morning you go shopping in the fresh food market. There's a 7-eleven and a gas station.

Sunday Pak Tak Market

Unlike other Sunday markets in the area, Kapong's Sunday market takes place early in the morning and often in the fog. Few tourists venture there, yet it's quite an experience. DG 8.71704, 98.42395 /GMS N 8°43'1.344", E 98°25'26.22"

Hug Kapong Café

Cute café in a photogenic white hut – perfect for a stopover en route to Kapong, Lamru Waterfall or the Hot Springs. Beautiful view of the countryside from the open seating platform, fine pastries (homemade) and drinks (hot or cold). Both to drink here or to take away.
Off 4090, just north of the Lam Ru Waterfall turnoff.
DG 8.64771,98.40959/ GMS N 8°38'51.756",0 98°24'34.523"

N Plai Wa Café

A coffee house in the middle of a small lake with water lilies. Parking spaces (free) for motorcycles and cars, Campsite next to it. Modern, new coffee house on a platform in the lake, with various seating options next to it. In addition to coffee and tea specialties and soft drinks, there are homemade pastries and snacks. Free WiFi. A pretty and well-located stopover. On Road 4090 between Kapong and Takua Pa. DG 8.72878, 98.38339 /GMS N 8° 43' 43.608", E 98° 23' 0.204"

Lam Ru Waterfall

The quite pretty and easily accessible Lam Ru Waterfall is located 35 km from Khao Lak, near the village of Kapong. It is part of the Lam Ru National Park, which stretches from the coast to here.
The seven-tiered waterfall has its source in the Kapong Channel and is embedded in bamboo, rattan, palm and fern forests. It carries water all year round. A narrow footpath on the right takes you to the top step, where you can also swim. This step is completely horizontal and resembles a paddling pool.
From the 4090 through Kapong, turn onto the small, paved side road (3045) – the path is only marked in Thai. After 4.5 km the sign 'Lumru Waterfall 800 m' points right onto a narrow concrete road. You drive to the small parking lot at the national park station. Here you would have to pay an entrance fee for the Lam Ru National Park, but mostly nobody is to be seen. After a two-minute walk on the right past the small dam you come to the waterfall.
DG 8.43654, 98.30888 / GMS N 8° 26′ 11.544″, E 98° 18′ 31.968″

Hin Lahd Waterfall

Hin Lahd waterfall is located 8 km north of Lam Ru waterfall. It is fed by three rivers. Apart from the crystal-clear waters and the rocky back wall that looks like it was built with bricks, the waterfall offers nothing spectacular. It is a meeting place for the children of the neighbouring villages, who come here to cool down in hot weather.
DG 8.65697, 98.46211 /GMS N 8°39′25.092″, E 98°27′43.595″

Sang Thong Waterfall (Kapong)

There are 3 waterfalls at this location – west of the town of Kapong. The falls are medium sized and surrounded by a shady forest. On some of the 11 steps you can swim all year round. To get here, coming from the south on the 4090, turn right almost opposite Kapong Hospital. Follow the road to the end, even after it is no longer paved. You cross 3 bridges. At the end of the road there is a small open space next to the river. The falls are on the right. To get to the first fall, cross the river and follow the path next to it.

Tubing at Kapong

You can (if there is enough water) float down the river on tires for 40 minutes. This is offered along with other activities such as jungle

trekking, bamboo coffee drinking, waterfall and lunch (and possibly elephant bathing) by Kapong Tubing Nature Tour:
kapongnaturetour.com

Wat Inthaphum

The classic temple has a resplendent Chedi stupa and Naga snake staircase.

Wat Pak Mok

The temple complex a little further north has a beautiful gate to the street, a thick, golden Chinese Buddha and plaster figures such as a Thai Buddha overgrown by a tree. DG 8.71704, 98.42395 / GMS N 8°43'1.344", O 98°25'26.22"

Kapong Hot Springs – Plai Poo Hot Springs

The hot springs are called Plai Phu or Plai Poo by the locals. They are located inland, have their source in a small river and are almost completely undeveloped – apart from a few stones in the river that have been piled up to form troughs for bathing. There is now a stall by the parking lot where you can buy drinks – and eggs with a basket for cooking in the springs. 4 eggs cost 22 baht – cooking time is 20 minutes. The basket is to be returned later. The hot springs are anything but overcrowded. Even on weekends you meet mostly local visitors. Take your bathing gear, if you want to soak in them.

Follow the good road 3002 north at the northern end of Kapong, then follow the "Hot Spring" signs (which are occasionally amusingly misspelled) onto 5014, which turns right. Stay on the road until it ends somewhat abruptly in a sandy path. The hot springs aren't signposted any further, but if you get out at the parking lot, it's a right turn down to the hot springs.
DG: 8.66979 98.47132 / GMS N 8° 49' 11.244" E 98° 28' 16.752"

Lam Ru Wasserfall

Kapong Hot Springs

Grand Canyon Kapong

Wat Pak Mok

Kwan Puk Baumtunnel

Grand Canyon Kapong

The gorge or canyon is not as impressive as the name suggests, but it is one of the local attractions. The river has dug its way meters deep into the soft ground here and has formed steep, jagged walls. In the riverbed you can occasionally see people panning for tin. Where it is wet enough, rare pitcher plants are growing.

Accessible via a gravel road, without rain, this should also be doable with a normal car.

DG 8.74998, 98.38038 / GMS N8°44'59.928", 098°22' 49.368"

Narai Historical Park

The Park and Temple Wat Narai Nikaram Park off the 401, the road to Khao Sok, contains antiques alongside bric-a-brac from the history of "Ta Go La", which is the old name of Takua Pa. There used to be a lot of trade here with India. The Vishnu and Lksmana statues are replicas, the originals are now in the National Museum in Phuket. According to information, a stone inscription shown here is between 1300 and 1400 years old. It was found at the top of Leang Mountain.

DG 8.77569, 98.41581/ GMS N8°46'32.484", 098°24' 56.915"

Other sights in the Kapong district

Phutajor – the viewpoint over the sea of fog belongs to the province of Kapong – but is located in the Klong Panom National Park behind another (impassable) range of hills even further east than the hot springs.

Rommannee Hot Springs – public hot springs with infrastructure on the way to Khao Sok.

Tree Tunnel Kwan Puk – At 401 at level with Takua Pa. Most beautiful if passed from the southern side. Described in the chapter Takua Pa.

Kapong has a **Sunday market** which, unlike other Sunday markets, takes place early in the morning and often in fog.

Kapong has a Sunday market that, unlike other Sunday markets, takes place early in the morning and often still in the fog: Sunday Pak Mak Market. Hardly any tourists find the way here, but it's quite an experience. DG 8.71704, 98.42395 /GMS N 8°43'1.344", O 98°25'26.22"

Half Day Tour Kapong:

A nice half-day trip through green countryside with interesting attractions off the usual tourist routes. Can be done as a self-drive or by minibus with a Thai driver. Also possible with a motorbike – but then you need to plan more time.

Khao Lak – Kapong: directly via the 4090 or more scenic via 4003 – stopover at Hut Kapong Café – bathe at Lam Ru Waterfall – visit Wat Pak Mok – boil eggs in the Kapong Hot Springs – Grand Canyon of Kapong – Kwan Tree Tunnel Puk – Takua Pa Old Town – have something to eat or drink – return via road 4005 through pretty countryside to Khao Lak.

You can add more sights at Takua Pa and make it a full day trip. The "bling bling temple" Wat Kongha Phimuk, the Iron Bridge and Bangmara Hill with its view are close by, Little Amazon and the Tsunami Museum and Memorial at Ban Nam Khem not much further. Here the return via the main road 4 would be easier.

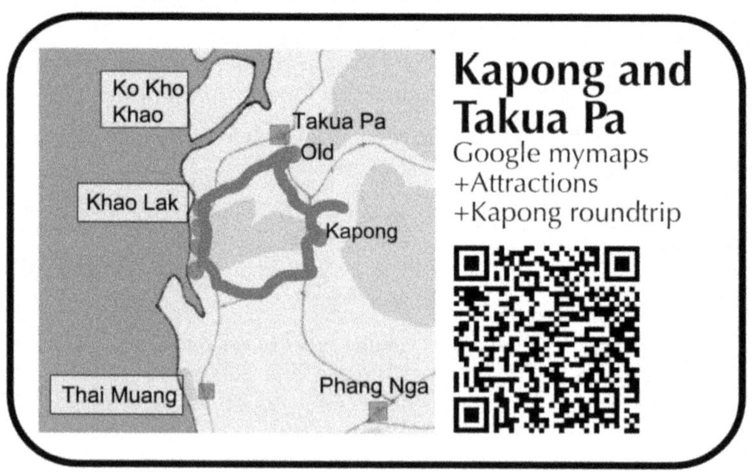

KHAO SOK NATIONAL PARK

The very green National Park with a lake in a fantastic landscape is a popular tourist destination just north of Khao Lak (it takes about one hour to get there) and Phuket (about two hours) and is also visited from Krabi and Ko Samui. The focus is on eco-tourism and many activities are offered: **elephant riding (and washing), jungle-trekking on foot, canoeing, bamboo raft riding, tubing, boat safaris** ...

The 739 km2 large national park is covered by **the oldest rainforest** in the world, contains **steep limestone hills** (between 400 to 960 m high), deep valleys, breath-taking lakes, dark **stalactite caves**, wild animals and rare plants such as **the Rafflesia** – a very large carnivorous flower. You can see these wild animals there: hornbills, elephants, Asian oxen, monkeys, gibbons, snakes ... The climate is often more humid and rainier than further south, even than in Khao Lak. Visits to the park concentrate on two areas: one **around the headquarters** (Khao Sok Village) and the other 67 km away at **Khao Sok Lake (Cheow Lan Lake)**.

The park entrance fee is 200 baht (per day) at the headquarters and 300 at the Pier for adults, 100 baht for children up to 14 years.

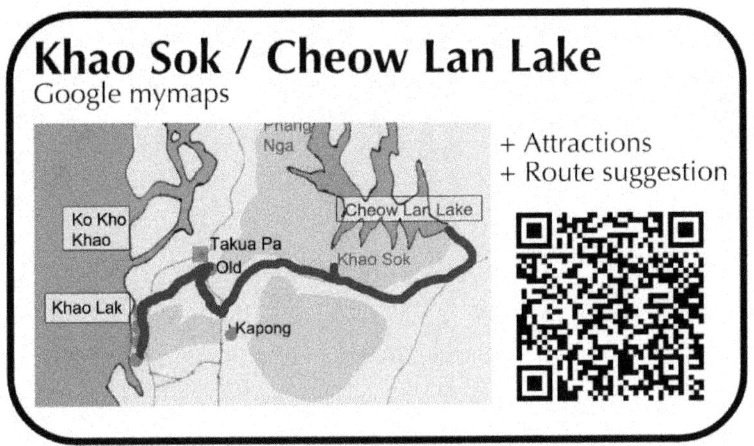

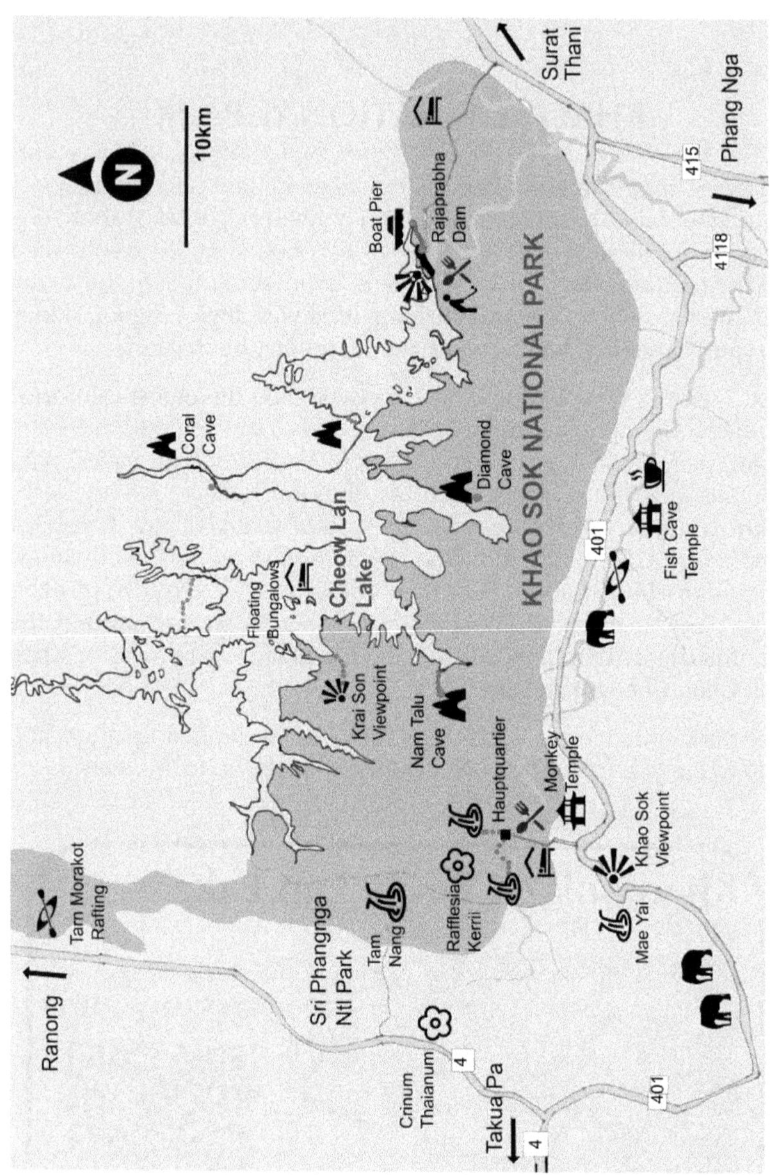

11-Map of Khao Sok and Cheow Lan Lake

Accommodation in Khao Sok

Accommodation is plentiful and of varying quality. You can either book directly – they also organize and offer tours and excursions – or you can book through providers in Khao Lak or Phuket. The park headquarters and visitor center stopped doing this in 2025. However, visitors must register there and pay the park fee.

Visitor Centre / Park Headquarters:

DG 8.91542, 98.52809 / GMS N 8°54'55.512", E 98°31'41.124"

There is a **main street** to the Khao Sok (headquarters) where most of the guest houses and bars are located. There is only one ATM and one gas station on that road and also a pharmacy.

Advance reservations for accomodation are usually not necessary. That also applies to the **tree houses** and glamping, only if you want to stay on in a **swimming bungalow** on the Cheow Lan Lake, it is advisable to book well in advance.

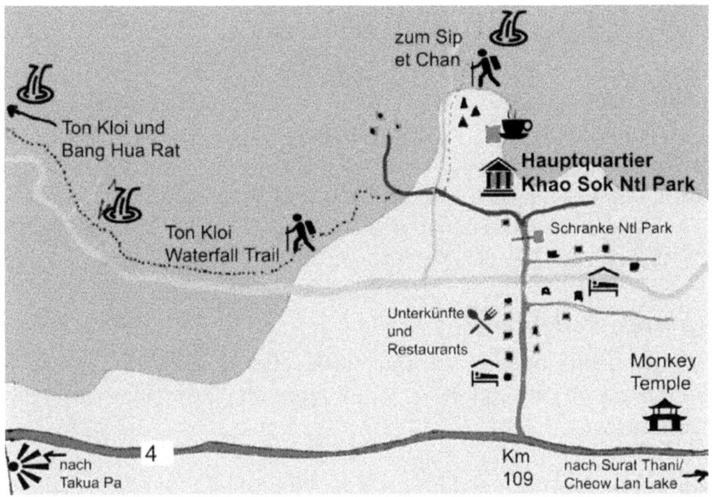

12-Map of the area around the Headquartes of Khao Sok

Restaurants at the Khao Sok

Most of the accommodation here have their own restaurants. The cuisine is a mixture of Thai and European dishes.

Nongsaw Thai Food

Affordable Thai food, ranging from mild to spicy. Friendly owner/chef.

Thai Herb

Cheap, good food and fresh shakes. The restaurant is clean and has an amazingly large menu. The food is Thai but adapted to the western taste (not very spicy).

Chao Italian Restaurant

Located just 100 meters from the park entrance on the main street. The best pizza we have ever had in Thailand – thin crust and from the stone oven. The restaurant has a newer branch further up with the same menu.

Khaosok Sunlight

A restaurant with a view, very close to the Khao Sok Viewpoint. Friendly owner, a great place for a break on the go, or to enjoy the sunrise or sunset in Khao Sok with a view. Open all day.

Bridge Hill Café

The Café in the middle of Khao Sok next to the bridge of the Road 401 over the river Sok is hip, offers great views of the landscape (including photo points like a white staircase to the sky) and besides dessert they also offer normal Thai food and accommodation (glamping). 💻 facebook.com/bridgehiicafe
DG 8.8501034, 98.3489306 / GMS N 8° 51' 0.372", E 98° 20' 56.15"

Wangwa Hope Restaurant

Thai and European food, pizza and steaks. Good selection and well prepared. Restaurant on road 3062 to the reservoir / lake. 💻 wangwa-hope-restaurant.business.site

Kitchen Guilin

A quite large restaurant that caters for tourist groups near the lake. It is in the park, at the western end of the lake, near the golf course and the pier, where you can rent longtail boats. View of the dam and the lake. 💻 guilin99.business.site

Khao Sok Ntl Park

Hiking and Things to see in the Ntl Park

Hikers should wear shoes that are sturdy and firmly closed. Sandals invite leeches which occur on the ground and in the bushes in the park. The use of insect repellent is also recommended to fend off the leeches to some exent. A look at the weather forecast is important: some hiking trails and especially cave visits cannot take place when it rains. The rapidly rising water is dangerous. Many trails start from the visitor centre, others from the 401 road. Most require a guide, which is available from headquarters.

Ton Kloi Waterfall Trail:

The Sok River's single-tiered waterfall is about 7 km from the HQ. The way there is the main trekking path of the Khao Sok national park. The first 3 km before the checkpoint on a wide path can be walked without a guide. The next 4 km lead to the fall on small paths through the jungle. Along the way there are smaller falls (Wing Hin, Bang Hua Rat), a swimming area (Wang Yao Pool) and small side paths along the river.

Wing Hin Waterfall

The 20 m high fall is about 2.8 km from the HQ on the Ton Kloi Waterfall Trail and before the checkpoint: it can be visited without park admission. It lies on the other side of the Sok River, which you can easily cross here over stones.

Bang Hua Rat Rapids

Located on the Ton Kloi Waterfall Trail, about 3km from HQ. The rapids are not huge, but you can bathe your feet in the water next to the large boulders. Popular for rafting activities.

Tang Nam Gorge

Two high cliffs standing close to each other at the end of the Sok Channel. 6 km away from the headquarters on the Ton Kloi Waterfall Trail.

Than Sawan Waterfall

Sok tributary waterfall 6 km from HQ, next to Ton Kloi Waterfall Trail. The way here is strenuous and the last part goes through the riverbed, which you must wade through.

Sip Et Chan Waterfall

Stair-like waterfall over 11 steps with a large pool where you can swim. 4 km from the headquarters. The way there starts from the northern end of the campsite. The first approx. 500 m lead over a wooden promenade and can be walked without a guide.

Khlong Pae Nature Trail

About 10-12 km east of the headquarters off the 401 starts a 6.5 km long trail that leads to Cheow Lan Lake. You need a guide. The visit to the lake can also be combined with a boat trip and other attractions around the lake.

Bang Hman Trail

Long and demanding but interesting Trail. Steep, then you hike through a river, then in the water through a cave, then back to the ranger station. The path urgently needs a guide and when it rains you are not allowed into the cave.

Rafflesia Kerrii Meijer

Giant flower, approximately 1 m in diameter. It is a parasitic plant that is very rare. It takes 9 months for it to bloom and the flower only keeps about 7 days – so you have to be pretty lucky to see it. It blooms between November and January and is visited on trekking trips.

Mae Yai Waterfall Khao Sok

The only waterfall in Khao Sok National Park that can be reached by car and without a long walk – maybe this is why it is called „grandmother". It is located next to the Suratthani-Takuapa road (at km 113), 5.5 km away from the headquarters. There is no sign, but you can get off the road and park your car. The waterfall is only one-stage, about 30 meters high. Best visited during the rainy season, otherwise there may be little water. You can't swim here.

In the steepest curve in a valley on the way to the Khao Sok National Park. DG: 8.8835, 98.49848 / GMS N 8° 53' 0.6", E 98° 29' 54.528"

Viewpoint Khao Sok – San Yang Roi

The viewpoint is located on the hill directly after the Mae Yai waterfall about 5.5 km west of the main entrance to the park. It is not signed, but you can see the parking from the road 401. Larger tour buses usually pass it, smaller ones stop occasionally. It offers the best view of the green landscape and a good photo opportunity.
DG: 8.88534, 98.50255 / GMS N 8° 53′ 7.224″, E 98° 30′ 9.179″

Wat Tham Phanthurat or Monkey Temple

A temple at Khao Sok National Park (near the HQ) with macaques. Besides the newly built temple there is a cave (more like an overhang) with Buddha statues under one of the steep cliffs. There is a kiosk where you can pay the entrance fee and buy food to feed the resident (mostly friendly) macaque monkeys. Beware of your removable small parts such as glasses or cameras!
DG 8.91157 98.52043 / GMS: N 8° 54' 41.652" E 98° 31' 13.548"

Wat Tham Wararam or Fish Cave Temple

The temple with a tunnel that runs under one of the limestone cliffs, is an insider tip in Khao Sok. For 10 baht you can buy fish food for feeding the colourful fish here and do something for your karma at the same time. To reach the fish, you cross the rock through a cave tunnel to the other side, where a river and a lake with small platforms invite you to linger. Just off the main road, it is easy to reach, for example on the way to Cheow Lan Lake.
DG 8.8501034, 98.3489306 /GMS N 8° 51' 0.372", E 98° 20' 56.15"

Kayaking (or Bamboo-Rafting) on the Sok River

The river Sok is the main river in the Khao Sok National Park. The link road 401 between Takua Pa and Surat Thani is located in its valley and crosses it several times. The river is surrounded by beautiful scenery with high limestone cliffs and greenery. Various activities such as kayaking or bamboo rafting are carried out on and in the river and its tributaries. The river is quite tame in the dry season (high season) and at the end of the dry season in April it may have very little water. On the quiet ride along the river you can enjoy the landscape, see birds and monkeys, various amphibians and reptiles – but no crocodiles, even if the guides sometimes joke about that. Some trips will stop for a tea or coffee (prepared on a fire next to the river) or for a swim. Occasionally there are ropes hanging from the trees, from which you can let yourself drop into the deeper parts of the river or feel like Tarzan. Fun for the whole family!

Zipline / Rope Park

The Tree House Sky Trek at Khao Sok is a zipline with 12 stations. A tour lasts between 45 minutes and 1 ½ hours. It takes place under the supervision of the staff of the Tree House Resort, to which this attraction belongs. It is is located near the entrance on the main road to the Khao Sok headquarters. 💻 khaosoktreehouseresort.com

Emerald Pool at Watershed Forest / Ban Nam Rad Watershed Forest

The place is close to Cheow Lan Lake. We went there after seeing pictures of a natural lake with clear water in the forest. It was... not quite what we expected. It is a public, natural swimming pool in the forest. The path there seems to lead to nowhere and since we took the wrong (second) exit, the last part was unpaved. Tip: follow the sign for the waterfall, not the river. The facility is a local attraction and has been developed accordingly. It attracts many (Thai) visitors, so access has been restricted. Large parking lot (20 baht parking fee), food stalls, coffees, information signs. In the park itself it is forbidden to take with you: food, soap or shampoo and alcoholic drinks. The left path from the parking lot leads through the forest for about 100m. At the stand you pay 100 baht per person to enter the pool (less if you just want to look, more for activities like "rowing"). You are not allowed to take any bags with you – but there are free lockable compartments at the next stop where you can leave your stuff. There is a toilet or changing room, followed by strict entry controls to the "pool area". Another 50m further you finally reach the pool. The Emerald Pool is a natural lake with a white sand bottom, clear water with fish, surrounded by concrete. Somewhere in the back there is the opportunity to go boating and have your photo taken. When we visited in February 2024, we were the only European tourists for miles. The many Thai visitors were dressed classically conservatively – no bikini in sight, and many of the men also wore bathing shirts and hats. DG 8.72878, 98.38339/GMS N 8°43'43.608", E 98°23'0.204"

Rajjaprabha Dam

Cheow Lan Lake

Khao Sam Kloe

Floating Bungalows

Suspension Bridge on the Heart-Shaped Mountain

An unknown landmark near the lake. A long suspension bridge for pedestrians and motorcycles, a temple by the river, a place to eat, campsite. DG 8.71704, 98.42395 / GMS N 8°43'1.344", O 98°25'26.22"

Cheow Lan Lake

Cheow Lan Lake or Khao Sok Lake is a reservoir which is 165 km2 large and about 200 m deep and has a colourful history. Steep limestone cliffs towering up to 900 m out of the water – a similar sight to the Phang Nga Bay, only with fresh water and almost more impressive if that is possible. The dam of the lake was built 1982 to generate electricity for the (quickly) developing region. Thailand's King named it the Rajiaprabha dam – the name means "the light of the kingdom" – in an opening ceremony on his 60th birthday. Except for generating electricity, it also serves as flood control and is used for irrigation and fish farming.

It took about one year for the lake to fill and nearly 400 families from a submerged village had to be resettled. There were projects to resettle the animals by boat and helicopter – but many died because their habitat was so suddenly limited. Nevertheless, many partly endangered species can be found (again) in the national park and the lake today.

You can **visit the lake on your own**. On the lake itself, however, you need a guide because it is part of the national park. Entrance to the park costs 200 baht. Tours are bookable directly at the parking lot and pier to the lake. A private boat with guide is available for about 1500 baht for a 3-hour excursion, accommodating up to 6 people. You should set the price first, otherwise it could rise.

Pier: DG 8.97717,98.8205/ GMS N 8°58'37.812", E 98°49'13.799"

Rajiaprabha Dam

Rajiaprabha Dam – which means light of the kingdom – got its name in an opening ceremony from Thailand's king on his 60th birthday. In addition to the production of electricity, the dam serves as flood control, for irrigation and for fish farming. It took about a year to completely fill the basin and almost 400 families from villages had to be relocated. There have been projects to relocate the animals by boat and helicopter – yet many died because their habitat suddenly was so much smaller. Today there are (again) many wild, partly

endangered species in the national park and at the lake. At the dam itself, there is a lookout with a large parking lot and beautiful views of the dam and the lake. Viewpoint Dam:
DG 8.97247, 98.8057 / GMS N8°58'20.892", E 98°48'20.52"

Khao Sam Khloe

Emerging from the turquoise waters, the three pinnacles of Khao Sam Khloe are the most-photographed attraction on Khao Sok Lake and a must-see. It is also called the Guilin of Thailand as it is reminiscent of the well-known Chinese landscape.

Diamond Cave – Pra Kay Petch Cave

Cave with stalactites right by the lake, about 18 km from the pier. It can only be reached by boat. It is one of the most beautiful and impressive caves in the national park with giant spiders and bats. Take a flashlight with you.

Nam Talu Cave

30 m wide entrance and a small river that leads through the 500 m long stalactite cave. The visit is very adventurous and only feasible in the dry season / when it's not raining, as you wade directly through the running water that partially reaches up to the chest. The cave can only be reached by boat and a 3 km hiking trail from the lake, although it is far from the pier and closer to the headquarter (as the crow flies). Open from December 14th to around May.

Coral Cave – Pakarang Cave

The cave is located on a small side lake next to the Cheow Lan Lake. It can be reached by boat by entering the nearest branch of the reservoir, taking a short hike over the separating hill and then taking the bamboo raft directly to the cave. Despite the effort required, this is one of the most popular caves in the park. Fossil corals were found here and it served as a shelter for communist rebels between 1975 and 1982.

Floating Bungalows

There are floating bungalows on the lake where you can stay overnight – the operators have to be relatives of the original landowners to get a license for it. The bungalows are of varying

quality – from very basic wooden huts (like *Ton Tuey*) to barrel-like floating modern rooms (with toilets on land) and luxury tents on rafts (with toilets inside the tents like the Lake Camp of *Elephant Hills*) … everything can be found here. You get what you pay for, but a stay is always an unforgettable experience!
Watching the sunrise over the steep cliffs and the tranquil lake is an unforgettable experience. You can swim and kayak in the lake and there are evening and morning wildlife viewing excursions.

Selection of accommodations on the lake:
500 Rai Floating Resort: Modern, highly organized, located far back, decorated in dazzling white. The Honeymoon Suite is somewhat awkward because it can only be reached by a noisy water taxi from the main complex.
ToneTeuy Raft House: One of the oldest accommodations, located on a narrow side channel near Nam Talu Cave. Very simple wooden huts without amenities (hard flooring, no electricity, toilet on dry land).
Panvaree Resort: The Greenery: Beautiful location, relatively central to the lake. Well-equipped two-story bungalows.
Elephant Hills Lake Camp: Luxury tents with fans, shower/toilet, and comfortable beds.
Phutawan Raft House: On the same section of the lake as the Elephant Lake Camp, round bungalow-like huts, toilet on dry land, popular with Asian visitors.
Smiley Lakehouse: Very large complex with various bungalows, all connected by a single jetty. Popular with Asian visitors.

Examples of (guided) tours exploring Khao Sok Park:

It should be noted here that (apart from visiting the lake and some trekking tours) you are usually **on the edge of the national park** and not in it. This means the guides do not have to pay any entrance fees. The landscape is still very worth seeing.

Night Safaris

Excursions in the evening or at night, which are offered (with a guide) are exciting. You can watch animals that are nocturnal and cannot be seen during the day. Because of the snakes you shouldn't try it alone.

Jungle Cooking Class

Khao Sok Jungle Cooking Experience offers the opportunity to take a cooking class in the great outdoors at Khao Sok (near the Khlongphanom National Park Gate) and to grill and cook traditional meals over the fire. 💻 facebook.com/junglecoooking

Day trip Khao Sok

Pick up at the hotel. Drive to the Khao Sok with a stop at the local market (in Takua Pa). Elephant riding by a river. Feeding and photographing of the elephants. Stop at the Khao Sok viewpoint. Thai lunch. Afternoon kayaking on the Sok River. Swimming in the Sok River. Visit to a local temple with monkeys. Stop at a waterfall. Back at the hotel at approximately 5 pm.

2-day trip Khao Sok / Park

Pick up at the hotel. Drive to the Khao Sok with a stop at the local market (in Takua Pa). Elephant riding at a creek. Thai lunch. Afternoon kayaking on the Sok River. Swimming in the Sok River. Check in for your Bungalow at the park. Day 2: Trekking in the Khao Sok National Park. Here you have the possibility to see gibbons, langurs, birds and various reptiles. Bathing under the waterfall. Back to the resort and lunch. Ride back after an afternoon rest.

2-day trip Khao Sok / Lake

Drive to the Khao Sok National Park. Stop at the Viewpoint. Visit the headquarters. Drive to Cheow Lan Lake (Ratchaprapa Dam). Ride by longtailboat through the fantastic scenery. Arrive at the Raft House (floating hotel). Thai lunch. Afternoon relaxing at the lake. Guided kayak tour. Dinner at the Raft House. Night Safari on the lake.
Day 2: Kayaking, morning meal at the Raft House. Trekking through the jungle to a cave and a small lake. Lunch and relax at the lake and return to Khao Lak.

Cheow Lan Lake Day Tour

Panorama of the Cheow Lan Lake seen from a longtail boat ride. Hike in the jungle. Bamboo Boat Ride in Hidden Lagoon. Discover a coral cave (with stalactites). Lunch buffet. Kayaking on the lake. Back.

2-day trip Cheow Lan Lake

Transfer. Viewpoint stop. Headquarters visit. Drive to Cheow Lan Lake, take a longtail boat ride through the fantastic landscape. Arrive at the Raft House. Thai lunch. In the afternoon relaxing at/in the lake. Excursions by kayak. Dinner at the Raft House. Night safari on the lake.

Morning: Kayak excursion, breakfast at Raft House. Trekking with a guide through the rainforest to a stalactite cave and a small lake. Relax in the afternoon and drive back.

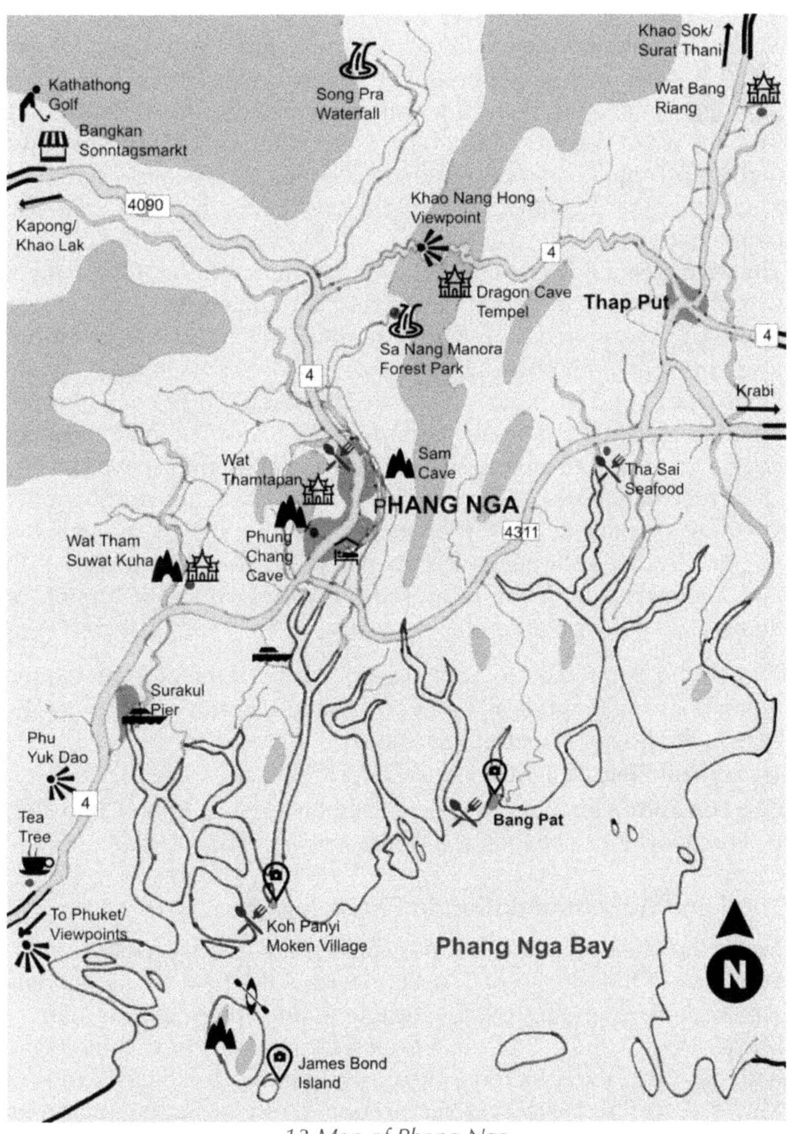

13-Map of Phang Nga

PHANG NGA AND PHANG NGA BAY

The Phang Nga Bay / Ao Phang Nga National Park

This wonderful, large bay (401 km2 is the part of the national park alone) with mangrove forests on the shores and steep karst formations (limestone hills) protruding from the water is only an hour by car from Khao Lak. The best-known part is Ko Tapu – commonly known as James Bond Island – but there are many other beautiful rock formations, caves, beaches and rock paintings.
The Phang Nga Bay is a UNESCO World Heritage Site. Originally it was shaped from the coral deposits of an ancient sea, which was raised by folding and then largely removed again by erosion. It has thus the same origin as Halong Bay in Vietnam with the iconic landscape – and it shows. There are 42 islands in the bay and the unique views attracts many tourists every year. The national park covers an area from land to sea and some islands in the bay. The HQ is in the mangroves south of Phang Nga town but doesn't offer anything of interest nearby apart from a nature trail through the mangroves. The national park is open from October 15th to May 15th and is closed during the rainy season. Admission is 300 baht for adults, 150 baht for children 3-14 years.

Those who don't want to book a guided tour of the bay can simply rent a boat with a guide at a pier on a mangrove arm and explore the bay on their own. Caution: Pay attention to the tides!
Surakul Pier: DG 8.39005, 98.46033 / N 8°23'24.18", E 98°27'37.187"
Ban Hin Romi Pier (directly below Samet Nangshe), **Boon Choo Pier, or Pracharat Pier** between the viewpoints and Phang Nga.

Food and Accommodation in Phang Nga Bay

Inside the National Park: It is possible to stay in a few hotels on Ko Panyii or in the village of Tha Dan, where the park's headquarters are located. Camping on the beach is only permitted as part of booked tours. Since there are no restaurants on the islands in the national park, tours include meals and drinks. The large islands of Kho Yao Noi and Kho Yao Yai are only partly in the national park area and are inhabited, offer hotels, camping, glamping and restaurants.

Kayaking Phang Nga Bay

Ko Tapu - James Bond Island

Ko Panyee

Phang Nga Bay Tour

I would recommend booking a tour or a guide to visit here. An example of a day tour:

In the morning pick up at the hotel is around 8 am and then you drive south – about one hour, to a small pier in the mangroves in Phang Nga Bay. Depending on the tides you ride in a long-tail boat through the mangroves. Not all waterways are open at low tide. The sea here is only a few meters deep – which is why there are rarely high waves in the bay. Nevertheless, it is good to protect your camera and other electrical appliances from the water. You explore James Bond Island, go kayaking, have lunch in the sea gypsy village and back on the mainland you visit the cave temple with monkeys: Wat Suwanakhua. The tour has something for everyone (landscape, culture, local people, good food) so I highly recommend it.

Included in the tour: transfers, national park fees, life jackets (especially for children), lunch and (non-alcoholic) drinks, guide.

Things to bring: sunscreen, hat (at least for the canoe trip, but also otherwise), camera in a waterproof bag, towel, and bathing gear.

There are now tours that start earlier, so you can stop by the viewpoint and see the sun rise over the Phang Nga Bay (and avoid the rush). Or book a private tour into the bay and choose your own stops.

Ko Tapu – James Bond Island

The most famous stop on a tour is Ko Tapu or (as it is called) James Bond Island. The 20 m high rock that stands lonely in the sea was shown prominently in the 1974 James Bond film "The Man with the Golden Gun". But those who hope to find the hiding place or the great Villa of the villain Scaramanga here are disappointed. It even cannot be found in the crevice with the commemorative plaque. A narrow path leads up on the right side and halfway around the island to the remains of a pier (which has been washed away) and a small sandy beach. In the middle of the island a lot of small souvenir shops have been erected, where you can also get ice-cream or something to drink. One should take care not to buy shells and coral on offer here – it is forbidden to take them out of Thailand. You are never alone here ... except maybe if you organize a private tour in the early morning or the evening – after 5 pm.

Kayaking in the Phang Nga Bay

You continue your tour by longtail boat to a canoe station, which consists of a bigger ship fixed near some cliffs with caves. There you can get a canoe and paddle with a guide for about 30 to 45 minutes through the mangroves and caves.

Rock Paintings

On the way with the longtail boat in the bay you pass some paintings on the rock walls: fish, dolphin and geometric structures are recognizable. Unfortunately, the age of the drawings is unknown.

Shell Graveyard

Deposited layers of shells and mother-of-pearl from times past. The place is only accessible to authorized guides and visitors. Right next to it are ancient rock paintings that are attributed to the Khmer and which supposedly show a treasure map to their gold hidden in the bay.

Ko Panyi – Sea nomad village

In the fishing village of Ko Panyi you have a short guided walking tour. The 300-year-old village is almost entirely built on stilts; with only a small part (where the mosque is) standing on the land. On the seaside of the fishing village there is a row of tourist-restaurants and a variety of shops inside. They even have a soccer field on the water! In spite of the precarious location not one of the inhabitants perished in the 2004 Tsunami. Some elders who knew what it means when the sea retracts, warned everybody and the villagers fled to higher ground.

Phang Nga Bay on a Chinese Junk

A trip for romantic moments is the Sunset Dinner Cruise, which is a dinner aboard a Chinese junk in the picturesque Phang Nga Bay at sunset. Pick up from the hotel in the late afternoon. You are driven to the Marina in (northern) Phuket. Dinner is served on June Bahtra, a traditional Chinese junk. In the evening, the bay is practically deserted and provides beautiful views. 💻 asian-oasis.com/june-bahtra

Twilight Sea Canoe (Phang Nga Bay)

Experience Phang Nga Bay at night – if you're lucky, you'll find bioluminescent plankton in the dark sea while paddling through a tranquil lagoon. The excursion also includes sunset over the bay and refreshments. 💻 twilightseacanoe.com

Ko Yao Noi

The "long narrow island" – which is the translation of its name – with its often luxurious accommodation and relative seclusion in the middle of Phang Nga Bay attracts upscale tourists – and also many weddings or honeymooners. Alternatively, you can stay in a homestay with locals. 💻 kohyaohomestay.org. Ecotourism is very important here. The island offers rolling green landscapes, mangrove forests, beaches and Muslim villages whose residents go on with their lives as if the tourists weren't there. The east side is completely covered by trees. A main road encircles the southern part of the island, where all the developed tourist spots are located.

You get there by ferry (once a day) or longtailboat from Phuket (from Bang Rong Pier), landing at Manoh Pier in the southwest; or from Krabi, then you land at Tha Khao Pier on the east coast.

Ko Yao Yai

This is the largest island in the Yao archipelago in Phang Nga Bay. It has sandy beaches, mangroves, rubber plantations and small fishing villages. The island is surrounded by coral and diving sites such as the King Cruiser Wreck and the pillars at Shark Point. Ko Yao Yai is next to the smaller island of Ko Yao Noi, which is better developed for tourism. Yao Yai only has some smaller bungalows and one larger resort. It has a paved road from the pier to Prunai, the largest village on the island, with food stalls and small shops and, since 2016, a 7-Eleven. The rest of the roads leading from this village to other parts of the island are gravel roads. The most beautiful beaches can be found on the west coast. Lo Pared Beach is a sandy beach suitable for swimming. Ao Som in the north of the island offers a view of the rocks of Phang Nga Bay, Hua Laem Beach is very lonely, with a beautiful sandy beach.

Samet Nangshe Viewpoint

Wat Suwan Khuha

Dragon Cave Temple

Attractions Phang Nga City and Coast

Phang Nga Town

Located in stunning surroundings, **the city Phang Nga** itself is not very remarkable. It does not have an Old Town, but it has plenty of opportunities for accommodation and some restaurants. An overnight stay is usually not worthwhile, because the city is easily accessible from Khao Lak and Phuket. It's not a beach destination either: the shoreline to the bay here is dense mangrove forest throughout. The city is surrounded by steep green hills and close to the mangrove coast and serves primarily as a starting point for tours to the Phang Nga Bay and its attractions, but the surroundings do have lots of attractions,

Phang Nga Museum

The museum in the city of Phang Nga is located in the old city hall, which is built in the colonial style. On the facade there is a Garuda (mythical creature animal-human). The history of the city is shown in a permanent exhibition on the spacious floor area. Other topics are culture, economy, and local knowledge. Near Phu Chang Cave in Phang Nga Town. m-culture.go.th/phangnga (website in Thai only).

Phung Chang Cave

Phung Chang Cave or Elephant Belly Cave is worth a visit. The rock in which it lies looks like an elephant silhouette – so the cave is in the belly. Inside the long cave there are beautiful stalactites and stalagmites, some of which resemble elephants, tusks, and other things. You can do a 40-minute tour for 500 baht per person. Since most of the tour takes place in the water, it is advisable to wear shorts and waterproof shoes. If you do not have any with you, you may purchase flip-flops where you buy the tickets. Headlamps are provided free of charge. Unfortunately, you are not allowed to take pictures inside – but at the entrance you will be photographed, and you can buy the picture after the tour. The cave tour is worth the money: you paddle to the first platform with the kayak. There you switch to a bamboo raft, which is pulled through the water to the next platform, from where you can wade in the now low (calf-high) water. Since the cave is built up like a long tunnel, you go back the same way, crossing the entering visitors.

The cave is located just off the main Road 4 –in Phang Nga itself.
DG 8.44217, 98.51684 / GMS N 8°26'31.812", E 98°31'0.624"

Sam Cave / Tham Sam

This cave has ancient wall drawings, which are believed to have originated at the beginning of the Rattanakosin era (between 1782-1932). The Department of Fine Arts has identified them as original ancient remains. The outer hall is a long, covered area with a smooth ground. The walls of the cave are covered with drawings over a length of 70 m. They are depictions from Buddhism, sceneries and the way of local life in earlier times. In the front part of the cave there is a Buddha figure sculpted in stone. Next to the H3027 in Phang Nga. From Rong Ruea Road it is 1.1 km east of the city centre, located on a beautiful lake. It is a secret tip, even the locals often don't know about this magical looking place.
DG 8.46456, 98.53877 / GMS N 8° 27' 52.416", E 98° 32' 19.571"

Wat Suwan Kuha

It is sometimes also called Wat Suwannakuha or Wat Tham, also known as "the Temple with the Great Buddha in the cave". Many tours and tourists visit this temple, which is why a whole infrastructure of small shops has formed in the parking lot. In addition to drinks, ice cream, T-shirts and other souvenirs, they also sell peanuts for the many monkeys here. But take care, the monkeys are quite obtrusive – tour guides use slingshots to keep them at bay, individual tourists must be attentive so that the monkeys do not steal anything.

The entrance to the cave with the Buddha is on the right side of the parking lot through a beautiful (blue) painted gate. In the cave itself (you pay entrance), you can see the 15-meter-long reclining Buddha statue and some smaller golden statues. There is also the opportunity to be told your future by a machine – which unfortunately is only in Thai. A staircase leads up (and outside) at the back of the cave. Follow the staircase to get to a plateau where another staircase on the left leads down to a pretty limestone cave.

If the turn-off of Highway 4 (to the left) is signed, follow the sign for the Raman Waterfall National Forest. After about half a kilometre you get to the large parking lot of the temple on the right.
DG 8.42884, 98.47056 / GMS N 8° 25'43.824", E 98° 28' 14.016"

Wat Thamtapan

This temple is a little ... different. It is located at the end of Soi Thamtapan, a small side street in Phang Nga. At first you may think you have surprisingly landed in a somewhat abstract Disneyland. There are not only animal figures there, but also disturbing statues of how the Thai imagine hell. You will descend to hell by a dragon mouth (and a long passage going downhill behind it) – or if you take the path on the left along the rock wall – to a monk under a rock overhang, which will bless even a farang (non-Thai) for a in return for a gift. Buddhist Hell is called Narok in Thai and if you see its images here, you understand that it is a good idea to be "good" in life. If you go past the dragon and to the back of the temple area, you find a row of commemorative statues of monks on the left and a large stone relief on the rock wall. On the right, tucked behind the huts, there is a wobbly and steep staircase going up to a viewing platform and a shrine on the top of the hill.
DG 8.45393 / 98.52807, N 8°27'14.148" / E 98°31'41.051"

Raman Waterfall Forest Park

Waterfall, places to bathe, toilet, jungle path. Only a few tourists visit this place, the path to the waterfall stretches up the mountain and the exotic vegetation gives the impression of a jungle path. On the right side the water rushes down with a roar and on the left you can marvel at wild begonias, ferns and other plants. Many exotic insects, well-camouflaged tree frogs and forest butterflies amaze everyone. It's clean but it may have leeches.
In the hinterland of Phang Nga, the road continues past Wat Suwan Kuha. DG 8.45132, 98.4472 / GMS N 8°27'4.752", E 98°26'49.919"

Wat Kaew Manee Si Mahathat

Temple complex with a central black statue of a monk. The large statue represents Por Than Klai, who died around 45 years ago at the age of 93 and was extremely famous – even to royalty – for his ability to predict the future. The temple complex contains a wax museum with images of gods from Thai, Indian and Chinese cultures and is very well maintained. On Highway 4 on the way to Phang Nga.
DG 8.33476, 98.42627 / GMS N 8°20'5.136", E 98°25'34.572"

Long Lae Market

Local Sunday market near Phang Nga. This Sunday market, previously known only to locals, offers a wide selection of regional foods, numerous food stalls, and live music. It's idyllically situated in the countryside. Eat and shop like the Thais do. Open from 7:30 am on Sundays. Just past Highway 4 between Sarasin Bridge and Phang Nga Town, near Wat Kaew Manee. DG 8.33146, 98.39318 (GMS N 8°19'53.256", E 98°23'35.448"

Samet Nangshe Viewpoint

Just over an hour's drive from Khao Lak and the best views of Phang Nga Bay from a height that makes you think you're flying, that is the Viewpoint Samet Nangshe.

The viewpoint has been greatly expanded (since we discovered it in 2017): Plafonated viewing area, seating, toilets, small restaurant, plus photo points such as swings or seats. You can stay in tents (for around 300 baht per tent). The place is popular with Thai and Asian travelers, but they usually disappear after 6 pm. The sunset with the changing light over the bay is beautiful, but the sun sets behind you. The most spectacular view is at sunrise early in the morning as the sun rises directly behind the islands in the bay.

Tour operators from Khao Lak or Phuket offer the viewpoint as a stopover, either during the day or early in the morning.

It's still not easy to find (it is best to enter the location into your GPS and follow the directions). Coming from Khao Lak, turn towards the bay (east) before the village of Phang Nga. Somewhat problematic is the fact that because of the divided Highway 4, you cannot turn directly, but must "overshoot" and then take the next U-turn and drive back. Luckily, it has more U-turn opportunities to do than the apps would have you believe. You drive through an attractive landscape and small towns to the mangrove fields. The viewpoint is signposted. Down the street there is a ticket booth where you have to pay a fee to visit: 30 baht per person to walk up. 90 baht for a transport up and down. Since 2022, you can no longer drive up to the Samet Nangshe viewpoint yourself. It is still a single lane gravel road.

DG: 8.23999, 98.44634 / GMS: N 8 ° 14 '23.964", E 98 ° 26' 46.824"

Samet Nangshe Boutique: Those who prefer a more comfortable stay can book accommodation at the nearby Samet Nangshe Boutique.

The hotel has a restaurant that offers fine dining with a great view at expensive prices.

Beyond Skywalk Nangshi

The new Skywalk opened in 2024 right next to the Samet Nangshe Viewpoint. U-shaped glass-floored walkway (on high, ugly concrete pillars) is part of the new *Beyond Hotel* here and is open from 6 am to 7 pm. Ticket prices (2025): Adults 750 baht (includes a 200 baht credit for food and drinks), students/children (60 to 130 cm) 450 baht (including a 100 baht credit for food and drinks), children under 60 cm are free. You are taken by taxi and elevator to the platform, where you must put on overshoes for the glass floor.
Also available in the Beyond Hotel: *Skywalk Café*, swimming pool with a view and pool bar, accommodation: luxury tents, pavilions, one-bedroom villas. 💻 skywalk-nangshi.beyondresort.com

Ao Toh Li Viewpoint

This viewpoint is just a little further south and has the same beautiful view of the bay. The way up is not signposted, but is tarred throughout and, although steep in parts, can be driven with a normal car – and here you are allowed to! The viewing platform is well secured, and has well-maintained photo points such as swings.
For us, this is (since 2022) the better place, because the view is just as great, you can drive yourself up there – and there are significantly fewer tourists.
You pay 50 baht to the owner of the private property. You can also book an overnight stay with him, either in a tent (500 baht for 2 persons), or small bungalow with or without air conditioning (1200 baht or 700 baht per person). Contact: ✆+66 89 591 0569 (only Thai).
💻 facebook.com/LohLiViewPoint
DG: 8.22637, 98.44472 / GMS: N 8°13'34.932", E 98°26'40.992"

Benyaran Museum

The small museum exhibits a collection of various antiquities divided into different zones. For example: utensils, traditional medicine, military equipment from the world war, fossils and tin mining. It has replicas of an old coffee shop and theatre. A somewhat curious collection, but one that makes for an interesting visit. 🕒 Daily 8am-5pm. Entrance fee 50 baht. 🚗 From Highway 4 towards Phang Nga,

turn onto Highway 1004 (Ban Lo Yung) and follow it for about 19 km. The place is about 9 km away from Samet Nang She Viewpoint.
DG 8.6067645, 98.2617416/GMS N 8° 36' 24.352",E 98°15'42.269"

Tao Thong Waterfall

Small, hidden waterfall down at Phang Nga towards Krabi. Coming from the Tao Thong Cave, the water falls over several smaller steps. You can swim in a lake and a suspension bridge offers a bit of adventure jungle feeling.
DG 8.4854, 98.5857 / GMS N 8°29'7.584", E 98°35'8.52"

Baan Bang Phat Fishing Village

The fishing village Baan Bang Phat in the mangrove forests on the coast of Phang Nga Bay is a spot still quite undiscovered by foreign tourists. The village is built on stilts in the water and can only be reached by a narrow, 150-meter-long bridge that only pedestrians and motorcycles can cross. Bang Phat itself is very intimate – much smaller and much more authentic than the famous sea gypsy village of Panyee in the Phang Nga Bay. There are some restaurants right by the sea (with guaranteed fresh seafood), a few home-stay accommodations and some souvenir shops. You can see some of the islands in Phang Nga Bay from here or you can have a look around the village. A small golden dome marks the location of the mosque.
At Phang Nga Bay, at the end of a road that winds idyllically from Highway 4 south of Phang Nga
DG: 8.36216, 98.57718 / GMS: N 8°21'43.776", E 98° 34' 37.847"

Eating and drinking in Phang Nga

Morning Market:

Located in Phang Nga next to the Rattanapong Hotel. Starts from 5 in the morning – a place to try sweet sticky rice, fried bananas and local fruits and vegetables and fish.

Night Market:

Near the hospital of Phang Nga in the city centre. With the usual wide selection of food and snacks. Every day from about 5 pm.

Tha Sai Seafood:

Outside the city on the way to Krabi. The restaurant is located directly on a mangrove arm with a nice view. DG 8.45372, 98.61246/ GMS N 8°27'13.392" O 98°36'44.855"

Ruean Phae Sam Chong Seafood

The restaurant is located on the Bang Lam River in the mangroves near Phang Nga on two floating platforms. It's popular with locals and a great alternative to the tourist traps on the Sea Gypsy Island (Ko Panyee). They offer a seafood menu with fresh daily catch. The fried bass with 2 sauces is recommended by Michelin Thailand 2022.

Only 5 km from Road 4, about halfway between Sarasin Bridge and Phang Nga town. DG 8.6067645, 98.2617416 /GMS N 8° 36' 24.352". E 98° 15' 42.269

New Fern Restaurant (and others) on Ko Panyee

The row of restaurants on the main piers on the island of Ko Panyee offer mainly Thai buffet lunches for the (many) tourist groups that stop here. They also have à la carte menus for the rest of the visitors. The view of the bay is particularly beautiful thanks to its location. The prices are accordingly (high): if a smoothie on the beach costs 50 baht, it is 100 baht here.

Tree Cups Phang Nga Coffee

A Coffee Shop in a very special location: high on an old tree. You can drink your coffee on the platform and enjoy the panoramic view. 12.30-5.30 pm. Something for a stopover on a Phang-Nga trip, though somewhat difficult to find. facebook.com/TreeCups

Take the road into the hills for approximately 900 m at the junction. DG: 8.36427, 98.44489 / GMS: N 8°21'51.372", E 98°26'41.604"

Attractions around Phang Nga: Inland and towards Krabi

Sa Nang Manora Park

About 5 km north of Phang Nga is the Waterfall Forest Park Sa Nang Manora. A 2 km nature trail, a Bat Cave and a Shell Cave are posted in the park. You reach a couple of pools and waterfalls after a short walk through the trees. On a hot day this is a nice detour to take a picnic and cool down. The waterfalls are not spectacular, but with its green setting and the tranquillity, this is a small paradise. If you

Street Art by Alex Face

Sa Nang Manora Forest Park

Thap Put

Tham Sam Rock Art (Sam Cave)

Wat Bang Thong

continue walking, you should know that the paths across the river are often adventurous, as there are no bridges. You will have to skip from stone to stone or scramble over fallen trees. Follow the signs and the road after the junction of the main road 4 to the right (coming from the south) DG 8.49414, 98.51524 / GMS N 8°29'38.904", E 98°30'54.864"

White Water Rafting and Quad (ATV)

White water rafting is generally offered as a day trip, along with other attractions (such as ziplining or elephant riding or quad biking) including transportation and food. Children can participate, but it is recommended that they are able to swim (in spite of the obligatory life jacket). Start is at the **Ton Pariwat Wildlife Station** after a short introduction. With the inflatable boat for 5 persons and an experienced guide, you float down 5 km on the relatively narrow river Khlong Song Phraek over a few rapids and past rocks. The journey takes about 45 minutes and is possible to do all year round, although it is more exciting in the rainy season. In the dry season, they dam the water and release it along with the boats. Compared to white water rafting elsewhere, this is pretty tame but still fun.
Quad biking (ATV) is also taking place at Ton Pariwat Station. After a short introduction you ride on the winding paths over a hill, through a valley and through and along the river Song Phraek. The landscape ranges from picturesque to wild, the equipment well maintained, and riding is easy and fun – children can ride with a parent.

Ton Pariwat Wildlife Sanctuary

The park consists of 224 km2 of green forest and hills above Phang Nga.
Headquarters: DG: 8.61123, 98.55054 / GMS: N 8 °36'40.428', '0 98°33'1.943"
In the park, about 100 m from the headquarters, there is a waterfall: **Namtok Ton Pariwat**, better known as **Namtok Song Phraek**. The low falls have a plunge pool where you can swim. Iron deposits are visible in the rocks – there used to be mines in the area. In the rainy season, the river carries a lot of water.

Khao Nang Hong View Point

The road between Phang Nga and Krabi is one of the most beautiful in the area (although very, very winding), the viewpoint is nothing more than a short stop on the way to Wat Bang Riang for example. There is a small parking lot, but we didn't see a restaurant. A path goes up the hill to the viewpoint, which was not passable when we visited. DS 8.53515, 98.5593 / GMS N 8°32'6.54", E 98°33'33.479"

Dragon Cave Temple (Praya Nakarach Cave Temple)

You reach the cave temple via a very long staircase with 235 steps of different heights that lead into a cave vestibule. From here you have a good view of the valleys and hills in the area. The cave can be explored up to about 100 m and there is a feeling of absolute silence and peace inside and at the Buddhist altars. The monastery was lovingly integrated into the mountain and is laid out on several levels on and in the mountain. There are many Naga statues (dragon-snakes), Buddha figures and golden monk statues. The monks here sell tea and ointments. Visits are free, but a "merit" (donation) is requested at the staircase for maintenance. Just south of the Highway 4 between Phang Nga and Krabi.
DG 8.6067645, 98.2617416/ GMS N 8°36'24.352", E 98°15'42.269"

Thap Put Stone Quarry, Thong Lang Cave

A local attraction because the water of the lake in the former quarry here is an extreme turquoise blue. You can hardly believe photos you see, but it is true. Thais describe it as almost alien, in any case it offers a nice contrast to the grey rocks and harmonizes with the surrounding green pine trees and the green algae in the water. It is close to Road 4 and is easy to find if you navigate by GPS. There are a few stalls along the way selling drinks and snacks and souvenirs from local vendors. There are no toilets. Access is free (as it is public land) and there are no barriers. Signs warn not to slip on the short path to the edge of the lake and fall down the steep edge into the lake and swimming is prohibited... it is probably very difficult to get out again. On Road 4 between Phang Nga and Krabi (before the turnoff to Wat Bang Riang) DG 8.54397, 98.59733 / GMS N 8°32'38.292", E 98°35'50.387"

Wat Bang Riang

This temple is also called Wat Rat Upatam. It consists of different parts: a big temple at the foot of a hill and smaller temples and statues in different styles located on the top of the hill. Most tours drive right up and miss the beautiful temple in a small lake in form of a dragon boat. The part on the hill includes a combination of three different temple styles: Thai, Chinese and Chedi pagoda. A tooth of Buddha is

kept in a shrine. The temple is located quite far from the coast, 40 km north of Phang Nga. A large seated golden Buddha statue high on the hill is looking over the country. It has a lot of stairs, but the view over the green hills is worthwhile. The temple is visited mainly by Thai tourists and some tours, but still worth seeing. A visit to the pompous temple on the hill with the chedi is possible in appropriately decent clothing (you can buy overcoats here) and only costs 20 baht. Once inside the temple, do something for your karma and donate coins at the various Buddha statues. The temple is located far inland, 40 km north of Phang Nga
DG 8.59346, 98.66891 / N 8° 35′ 36.456″, E 98° 40′ 8.075″

Wat Bang Thong

Also called Wat Maha That Wichiramongkol. A new temple in Phang Nga (towards Krabi) with an almost 70 m high, golden central tower, that can be seen from afar. In addition to the tower, you can also see a 30 m high statue of the immortal monk Luang Pu Thuad and a statue of the famous king cobra, which is said to have spat a magical crystal ball at him. The temple complex is huge and decorated in detail – definitely worth a visit. Entry costs 50 baht per person. You should dress appropriately and take off your shoes before entering the complex, as well as your hat for the interior of the central tower. In the temple tower you can decorate the central Buddha statue with golden cloths in a ceremony. Of the many golden monk statues in the surrounding shadow corridor, only one does not look straight ahead, but (distracted?) to the top right.
DG 8.6067645, 98.2617416 / GMS N 8°36'24.352", E 98°15'42.269"

KRABI

You can find Krabi on the map at the height of Phuket on the other side of the Phang Nga Bay. With its beaches facing west, it benefits from both the direct view of the sunsets and the fantastic view of Phang Nga Bay. For a day trip it is (in my opinion) quite far away from Khao Lak, even if some providers offer tours there.
Krabi has an **airport** that can be used as an alternative to Phuket Airport. There are also **ferries to Phi Phi Island** In general, Krabi is popular with island hoppers.

Krabi is on the mainland, about a 3-hour drive from Khao Lak. The drive takes so long because the landscape there slows down the journey. Along the way it has some very interesting attractions that can be visited. **QR code to Googlemaps with the route and points of interest on the way to Krabi**.

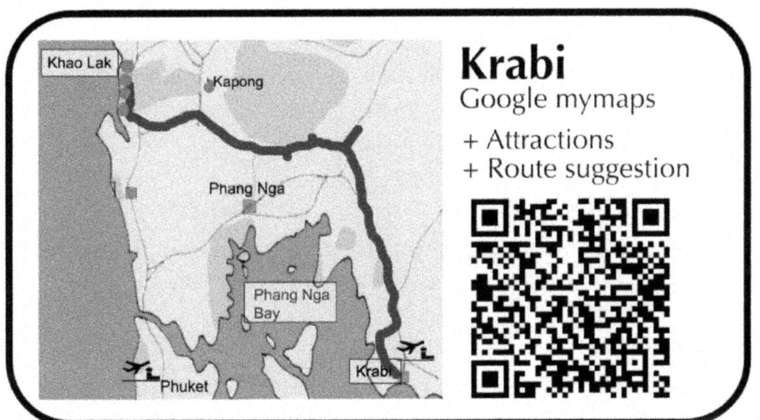

The main attractions of Krabi are:

Ao Nang Beach

Like Patong, but with a view of the Phang Nga Bay. Numerous shops and bars and restaurants and tailors and tour operators. Something for the tourists that like the hustle and bustle.

Railay Beach

Railay Beach, which is only accessible by boat, is quieter, although it is located directly between the busy towns of Krabi Town and Ao Nang Beach.

Phrang Nga Cave Beach

Often cited as one of the most beautiful beaches in the world, Phrang Nga Cave Beach boasts white sand, turquoise water, and steep cliffs that provide shade. The cave contains a temple.

Tonsai Beach

This beach is especially known for its cliffs, where rock climbers can test their skills.

Tiger Cave Temple

The Tiger Cave Temple is decorated with golden Buddha statues and skulls in a long cave.

Khao Khanab Nam

The two approximately 100m high rocks in the sea and mangroves are the gateway and landmark of Krabi. There is also a stalactite cave that can be visited after a short boat ride.

Krabi Town Night Market

This is where Thais eat and shop. The night market in the main town is open Friday through Sunday from 5 pm to 10 pm.

Princess Cave

The cave contains a temple shrine dedicated to a mythical sea princess who is said to protect fishermen. It features hundreds of carvings and drawings of lingams (penises), which symbolize fertility and prosperity.

Ao Thalane Mangroves

Impressive mangrove forests surrounded by steep, 100-meter-high cliffs. The narrow channels and open lagoons can only be explored by kayak. You might spot macaques and kingfishers along the way.

Thapom Klong Song Nam

Known as the Two-Water Canal, this is where freshwater from springs mixes with the saltwater of the Andaman Sea. As a result, the water colour changes from crystal clear at low tide to turquoise green at high tide. An elevated wooden walkway winds through the natural landscape.

Klong Root (Clear Water Canal)

A tranquil, crystal-clear canal in a wooded area. It is fed by underwater springs and springs along its outer edges. Kayaking, fishing, and swimming are all possible.

Emerald Pool

The Emerald Pool is an incredibly blue pond, fed by a hot spring. You can swim in there.

Hot Springs - Khlong Thom

Around Krabi there are several natural hot springs where you can bathe. Some offer "contrast bathing": alternating between the hot spring and the cool river.

Krabi

Phi Phi Island

PHI PHI ISLAND

The very beautiful Phi Phi islands are located below Phuket and day trips from Khao Lak are possible – although I think, the time spent there is too short. To get there you transit from *Phuket* (*Rassada Pier*) or *Krabi*. Speedboats reach the islands in 50 minutes. The ferry costs 400-500 baht one way per person, a private tour / day trip between 6000-8000 baht. In the rainy season, cancellations and postponements of tours are possible due to the weather.

Hat Nopparat Thara – Mu Ko Phi Phi National Park

The islands are open all year round, the national park is closed between June 1st and July 31st. The park comprises two areas totalling approximately 388 km^2: one part off the coast of Krabi, the other around the Phi Phi Islands. Admission: adults 200 baht, children 100 baht. Divers pay 200 baht extra.

Phi Phi Don

On the main island of Phi Phi Don there are numerous places to stay and eat on the strip between the two bays (*Ton Sai Bay* and *Loh Dalum Beach*). There is no traffic, neither cars nor scooters – everything is within walking distance. Prices are slightly higher than in the rest of Thailand, especially in the high season from November to March. There are restaurants, bars, diving schools, tattoo parlours, souvenir shops, tour providers.

Phi Phi Viewpoint

Three consecutive places with a spectacular view on the islands. You have to climb yourself. Entry for the first two points is 30 baht per person, for the third you pay another 20 baht.

Laem Tong Beach

The northernmost beach on the main island. Secluded and only accessible via a steep hiking trail or water taxi. Coral reef right in front of the beach, where people like to dive and snorkel.

Viking Cave

The cave can now only be viewed from the outside. Countless birds nest in the cave, especially swallows, and there are historical murals on the walls.

Phi Phi Leh and the Maya Bay

Phi Phi Leh is the second largest island and is home to the famous Maya Bay as known from the movie The Beach in 2000. It became a hyped tourist magnet and when we visited a few years later the corals were not looking good because of the tourists trampling on them. The Maya Bay closed in June 2018. First it was only for the summer months so that the ecosystem could recover during the break, then for an indefinite period. In 2021 it was reopened after regeneration measures. Access is now time-restricted, Maya Bay is open from 7am-6pm and you can stay a maximum of 1 hour. A maximum of 4000 people per day was set and you are no longer allowed to swim or bathe here. Currently (2023) recovery periods are planned, and the bay is closed during the monsoon season from August 1st to September 30th.

Bamboo Island and Mosquito Island

2 lonely islands near Phi Phi. Mosquito has a small beach that is close to high cliffs and therefore often in the shade. Bamboo Island is completely surrounded by the white sandy beach - tours like to come here for picnic lunches.

Diving and snorkeling around Phi Phi

Next to Surin and Similan, the best diving and snorkelling areas in Thailand can be found here. Crystal clear water (from November to May), large coral reefs and diving areas close to the accommodations.

Phi Phi Island Excursion (8-9 hours)

Early start to Phuket around 5am - Speedboat ride (2 hours) – Stop at Phi Phi Leh Island with the beautiful Maya Bay (known from The Beach) and Phi Phi Leh Lagoon – Swimming break in the Lagoon – Ride to Phi Phi Don – Climbing the striking viewpoint on Phi Phi Don – Sightseeing around the island: Viking Cave, Monkey Beach – 2 snorkelling stops – Visit to Bamboo Island and picnic lunch and beach time – Speedboat return to Phuket.

BETWEEN KHAO LAK AND PHUKET – THE OVERLOOKED SOUTH

The area south of Khao Lak has been neglected so far, but it is popular with Thai visitors because of its natural beauty. For European visitors, a lot is still "uncharted territory", few of the attractions are signposted and if so, then not in English. Nevertheless, the area is ideal for private tours or self-drive excursions and those taking a trip to Phuket can stop at some of the attractions along the way.

Khao Khai Nouy

Or Khao Khai Nui: The viewpoint is mainly known by Thais – but hardly by foreign visitors. The view is wonderful early in the morning when the hills are covered in a light morning fog called Talak Noi (Sea of Fog). The real sea is 7 km to the west. Northern Thais are reminded of their homeland – but they like to visit the better-known Phutajor viewpoint, although Khao Khai Nuoy is easier to reach and just as beautiful. From the approximately 300 m high hill you have a beautiful view at any time of the day. There are different platforms – the nicest is at the top and faces the inland at sunrise, the one a little further down has a view of the seaside. They have tents and bungalows to rent for overnight stays. The viewpoint is about 30 minutes south of Khao Lak and is only signposted in Thai. The road goes up from the top of the 4240 road triangle. It starts out paved, but that soon wears off. With a normal PW it can be very difficult, especially if it has rained, better use a 4WD or scooter. Or you can be transported up by their pick-up service. DG 8.55965, 98.29488 / GMS N 8°33'34.74", O 98°17'41.568'

Khanim Waterfall

This waterfall is especially worth visiting during the rainy season. It's located very close to Highway 4 between Khao Lak and Phuket – even further upstream than Lampi Waterfall (so closer to Khao Lak) – yet you'll usually have it all to yourself. DG 8.49715, 98.28311 / GPS: N 8°29' 49.74", E 98°16' 59.195")

Across Highway 4, *Chiavisas Nature Farm and Restaurant* is worth a visit for a snack or a drink (Closed wednesdays).

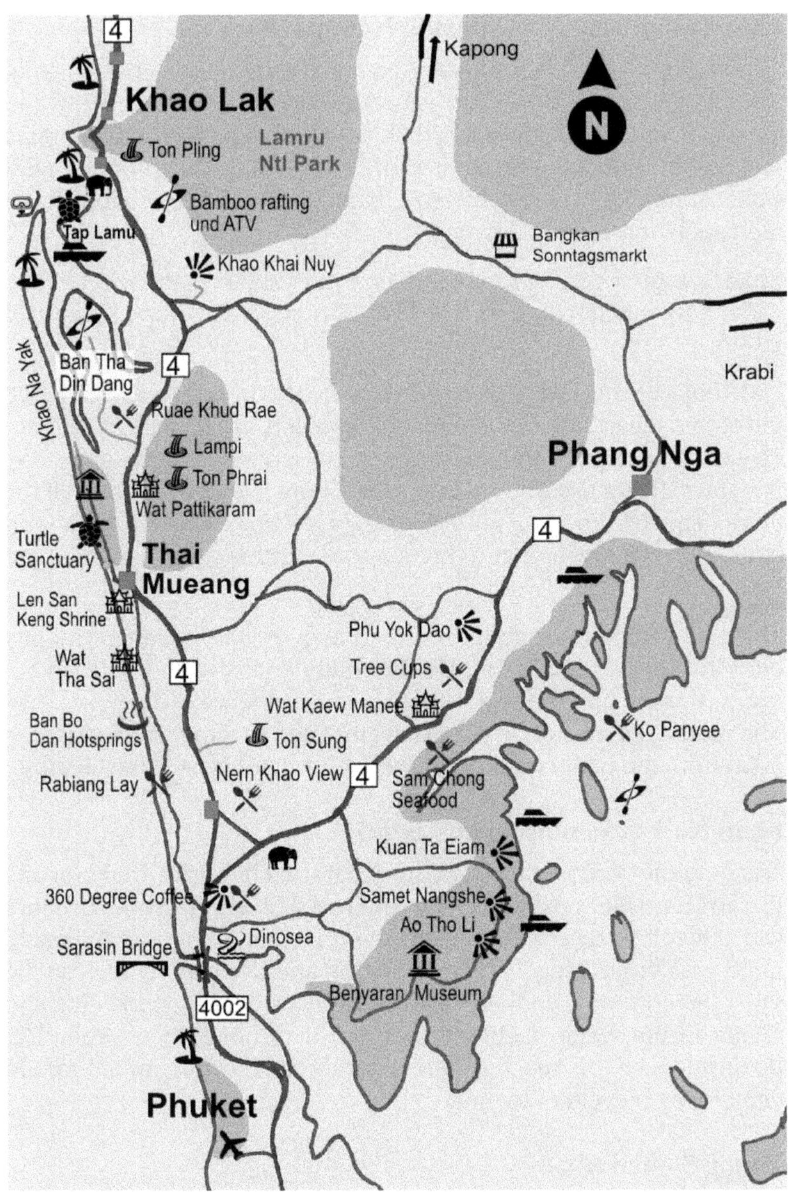

14-Map of the area between Phuket and Khao Lak

Khao Lampi Hat Thai Mueang National Park

Khao Lampi – Hat Thai Mueang National Park in the Thai Mueang district of Phang Nga province was established on April 14, 1986 and covers an area of 72 km2. It is divided into two parts: Khao Lampi, a range of hills on the east coast and Thai Mueang Beach on the west side. Admission for adults 100 baht – the ticket is applicable repeatedly throughout the day.

Khao Lampi is covered by evergreen forest with plant species like yang, fern, rattan, bamboo. The highest point is Yoz Khao Khamin at 622 m.

Hat Thai Mueang has white sandy beaches to the west and mangrove forest to the east where the park headquarters are located. There are civets, horse deer, red junglefowl (the colourful chickens) and more. Stingrays, flying fish and many species more live in the corals off the coast. The 13 km long sandy beach is suitable for swimming and bathing. From November to February sea turtles come ashore to lay their eggs.

The main office is on the beach road above Thai Mueang. You pay entry to the park and can visit other attractions of the park for 72 hours. Camping in the park is possible.
The **rusted remains of an old excavator** used to mine tin can be seen 5 km from the park entrance, along with a giant gear wheel nearby.

Khao Na Yak peninsula and beach

The long offshore peninsula in front that stretches from Thai Mueang to Tap Lamu Pier is Khao Lak's house reef. It is very pristine (because it is difficult to reach), with clear sea, miles of lonely sandy beach, lined with bright blue water on one side and dense pine trees on the other. Swimming is partially possible from the beach, snorkelling and diving in the water up to a maximum depth of 9 m as well. The peninsula can be reached via a sandy drive with an all-terrain vehicle, by bicycle or by boat.

Thung Samed Khao

A stretch of grassy landscape on the peninsula reminiscent of the African savannah. 5 km from HQ with a wide variety of bird species. Visitors will need a four-wheel drive vehicle or a mountain bike that can ride over sand.

Lampi Waterfall

Located in Khao Lampi Nationalpark 19 km from the Park Office. The waterfall has 4 floors. There is a large natural pool at the lowest.

Ton Phrai Waterfall

Inland in Khao Lampi National Park. Only one level, but with water all year round. From the visitor centre there you walk about 600 m along a nature trail past rare plants. The surrounding area is a lush evergreen forest.

Phang Nga Coastal Fisheries Research and Development Centre / Turtle Sanctuary

The Marine Life Research Station is located on Thai Mueang Beach close to the HQ. There are lots of sea creatures that are kept in tanks to see and learn about. In March each year, the hatched sea turtles are released back into the sea in a tradition called the *Sea Turtle Releasing Festival.*

Ban Tha Din Daeng

A small town well off the (western) tourist track, not so unknown to Thai visitors. The Muslim community mainly works in agriculture and is engaged in ecotourism. Here you can rent a longtail boat or kayak and explore the mangroves, hike through nature, visit the remains of old copper mines and swim on the beautiful, natural sandy beach. Pay attention to the tides when visiting. Contact: 💻habeedeen@hotmail.com, ✆+66 86 273 0823

Ton Sung – Phu Pha Sawan Waterfall

The fall flows from a high, steep cliff in the middle of the forest into a stream where you can swim. Very remote from everything, yet easy to reach via a new concrete road. Located outside the national park. DG 8.47513, 98.2655 / GMS N 8°28'30.468", E98°15'55.8"

Leng San Keng Shrine

Behind the Chinese gate in the village of Thai Mueang is a very pretty little Chinese temple. The visit is worth a stop to soak up the atmosphere and marvel at the colourful decoration.

Khao Khai Nui

Lampi-Hat Thai Mueang NP

Wat Tha Sai

Ban Tha Din Daeng

Khao Na Yak

Wat Tha Sai / Tha Sor / Tesdhammanava Tempel

In Thai Mueang, 40 km south of Khao Lak, there is this beautiful temple made of dark wood with gold inlays - instead of the usual white-red-golden ones. It is located directly on the beach with palm trees and sea view. On weekends there are many Thai visitors.
The beach in front of the temple has nice shade from the trees, but due to the currents and the rapidly sloping shoreline, it may be dangerous to swim. The gently sloping beaches further north are better for families with children.
DG 8.8501034, 98.3489306 / GMS N 8° 51' 0.372", E 98° 20' 56.15"

Ban Bo Dan Hot Springs

Beautifully framed and maintained hot springs, a 40 minutes-drive south of Khao Lak, just below Thai Mueang. They contain many minerals (including iodine), belong to the Hot Spring Beach Resort and Spa, and are surrounded by lush greenery. Cold water pool, gym, beach and restaurant are also available and accessible to day visitors.
🕒 Daily from 8 am to 10 pm. Day entrance costs 400 baht for adults and 200 baht for children. 💻 thehotspringbeach.com
South of Khao Lak, about 10 km below Thai Mueang
DG: 8.30735, 98.27383 / GMS: N 8° 18′ 26.46″ E 98° 16′ 25.788″

Natai and Natai Beach

The village lies between two major tourist destinations (Phuket and Khao Lak), yet it feels as far removed from mass tourism as possible. No hustle and bustle, no noise, 10 kilometres of sandy beach, local restaurants and shops. Accommodations are mostly small resorts or privately run villas. Behind the beach are mangrove forests and small streams. Thailand as it used to be. Most tourists don't even see the village, as they simply drive past it on Highway 4. The next town is **Khok Kloi**, about 2 kilometres inland on the main road (where it forks towards Phang Nga and the traffic lights are): an authentic Thai town with affordable accommodations, traditional restaurants, and local markets.

Eating and drinking between Khao Lak and Phuket

Rhuea Khud Rae – Ruekhoodrae Restaurant

A new modern styled restaurant on the road between Thai Mueang and Khao Lak. Good food and place for a stopover on a trip. They serve the (cold) drinks in clear cans with their logo on them. Thai Iced Tea is very good and can also be made less sweet. 🕒 Wednesday - Monday 10am-8pm. DG 8.47513, 98.2655 /GMS N8° 28' 30.468", 098° 15' 55.8"

Makai Cafe and Space

A charming Japanese-style café on the road through Thai Mueang. A café by day, a pub with draft beer and movie nights (in Thai) by night. 💻 facebook.com/makaicafeandspac

Nern Khao View Talay

The restaurant, in the heart of nature and in the hills behind the coast, offers a good view of the sea thanks to its altitude and natural cooling from the light breeze during the day. It is in a wooden pavilion decorated with wagon wheels, lanterns and an artificial waterfall. The spicy seafood soup is recommended by the Thai Michelin Guide. 🕒 9am-9pm. 💻 nernkhaoviewtalay.rnanagrand.com

Rabiang Lay Restaurant

A good Thai restaurant in a great location right on the beach. Well located for a stopover on route to Phuket or Phang Nga. The panoramic road along the sea is recommended for those who are not in a hurry and do not want to take Highway 4 between Phuket and Thai Mueang. DG 8.29267, 98.27263 / GMS N 8° 17' 33.612", E 98° 16' 21.468"

The Sea Light Cafe and Restaurant:

New restaurant right on the beach next to Wat Tha Sai. Very new, modern, but the service seems inexperienced.

360 Degree Coffee – Andaman Viewpoint Sky Crane

Another place that seems to be known mainly to locals. It is a viewpoint between Phuket and Khao Lak with a Coffee / Restaurant as well as a playground and a small water park. Suitable for children. On weekends there is a crane with a hanging "basket" for the 360-degree panoramic view. The restaurant offers inexpensive rice dishes and iced coffee as well as a selection of cakes. 💻 facebook.com/AndamanViewPoint A few km north of the Sarasin Bridge. Easily accessible from Highway 4.
DG: 8.24004/ 98.30088, GMS: N 8°14'24.144"/ E 98°18'3.168

PHUKET

Phuket is Thailand's largest island with 576 km2. It gained wealth from tin mining and rubber export. Today the main income comes from tourism. There are lots of things to see and do.

Phuket Excursions: All tour operators offer day trips to Phuket from Khao Lak – often allowing you to customize your itinerary. Not driving yourself on Phuket can take away a lot of the stress. The guides are often very flexible when it comes to planning – especially for small groups. I don't recommend driving yourself in Phuket – the traffic is horrendous. Phuket's roads are often congested (not just during rush hour), so it can take two hours or more just to get from one side of the island to the other. It's much more relaxing to be driven.

Phuket Smart Bus is an affordable option for travellers getting from Phuket Airport to the most popular destinations on Phuket itself (including Patong, Karon, and Kata). Tickets cost 100 Baht per person, payable on the bus (luggage is included), or you can choose the day pass to explore Phuket with hop-on hop-off service. 💻 phuketsmartbus.com

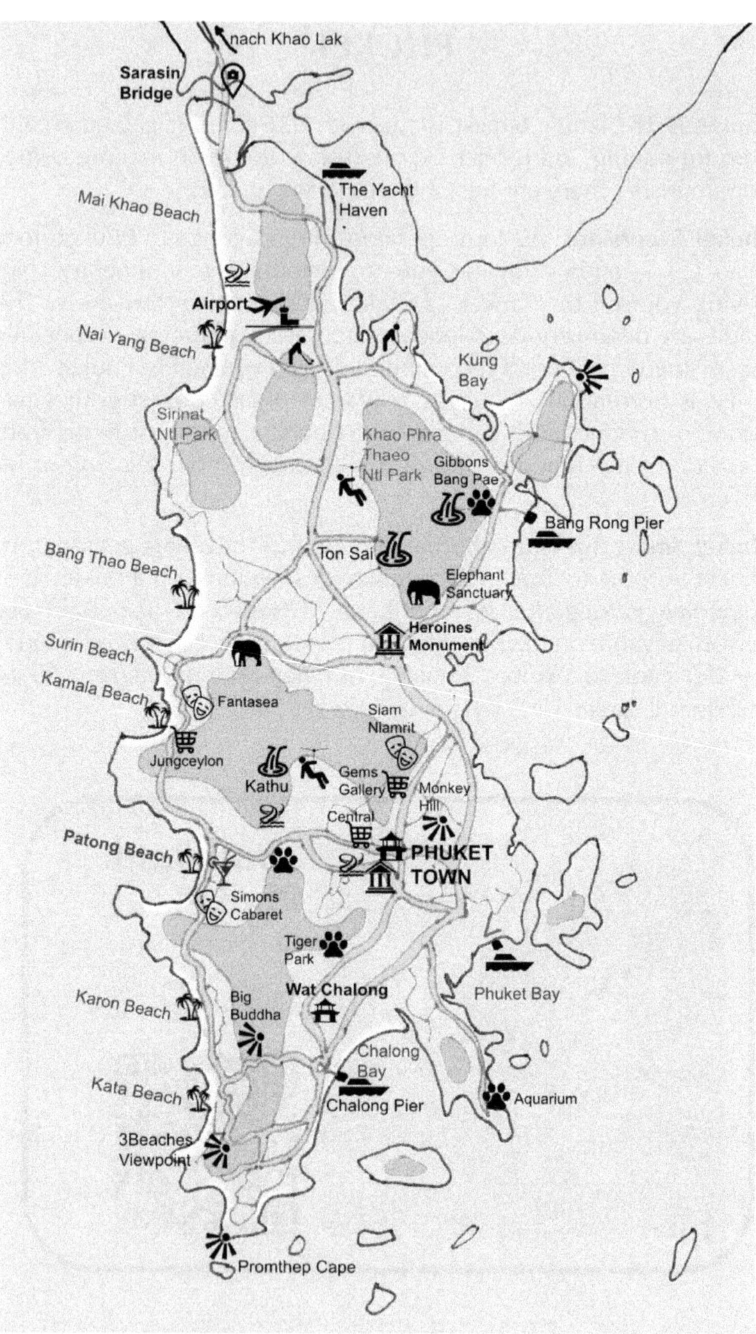

15-Map of Phuket

Sarasin Bridge

Since Phuket is so large, you often do not feel to be on an island when there. Phuket is separated from the mainland by water – but only about 500 meters and there is a bridge that connects these two parts of the country. It is now the third bridge here at the same place. The first bridge was built in 1967 and was named Sarasin after a now forgotten local politician. Because traffic (and increasing tourism) in the 70s was too much for the first small bridge, a second bridge was built there in the 80s. And then 2011 came the newest version: this one is called Thepkasattri Bridge, but most people still talk of the Sarasin Bridge. The old bridge (the 2nd) is still there and was provided with a pretty building on it – today it is regarded as a minor tourist attraction that can be walked on by foot.

It is especially nice to view the sunset from the small platform in the middle of the second bridge. In addition to tourists you can also see anglers in the evening. On the Phuket side there are small stalls with drinks and food. On the Phang Nga side there are several popular small stores where you can buy dried fish, T-shirts and toys. Here is also the best parking option for a visit to the bridge.

DG 8.20165, 98.29795 / GMS N 8° 12' 5.94", E 98° 17' 52.62"

Northeast Phuket

Do a self-drive trip with views of the Phang Nga Bay, non-tourist areas, a floating restaurant and more. Phuket has become very touristy and overcrowded. The last time when we were driving around there, I got the feeling that there are more cars on the road than residents. All the more surprisingly, there are still off the beaten track areas and untouched routes and spots left to discover. If you want to see a bit from the Phuket of earlier times, you should make this trip.

Panorama Roads

In the northeast of Phuket are two "loops": roads that make a big detour to return to the main path. In this case the main path itself is more a side road.

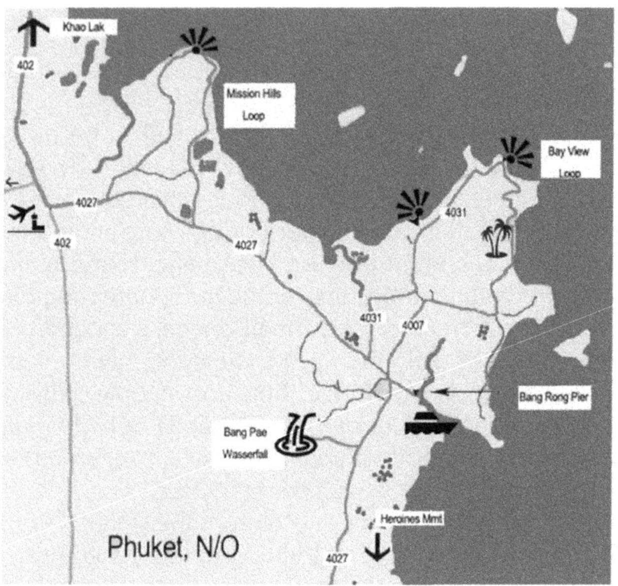

16-Map of North-east Phuket (Detail)

Mission Hills Loop
Approaching from the North: From Thepkasatri Road (the Highway 402, main connection axis through Phuket) take the small road 4027 just south of the turn-off leading to the airport. Caution: the entrance to the street here is narrow, it is not signposted and easy to miss. Once you've made it, you'll find yourself on a well-paved road that gets less and less busy the further you go. Take the turn off road to Baan Laem Sai (to the left) for good views of the bay. At the end of the loop you come out at Mission Hills Golf Course. There are large pineapple plantations in the area palm trees and rubber are grown.
Laem Sai: DG 8.11624, 98.37381/ GMS N8°6'58.464", E 98°22'25.716"

To get to the **Bay View Loop** and Laem Khat with its viewpoint into the bay and opportunities for swimming, there is also the easy option of approaching it from the south: From the roundabout at the Heroines Monument take the 4027 and turn 12 km later towards Ao Po Pier turn right, after another 3 km take the fork to the right again. Follow the road and you will get onto the loop, which brings you back to road 4027 after deserted beaches, spectacular views of the rocks and islands in Phang Nga Bay (Pa Klok Viewpoint, Laem Khat) and some steep turns and roller coaster-like elevation changes.
Laem Khat: DG 8.09804, 98.43248 / GMS N 8° 5' 52.944", E 98° 25' 56.927"

Bang Rong Pier

The area is a Muslim community, so you can see veiled women and men in Muslim clothing on their daily chores. The road to the pier is easy to find. From road 4027 turn off at the mosque and follow the signs to Bang Rong Pier.

DG 8.0498, 98.41583 / GMS N 8°2'59.28", E 98°24'56.987"

There is an entry gate – if you park there for a long time (for example to take the ferry to Ko Yao Noi), then you have to pay. But if you only come to see the place and have something to eat, parking is free. Monkeys can often be seen in the mangroves next to the road – they can be a bit cheeky, so be careful.

The pier is often a hive of activity, not only because of the ferry, but there are also fishing boats of the locals (large and small) and some cargo transport that is made over the waterway. If you turn left at the waterfront and follow the wooden boardwalk through the mangroves, you soon reach a floating restaurant. Although the small local restaurant has few tourists, they do have a menu in English available, and the food is good and very cheap. You cannot get alcohol there, but fresh juices and other beverages are sold. During the meal you can watch the activity on the water and observe birds and fish. From here you can make boat trips by kayak into the mangroves – just ask at the restaurant.

Phuket Gibbon Rehabilitation Project

Gibbons are endangered long-armed monkeys, which are unfortunately often misused to extract money from tourists, for example by offering to have a picture taken with them. Some are also kept as pets. This is illegal and captive gibbons have a miserable life – when they get older and more aggressive, they become useless for the owners. The gibbons which are taken away from their owners by the police, get a second chance at the Gibbon Rehabilitation Project. They go through a long period of rehabilitation before attempts are made to release them into the wild again. This does not work with all the animals. You are informed about the various gibbons and their stories on posters. The Gibbons are in large cages, some silent, some making their typical call, some climbing around.

DG 8.04242, 98.39326 /GMS N 8°2'32.712", E 98°23'35.735"

If you are offered to take a picture with a gibbon in Phuket or somewhere else in Thailand, take a picture of the owner and e-mail it with the information where it was taken to this project: 💻grp@gibbonproject.org. Or support them with a donation on the project site. By the way: the organisation does not get any money from the park entry fees here (200 baht).

Bang Pae Waterfall

Just beyond the Gibbon project, a path leads to the Bang Pae waterfall. You can stock up on drinks at the restaurant there – but please take the bottles back. The narrow footpath leads up a hill and down to the relatively small waterfall in a narrow mini gorge. This is said to be the largest waterfall on Phuket – perhaps it offers a more impressive sight in the rainy season? DG 8.04242, 98.39326/ GMS N8°2'32.712", E 98°23'35.735"

Khao Phra Taeo Wildlife Park

It is the last remaining evergreen jungle on Phuket. Highlights are the Ton Sai Waterfall and Bang Pae Waterfall. The highest point is the 442 m high Khao Phra. There is a 4 km continuous hiking trail from one waterfall to the other. A guide is required for this, which can be obtained from the Visitor Centre at Ton Sai Waterfall. Entrance fee to the park: adults 200 baht, children 100 baht.

Heroines Monument

A monument, that you will almost certainly see when you are visiting Phuket. It is dedicated to the two sisters Muk and Chan, who led the local population defending against an attack by the Burmese and managed to repel them. The monument is located in the centre of the island on the main axis between north and south – smack in the middle of a roundabout. You can see it well from the car, but on foot you have a real problem if you want to cross the road – especially with today's traffic.

DG 7.98097, 98.36391 / GMS N 7° 58' 51.492", E 98° 21' 50.076"

Phuket City / Old Town

Phuket Town was built at the time of tin mining, when the island benefitted from a great financial boost. Today the town is often overlooked by tourists, who mostly focus on the island's well-known beaches. That's a pity, since it's a mix of old and new, busy and quiet at the same time.

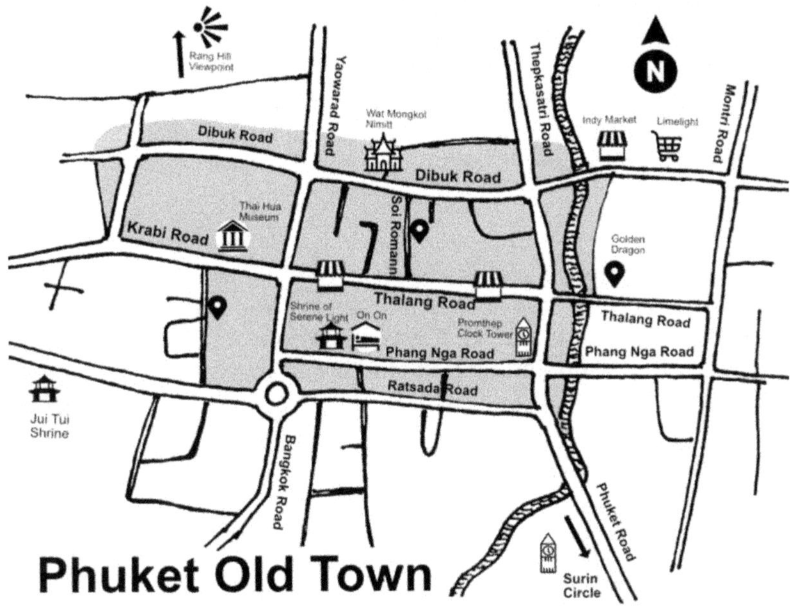

17-Map of Phuket Old Town

Phuket Old Town

In the **Old Town of Phuket**, you can see spacious Sino-colonial buildings built about 100 years ago. The quarter can be easily explored on foot. Five streets contain most points of interest: Thalang Road, one of the oldest streets, lined with many boutique shops and restaurants in its historic buildings today: **Phang Nga Road, Dibuk Road, Krabi Road** and **Ranong Road** and the narrow streets (Sois) around them. The buildings look nice because they have removed and replaced the above-ground lines that are so annoying everywhere else. Street art like from Alex Face (the Bangsky of Bangkok) can be found everywhere.

Promthep Clock Tower

The Promthep Clock Tower was built in 1914 as part of the police station building. For a long time, however, the clock tower had no clock. Initially, funds were lacking, and when they were finally raised after 40 years, the ship that was supposed to bring the clock from Penang, Malaysia, sank. It wasn't until another 20 years later, in

1976, that a clock could be installed thanks to a donation from the Phuket Lions Club. The completely renovated building now houses the tourist information office, where visitors can find information about the sights of the Old Town and excursions.
The new **Surin Circle Clock Tower** is smaller but stylistically very similar to the Promthep Clock Tower and is located nearby.

On On Hotel

The **On On Hotel** is well known. It is the oldest hotel in Phuket, (opened 1929) and was also seen in the movie "The Beach" starring Leonardo Di Caprio. In 2012 it was completely refurbished. Today it is called **The Memory at On On** and is no longer shabby, but clean and luxurious.

Temples and Shrines

In the heart of the old city, you'll find the Chinese **Shrine of the Serene Light**. It has been tucked away in a courtyard off Phang Nga Road since 1891, behind an entrance that is now adorned with a colourful Chinese gate.
Another Chinese temple is the **Jui Tui Shrine**, located just outside the old town at the corner of Soi Phuthorn and Ranong Road. The temple has been renovated several times and is well worth seeing (and colourful). The main deity worshipped here is Tean Huan Soy, patron saint of artists and dancers. A statue of him stands at the highest point of the main altar, accompanied by a chicken and a dog – apparently his favorite animals since childhood.
Wat Mongkol Nimit is a classic Thai temple located at the end of Soi Romanee.

Phuket Sunday Walking Street Market

This market takes place every Sunday from 4 pm to 9 pm. During the week, the 350-meter-long Thalang Street, with its many shops, restaurants, bars, and guesthouses, is bustling, but the highlight is the weekend event. The streets are closed off for the market, and additional stalls sell clothing, souvenirs, snacks, and drinks, while dance performances and live music are also featured.

The **Phuket Indy Market** is held on Dibuk Street on Wednesday, Thursday, and Friday afternoons.

Thai Hua Museum Phuket

Located in the old town on Krabi Road, the museum tells the story of Phuket and its first immigrants from China. The two-story colonial-style building is one of the most beautiful in the area and is a sight in itself. Open daily from 9 am to 5 pm, admission is 200 baht per person.

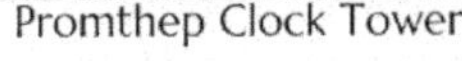

Promthep Clock Tower

Memory Hotel by On On

Walking Street

Shrine of Serene Light

Khao Rang

Rang Hill is the second largest peak in Phuket Town. It is in the north-western part of the city and covered by dense vegetation. There is a big golden Buddha (the first one they built in Phuket) and a fitness

circuit on the hill. In three restaurants you can eat. The hill has views over the city and the southeast coast.
DG 7.89274, 98.38009 / GMS N 7° 53′ 33.864″, E 98° 22′ 48.323″

Phuket Aquarium

A visit to this aquarium makes a nice trip with the family where you learn something about life in the sea. Hundreds of colourful exotic fish and other sea creatures can be seen in the 30 tanks here including an underwater tunnel between sharks, manta rays and other large fish. 🕒 8.30 am to 4 pm, 7 days a week. Admission: Adults 180 baht, Children 100 baht
Below Phuket town at the very end of a headland.
DG 7.80347, 98.40788 / GMS N 7° 48′ 12.492″, E 98° 24′ 28.368″

Wat Chalong

Also called **Chaithararam temple**. The most important temple on Phuket and one of the largest and most prestigious in the area. Magical powers are attributed to one of the revered monks here and many people come here to ask for help – if their desire is fulfilled, they burn chains of fireworks ... which often happens. The newest building there is the large Chedi, which you can climb up inside under the top. 🕒 Daily from 7 am to 5 pm. At the time around the Chinese New Year a big market takes place at the Wat Chalong. Then you cannot only shop and try different food, but you can also use simple fun rides.
After about 4 km on the right side coming from the roundabout in Chalong, after about 6 km on the left side coming from *Central Festival*. DG 7.84678 / 98.3369, GMS N 7°50′48.408″ / E 98°20′12.839″

Promthep Cape

The southernmost point of Phuket is a very popular destination, especially for sunset. Despite ample parking, it can get very crowded then. It is a nice place for the sunset, but to be fair this is great elsewhere on the coast as well. The point offers a view to *Naiharn*, to the *Racha Islands* and other small islands in the Andaman Sea, but I always found the (ever changing) huge collection of elephant statues most interesting. Laem Promthep can be approached from both Nai Harn and from Rawai. 🕒 Around the clock – before 5 pm there are way less people.
DG 7.76321, 98.3052 /GMS N 7°45′47.556″, E 98°18′18.719″

Windmill Viewpoint

The viewpoint not far from the *Promthep Cape* offers similar views to the southwest. On the hills are white windmills, which gave the place its name – in itself a rare sight in Thailand.
Between the beaches of Ya Nui and Nai Harn
DG 7.76972, 98.30672 / GMS N 7° 46′ 10.992″, E 98° 18′ 24.191″

Karon (Kata) Viewpoint: 3-Beaches Viewpoint

One of the most famous views of Phuket. You can see the beaches *Kata Noi, Kata Yai* and *Karon* and in the sea off Kata Beach the island of Ko Pu. Opening times: around the clock
DG 7.79722, 98.30226 / GMS N 7° 47′49.992″, E 98°18′8.136″

Sirinat Ntl Park

The small park on the coast is right next to *Phuket Airport*. It is best known for plane-watching: on *Mai Khao Beach* you have the landing planes directly approaching above you. Photography is now prohibited there. Sea turtles don't come here anymore – they are now further north at Khao Lak. There are many resorts in and around the park. Admission adults 200 baht, children 100 baht.

Phuket FantaSea

FantaSea is a theme park and show inspired by Thailand's traditions combined with new technology and special effects. The 70-minute show includes acrobatics, illusions, pyrotechnics, stunts and more with over 400 performers, 44 elephants, 3 tigers, 40 goats, chickens and 400 pigeons. there are also game halls, craft shows and shopping and a buffet restaurant seating 4000 guests on the premises. Tours going there are bookable with various providers, last 4 hours or longer and take place in the evening / at night. Combined tours with the *Chalong Temple* and *Patong* begin at 2 pm at Khao Lak. Possible for children over 4 years old.
Prices start from 1800 baht per person.
phuketfantasea.fun, Phuket, Kamala Beach,
DG 7.95638, 98.28751 / GMS N 7° 57′ 22.968″, E 98° 17′ 15.035″
Alternatively, go see the **Siam Niramit Phuket show**, which is similar (and newer). It takes place near Phuket Town.
siamniramitphuket.com

Skydance Helicopter Flights

Not for the vacation package tourist, but a recommendation for people who want to see the fantastic landscape from above. Skydance Helicopter offers various round trips from its base just below Phuket Airport. Included are transfer to the station (within 50 km radius) or parking at the helipad and drinks after the flight. Children under 2 fly for free on the parent's lap. People over 100 kg must book 2 seats. The helicopter is very well maintained, the pilot and the organization professional.

Contact: 💻info@skydance.aero, skydance.aero ✆+66 62 678 3333

Phuket Discovery: a 10-minute scenic flight down the coast (via Nau Yang Turtle Beach, Blue Canyon Golf Course) and back.

Phuket Scenic: 30 minutes scenic flight over Patong, Kata and Karon Beach, Promthep Cape and the Big Buddha.

Phang Nga Signature: 30-minute scenic flight over Phang Nga Bay overlooking the Sea Gypsy Village, James Bond Island, the mangroves.

Aerial Phuket & Phang Nga: 60 minutes, a combination of the two above.

More Things To Do and See on Phuket

Beaches: There are more than 30 beaches to choose from on Phuket, ranging from the most lively to the most secluded. The best beaches (from a tourist point of view) are found on the west side with beautiful sunsets and sand. The loneliest are in the Northeast.

Water Parks: If you haven't had enough water with the hotel pool, ocean, waterfalls, rivers and maybe Cheow Lan Lake, this is for you. *Splash Jungle Waterpark* near Phuket Airport, *Andamana Phuket* at Phuket Town, *Blue Tree Phuket.*

Phuket Wake Park: water park with possibilities to surf cable wakeboards and standing waves. Something for older children or young adults.

Chalong Bay Rum Factory: In the rum distillery, which is attracting international attention, you can book guided tours and cocktail workshops. The Michelin-awarded in-house restaurant is suitable for an extended stop. 💻 chalongbayrum.com

Tiger Kingdom – a newer attraction where visitors can have their pictures taken with living tigers (at your own risk and under supervision). I do not know how animal friendly that is, but when I think of the controversy with the Tiger Temple in Ayutthaya in northern Thailand (thankfully closed by now). I wouldn't recommend it.

Monkey Hill Viewpoint: View of Phuket town and lots of monkeys. You can drive up to a gate, from there it is a 25-minute walk to the viewpoint. Monkey food is sold on site, be careful with valuables and small items such as smartphones, glasses, handbags, bottles, which the monkeys like to steal.

Patong Beach: Very busy 2 km long beach with jet-skiing, parasailing, windsurfing and relaxing on the beach in between.

Patong nightlife: with lots of bars, transvestite shows, kickboxing and shopping. Most famous is the Bangla Road.

Simon Cabaret Show Well known show with transvestites and lady boys.

Big Buddha – exactly what it sounds like: a big Buddha, on a hill in the middle of Phuket, with a view. Due to landslides during the last rainy season, the access road was permanently closed in 2024; apparently, the ground is unsafe. So you can now only view it from a distance.

Shopping malls and outlet stores – Mostly Asian-inspired products and home furnishings etc. *Central Phuket, Jungceylon Mall, Central Patong, Limelight Phuket.*

Gems Gallery – Jewellery and jewels of good quality and with warranty. The prices are accordingly. The shop offers a Disneyland-like tour of the production process.

Even more to see and do:

Bungee jumping, Archery Shooting, Golf, Go-Kart, Monkey-/Crocodile-/Dolphin- or Snake Shows, Climbing Parks, Escape Room, Shooting Range, 3D Museum, Trick Eye Museum, Thalang National Museum, Thai Hua Museum, Baan Teelaka (Inverted House) ...

Phuket Airport

Sarasin Bridge

3 Beaches Viewpoint

Patong

Big Buddha, Phuket

Wat Chalong

WHAT FOR WHOM? TIPS AND IDEAS FOR EVERY TASTE

Tips for families with children

Children are curious and adventurous, so do not just stay on the beaches – as beautiful as they are. It's fun to try something new, so you can also expose the children to a bit of culture, such as a visit to a temple or a museum (as interactive as possible). And the food: it does not always have to be spaghetti, pizza or fish and chips (all of which are available): Tempura is great because the vegetables are hidden in the fried batter and a mild coconut milk soup (Tom Kha Gai) is possible as well – just don't forget to order it "mai pet" (not spicy).

More ideas for travelling with children:

- Build the largest sandcastle on the beach
- Find a waterfall and splash around! Sai Rung, Chong Fa, Sa Manora Forest Park, Si Phang Nga ...
- Take a bath with some fish in the Si Phang Nga Park
- Slide into a natural pool in the Sa Nang Manora Forest Park
- See the Police boat 813 and learn something at the Tsunami Museum in Ban Nam Khem
- Khao Sok excursions and activities
- Elephant feeding and/or bathing
- Bamboo Raft ride at Khao Lak
- Mini jungle trekking on the way to Small Sandy Beach at Khao Lak. Or a longer one at Khao Sok
- Get some jungle feeling in the "Little Amazon" at Takua Pa
- Go kayaking on a lake (Cheow Lan) or the sea (Phang Nga Bay)
- Take the Phang Nga Bay Tour
- Khao Lak Mini Golf (and Labyrinth)
- Visit the Turtle Conservatory at Thai Mueang or Lamru
- Do a snorkelling trip in front of Khao Lak: Khao Nay Yak, bigger kids on the Similans or Surin Islands
- Visit a cave with stalactites and water: the Phu Chang Cave at Phang Nga, a cave with a temple: Wat Suwan Kuha
- Do an easy bike ride around Khao Lak: to Ton Chong Fa or Sai-Rung waterfall
- Visit the Pet Cafe in Takua Pa: Burong Zone with parrots, rabbits and more
- Feed fish: at some creeks or waterfalls there are pecking fish and you can buy fish food: Sai Rung, Sri Phang Ga Waterfall, Fish Cave Temple at Khao Sok

• Visit a market and try local specialties: Bang Niang Market, Sunday market in the old town of Takua Pa, Sunday market at the river to splash around in Phang Nga: Bangkan
• ATV/Quad Biking – from the age of 12 you can drive yourself with instructions
• Eat with your feet in the river at Sai Rung Waterfall
• See monkeys (with due caution) at Wat Suwan Kuha (Phang Nga) or Monkey Temple at Khao Sok or "Little Amazon" at Takua Pa – or gibbons: if you're lucky on Cheow Lan Lake (preferably early in the morning) or down in Phuket at the Gibbons Retaliation Center
• Surfing lesson or skating or stand-up paddling. For example at Memories Beach
• Boil eggs in Kapong Hot Springs
• Relax and soak in the warm waters of Rommanee Hot Springs
• Play and Splash: Mini water park at 360 Degree Cafe
• Temple visit and some local culture: Khuek Khak Temple, Wat Phanat Nikhom at Bang Niang, Tha Sai Wooden Temple at Thai Mueang. Or a Chinese temple?
• Massage in the spa or on the beach – often works for children too and is then gentler than for adults
• Learn Thai cooking and then eat together in a cooking class at the hotel or restaurant
• Try mocktails – these are colourful, non-alcoholic drinks
• Eat ice cream – either rolled ice at the market or at an ice cream stand in the area. Tip: there are really great ice cream parlours at Takua Pa
• Handicraft or painting courses in the hotel
• Make your own batik / paint with the whole family at Batik Home
• A day at the water park: Forrester Khao Lak, Phuket or DinoSea
• Phuket Aquarium on a Phuket excursion
• Visit an interactive museum in Phuket: Trickeye Museum or 3D Museum or Upside down house
• Stay somewhere overnight in a different way: in a tree house in Khao Sok, on a floating raft on Cheow Lan Lake, or in a tent with a view of a viewpoint in Phang Nga Bay

Romantic things for couples

With its location on long, golden sandy beaches facing west, Khao Lak is predestined for romantic strolls on the beach and colourful sunsets into the sea. Khao Lak was voted No 6 for best honeymoon destination in 2024 by Travelers Choice.

Here are a few lovely tips:

• Seek and find a lonely beach
• Take a (private) photo shoot on White Sand Beach
• Stroll on the beach in the evening at sunset
• Romantic dinner on the beach. Restaurant recommendations: Krua Thai Restaurant (Bangsak), Boatyard Restaurant on Coconut Beach, Memories Beach Bar and Restaurant on Memories Beach, 8 Fish Bistro and Surf on Khuek Khak Beach, Nong Prew Restaurant on Bang Niang Beach, Lah Own Restaurant on Nang Thong Beach.
• Private dinner on the beach (can be booked in selected hotels: The Sands, La Vela, Marriott, Sarojin...)
• Private candlelit waterfall dinner (Sai Rung, Sarojin)
• Restaurants with special setting: Phu View with a view. Nai Mueang with decoration from tin-mining, Khaolak Blue Sky in the countryside, Laoleu Restaurant by the river, Pams Restaurant with a garden setting• Have a sunset dinner cruise on a Chinese Junk in Phang Nga Bay or on a boat off Khao Lak
• Book a massage or treatment at the spa
• Have a close encounter with an elephant
• Go on a bamboo raft ride in the green rainforest
• Have some cocktails at Moo Moo's Cabaret or any other bar
• Raise a sky lantern at night
• Soak in a hot spring: Natural ones at Kapong or with infrastructure at Romannee Hot Springs or Ban Bo Dan Hot Springs
• Have some dress or suit made for you by a tailor
• Enjoy delicious cakes or crepes (in the Coconut Café near the most beautiful beach in Khao Lak or with a view: in the Tree Cup at Phang Nga)
• Stroll through the Old Town of Takua Pa and try a Taosor Cake or some local Icecream in Takua Pa.
• Do a snorkel excursion to Similan or Surin Islands or Khao Nah Yak
• Cheow Lan Lake: stay overnight on the water
• Visit the Fantasea Show on Phuket
• Flowers from Me Style Flower in Khao Lak
💻 facebook.com/MeStyleFlowerKhaolakPhangNga
•Jewelry from Khaolak Gems&silver
💻 facebook.com/khaolakgemandsilver

Sporty Things for the Active and Adventurous

For people who like a bit more "action", Khao Lak offers a lot. With the many national parks in the immediate vicinity on land and in the sea, you can go straight out into nature for all sorts of adventures and leisure activities, alone or in a group. Many things are accessible by motorbike or e-bike, otherwise by paid taxis. The nightlife isn't that fabulous – party animals who need it take a trip down to Patong. What Khao Lak doesn't have are noisy jet skis or paragliding on the beach.

Tips for people who need to "get out":

- Do a diving course (short introductory courses or PADI training)
- Diving trips with liveaboards
- Snorkelling with turtles at the Similan and Surin islands
- Surfing or stand-up paddling on Pakarang Beach (also lessons)
- Skate Parks
- Trekking in the Lam Ru National Park or Khao Sok
- Kayaking in the mangroves north or south of Khao Lak. Rent a canoe and go exploring
- Explore a cave with a river through it: Phu Chang Cave near Phang Nga
- Quad biking (ATV) at Sai Rung Waterfall at Khao Lak or Phang Nga
- White Water rafting at Ton Pariwat
- Sport fishing
- Thai boxing training session
- Yoga lesson on the beach
- Horseback riding on the beach or in the hills
- Massage on the beach
- Visit a market and boldly try the fried insects and other specialties
- Moo-moos Cabaret
- Disco at the Build factory
- Try the many Bars with nice people
- Stay overnight in a tent and watch the sunrise at the Samet Nangshe or Ao Tho Li Viewpoint at Phang Nga (or take an early morning trip there)
- Go on a Phuket tour and see the Patong nightlife
- Try sport fishing or angling
- Take a trip into the Khao Sok and go trekking, especially Nam Talu Cave and Khlong Saen
- Zipline Sky Rock in Khao Lak or try one in Khao Sok or on Phuket
- Go on a bike trip on Ko Kho Khao Island
- Cycle to the Takua Pa Sunday Market
- Rock climbing on Ko Panyee in Phang Nga Bay
- Phuket excursion and Patong nightlife: Bangla Road, go go bars, ladyboys etc.
- Watch Fantasea or Siam Niramit Show in Phuket
- Phi Phi Island Overnight Tour – to sleep off the aftermath of the buckets.

Off the beaten path

Khao Lak lives from tourism and the offers are correspondingly broad (even if it is way more relaxed than Phuket). Tour trips of all kinds – mostly in groups – are offered everywhere. Many of the trips can also be made in small groups, as a private tour or even as a self-drive. To avoid the other tourists, it is sometimes enough to go somewhere outside of peak times: try going earlier in the morning or after 5 pm in the evening. And then, of course, there are places to discover that are not well known everywhere ...

Here are a few "secret" tips – go discover!

- Experience the sunrise over the sea of fog at Khao Kai Nui or Phu Ta Chor viewpoint
- Sunset picnic at a Phang Nga viewpoint
- Sunrise over Phang Nga Bay from the viewpoint (Samet Nangshe or better: Ao Tho Li)
- Private Phang Nga Bay Tour
- Private snorkelling tour (really lonely: Ko Kham and Laem Son National Park)
- Bike or motorbike excursions in the area
- Visit less well-known waterfalls (Ton Tham waterfall near Khao Lak, Ton Sung waterfall between Khao Lak and Phuket)
- Find a secluded sandy beach: above Bangsak or at Thai Mueang
- Kayaking at Ban Tha Din Dang: just south of Khao Lak in Khao Lampi–Hat Thai Mueang National Park
- Hot springs at Kapong and egg cooking in the hot springs
- Trekking in Khao Sok National Park (multi-day trips)
- Stay overnight on Cheow Lan Lake and go trekking in Khao Sok
- Wat Bang Riang in the morning if possible
- Baan Bang Phat – the other sea nomad village in Phang Nga Bay
- Self-excursion into the mangroves: Northeast Phuket and Kayak Rentals at Bang Rong Pier
- Go green in the Sa Nang Manora Forest National Park or in the Raman Waterfall Park near Phang Nga
- Alternative to the Sunday market in Takua Pa: Bangkan between Khao Lak and Phang Nga
- Discover the north: Si Phang Nga National Park, Tarn Morakot Rafting (Bamboo Raft), Kuraburi Pier
- Walk across the Dragon's Back Dune at low tide
- Day trip or overnight on Ko Yao Yai
- Biking on Ko Kho Khao or near Phang Nga
- Visit a morning market with the locals – Bang Niang Fresh Market, Kapong Sunday Market, Takua Pa, Khao Sok

• Restaurants: sooo many undiscovered places with fine and cheap food. Just try it!
• Take a cooking course – you get a lot of info about the local life
• Private tours of the area: the best way to see how Thai people live and work is to hire a local guide. Ideas: cashew nut factory, pineapple plantations, fishermen at the pier, donating food to the monks in the morning, visit a school.

For culture and history enthusiasts

For a "typical beach destination", the area around Khao Lak offers a lot of historical interest. In the Neolithic period, people left rock drawings. From the 7th century onwards, the area was an important trading hub and later part of the Silk Road. There were land and power struggles with the Khmer and Burmese. The discovery of tin in the 15th century brought about a strong economic boom in Takua Pa and the surrounding area. This attracted many Chinese guest workers and trade was carried out as far as Europe (with the Portuguese and British). During World War II, planes landed here on Ko Kho Khao. Between 1975 and 1982, the communist rebels hid in caves in Khao Sok National Park. Tourism discovered Khao Lak quite late – and then the tsunami came in December 2004 during the boom.

Historically interesting

• Cave paintings in Phang Nga Bay. Can be seen on a trip with the longtailboat
• Wall painting with Khmer/pirate treasure map: in Phang Nga Bay on an island (private tour necessary and guide who knows his way around)
• Shell cemetery. Not a burial place, but a depository where mother of pearl is still mined today.
• Sam Cave. Cave near Phang Nga with historical wall paintings of everyday Thai life and Buddha relief
• Narai Historical Park near Takua Pa – many replicas, the originals are in Bangkok
• Ban Thung Tuk Ancient City – excavation site on Ko Kho Khao
• World War 1 airfield on Ko Kho Khao (now just a grass field)
• Coral Cave on a side lake of Cheow Lan contains fossil corals and served as a hideout for communist rebels between 1975 and 1982.
• Rajiaprabha Dam – Dam on Cheow Lan Lake in Khao Sok. Opened by Thailand's last king on his 60th birthday.
• Phang Nga Museum – History of Phang Nga
• Benyaran Museum – Antiques from the area
• Mining Museum Phuket – Tin mining museum

Architecture and temples

- Takua Pa old town with Sino-Portuguese arcade houses
- Remains of the old city wall in the historical park of Takua Pa
- Phuket old town
- Heroines Monument on Phuket
- Wat Khomniyaket, new and classic Buddhist temple in Khuek Khak.
- Wat Tha Sai. Wooden temple near Thai Mueang
- Wat Khongkha Phimuk near Takua Pa. The chedi next to the classic red and gold temple in Thai style is gold-plated all around and the interior is completely lined with mirror mosaic.
- Wat Suwan Kuha – cave temple with a large, reclining Buddha near Phang Nga
- Wat Bang Riang on the hill between Phang Nga and Krabi.
- Wat Bang Thong. Huge new temple complex towards Krabi with an almost 70m high, golden central tower.
- Wat Chalong – Phuket's most famous temple

Tin mining remains

- Engine of a tin mining ship in the old town of Takua Pa
- Boon Soong Iron Bridge – built from the metal of a tin mining ship
- Remains of machines used for tin mining on the Khao Na Yak peninsula (Remains of Tin Dredging)
- Many of the small lakes around Khao Lak are remnants of open-pit tin mining
- the black sand of Nang Thong Beach – tin is the dye here

Memories of the 2004 tsunami

- Navy Boat 813 – the police boat that washed ashore is still in the same place in Bang Niang. A memorial park was built around it.
- International Tsunami Museum – the museum in Khao Lak is very small
- Memorial at the Navy Base
- Tsunami Memorial in Ban Nam Khen – large Buddha and wave-like memorial wall
- Ban Nam Knem Tsunami Museum
- Similana Resort: today a ruin, a lost place
- Saori Foundation Center

What to do when it rains? – Not only in the rainy season / low season

Of course, rain during the holidays is not nice, but it does make a difference whether it's wet and cold, or just wet because the temperatures remain at a pleasant (to hot) 22 to 34 degrees even in the rainy season – and rain usually looks worse than it really is. Weather forecasts and apps very often show rain – but this does not mean that it will rain all day, nor that it necessarily rains exactly where you are. It often rains in the evening hours, and it may be heavy, but short.

Therefore: go out anyway! Take an umbrella with you and possibly a dry bag.

• Swimming: When you're wet, you're wet. Swimming in the pool is always possible (except during thunderstorms: please leave the water immediately!). Swimming in the sea in the low season is often dangerous because of the currents and the waves. Please note the signalization flags on the beach.
• Surfing is better with the high waves of the rainy season. Cape Pakarang is best for it in Khao Lak. The Memories Bar also offers rental equipment.
• Too many waves? Try surfing on land: skate at one of the skate parks in Khao Lak.
• Snorkelling and diving is not possible in the low season: the national parks off the coast are closed. You can still do an introductory diving course in the hotel pool
• Visit the waterfalls: With water they certainly look splashing and you can bathe under some of them.
• Elephant watching or bathing and feeding. Elephants have no problem with getting a little wet – and are grateful for the food.
• Massages and Spa: treat yourself to a Thai massage or a wrap or scrub or a manicure ...
• Market visit: shop under umbrellas or in covered shops. Bang Niang Market on Monday, Wednesday and Saturday; the market at the Built Factory on the other days. Sunday market in the old town of Takua Pa. The fresh markets in Khuek Khak (and other places) are open daily.
• Visit a temple: it is always dry inside, but please dress accordingly.
• Tailor: Have a dress or suit made.
• Cooking course or cocktail course: Many hotels offer this, but you can also book outside and learn how to get the ingredients.
• Restaurant-hopping: try as many of the excellent restaurants in Khao Lak as possible. As more and more tourists stay during the low season, the choice of restaurants becomes larger.
• Excursions in the area: in the minibus you stay dry, in the Songthaew also (if they have closed the tarpaulins on the side) and Bo jeeps, otherwise open vehicles, can be made rainproof.
• Book a "Foodie tour" and not only get to know the area, but also the local specialities.
• Phang Nga Bay Tour: You can do that even in the low season if the waves are not too high.
• Royal Thai Navy Fleet Turtle Nursery: The pools are covered, so you can visit the turtles dry.

• Read: all the books you never had time for. If you do not have an e-reader or have taken books with you, you often find a hotel library or visit *Juice from Mars* and his mini–library.
• Watch shrill Thai television: Try it – it's almost a cultural experience.
• Use the gym in the hotel
• Rawai Muay Thai: attend a Thaiboxing class.
• Attend a yoga class. Some hotels offer classes, or you can join a yoga class outside or ask for private lessons.
• Have a bamboo tattoo done as a special souvenir
• Bowling for 150 Baht pp in the Graceland Hotel (north of Bangsak)
• Go fishing
In the evening:
• The sunset is even more spectacular with a few clouds.
• Moo Moo Cabaret – wet your throat (with some cocktails)– only in high season
• Watch a fight at the Thai Boxing Stadium (on Fridays)
• Visit bars and pubs: A chance to not only drink cocktails and beer, but also to meet some of the people living here (expats and locals).
• Island trip to Kho Phi Phi: possible even in low season when the waves are not too high.
Take a trip down to Phuket:
• 3D Museum on Phuket
• Phuket Aquarium (Mainly inside except for the outside nature trail that leads to the Turtle Hatchery.)
• Cinema: Unfortunately, there is none at Khao Lak, but down on Phuket: Multi-Screen Cinema at the Jungle Ceylon Mall in Patong and the Central Festival Mall outside Phuket Town. There you can also spend a few hours shopping and eating.

Route tips for self-drive or taxi

Whether by rental car or taxi (Songthaew or minibus): here are some easily feasible and worthwhile route suggestions with attractions in the Khao Lak area:

Temples and Caves – Tour, Phang Nga (day trip)

Khao Lak (Khuk Khak Temple) – Phang Nga– Wat Suwan Khuha – Phung Chang Cave – Wat Thamtapan – Sa Nang Manora Forest Ntl Park – Khao Lak

Kapong Tour: Nature and Culture (day trip)

Khao Lak – Khao Khai Nouy Lookout – Lam Ru Waterfall – Kapong Temple – Hot Springs – Takua Pa Old Town and Chinese Temple – Big Buddha – Sai Rung Waterfall – Khao Lak. (Attention: The viewpoint needs a 4WD vehicle).

Takua Pa Tour (half day or day trip)

Khao Lak – Andaman Viewpoint – Ban Nam Khen Tsunami Memorial – Little Amazon Takua Pa – Boon Soon Iron Bridge – Wat Khongkha Phimuk – Takua Pa Old Town – Big Buddha – Sai Rung Waterfall – Khao Lak

Everything about the water in the north (day trip)

Khao Lak – Sai Rung Waterfall – Ban Bam Khem Tsunami Memorial Centre – Ferry to Ko Kho Khao – Ko Kho Khao View and Relax on the Beach – Ferry Back – Takua Pa – Tam Nang Waterfall – Back to Khao Lak

Big round trip (day trip)

Khao Lak – Takua Pa – Khao Sok (Waterfall, Viewpoint, Restaurant) – Cheow Lan Lake – South Bang Riang Temple – Curvy Scenic Road 4 – Sao Manora Forest Park – Khao Lak.

That means a lot of driving, but you are on nice roads and you can always stop in between for attractions and something to eat and drink.

Khao Sok Tour (day trip, possibly with overnight stay)

Khao Lak – Big Buddha – Takua Pa – Mae Yai Waterfall – Khao Sok Viewpoint – Ratchaprapha Dam – Marina Cheow Lan Lake – boat rental and trip on the lake (at least 2 hours) – drive back to Khao Lak (Why don't you take a relaxing stop in the hot water on the way to the Romanee Hot Springs?) That's a long drive. Possible to spend one night at Khao Sok National Park, as there are many accommodation options in front of the national park headquarters. Then you could add a small hike in the park in the morning.

To the undiscovered North (Day Trip)

Khao Lak – Andaman Viewpoint – Takua Pa – Water Onion Conservation – Si Phang Nga Waterfall – Tarn Morakot Rafting – Kuraburi Pier – Boat to Dragonback Dune – Kuraburi Pier – Back to Khao Lak

The south on your own (half day to full day trip)

Khao Lak – Komols Corner: Bamboo Rafting – Ton Prai Waterfall – Mueang Thai – Leng San Keng Shrine: Chinese Temple – Wat Tha Sai: Wooden Temple – Phang Nga Coastal Fisheries Center – Khao Lampi Hat Thai Mueang National Park to the beach – back to Khao Lak

Phang Nga Tour (half day to day trip)

Khao Lak – Thai Muang (Turtle Sanctuary) – Coffee at Tree Cups – Surakul Pier (Mangrove / Phang Nga Bay Boat Cruise) – Wat Suwan Khuha – Bang Pat Fishing Village (Food) – Phang Nga – Phung Chang Cave – Sa Manora Forest Park – Khao Lak

If you start early in the morning, you can try to catch the sunrise at Samet Nangshe Viewpoint and have a drink there. If you drive at night allow more time – the roads are dangerous because there are many vehicles without lights on the streets.

Phuket, the north (half day trip)

Khao Lak – Andaman Viewpoint (360 Degrees Coffee) – Sarasin Bridge – Mission Hills Loop – Bay View Loop – Lunch at Floating Restaurant at Bang Rong Pier – Gibbons Rehabilitation Project and Bang Pae Waterfall– Phuket Elephant Sanctuary – Heroines Monument – back to Khao Lak

Phuket complete (day trip)

Khao Lak – Sarasin Bridge – Heroines Monument – Phuket Town – Wat Chalong – Promthrep Cape – 3 Beaches Viewpoint – Return via the Beaches: Kata – Karon – Patong – Kamala – Heroines Monument – back to Khao Lak. (Note: because of the heavy traffic on Phuket this is really a day trip and rather exhausting for self–drivers).

Excursions, tours and unforgettable moments

Memories are the souvenirs that last the longest. You can collect many beautiful memories in Khao Lak, be it on your own or through the numerous tour operators. Excursions can be booked in the hotel, on the Internet, at the small tourist information shops on site, even in some restaurants, bars or massage parlours. – the later organize this through local providers, but sometimes the risk is that these are not officially licensed, meaning you won't be insured. Those who book their tours online with getyourguide or Viator are probably insured, but they'll likely end up in the tourist traps of mass tourism.

We were a bit disappointed with the JW Marriott, because they obviously wanted to keep people in the hotel itself, and nowhere at the reception (or anywhere else) were excursions advertised, nor the usual scheduled transfers to Bang Niang or La On. There's a taxi stand in front of the hotel, where you can organize this yourself if you're not mobile (like us) and of course, there is internet connection,

to contact local tour operators. They all pick you up from the hotel, no matter how far away it is. Some even visit you at the hotel and show you what they have to offer.
Pro Tip: Guests of hotels where breakfast is included and whose tours start before breakfast are entitled to a free meal box. (Must be registered at the hotel the night before – and don't forget to get it in the morning).

A selection of tour providers in Khao Lak:

(Order without ranking)

Khao Lak Tour Plan – local, customized. 💻 khaolaktourplan.com,
Khaolak Land Discovery – 💻 khaolaklanddiscovery.com
Khao Lak Vista Tours & Travel –💻 khaolakvista.com
Green Andaman Travel – 💻 greenandamantravel.com
Khao Lak Private Travel – William Suwanchatree. Taxi, Transport, Tours. 💻 khaolakprivatetravel.com, whatsapp: ✆+66 96 896 3653
Khaolak Guru – (English/ French) 💻 /khaolakguru.net
Excursions Thailand – 💻 excursionsthailande.com longtime provider (French)
Khun Pond on Tour (german, English) local well known guide 💻 facebook.com/pond.beachbar.14 ✆+66 76 484 657
Discovery Travel Khao Lak – eco-friendly 💻 discoverykhaolak.com
Khao Lak Discoveries 💻 khaolakdiscoveries.com
Go on Tour Khao Lak – Gabi and Odty have their office in Bang Niang. 💻 goontourkhaolak.com
Go Travel Phuket Büro auf Phuket. (german, reliable), Contact per Whatsapp: Danijel +66 82079779 Charly: +66 847 440 482 💻 gotravelphuket.com und facebook.com/groups/167209203875424.
Khao Lak Adventures (german, English) 💻 khaolak-adventures.de
Nice Trip Khaolak – experienced French speaking travel agency. 💻 nicetripkhaolak.com
Toms Touren – 💻toms-thailandtouren.de tours with an individual touch.
t-*globe*–💻 khaolak.de & t-globe.com. Contact khaolaktransfer@gmail.com
Holiday Service Khao Lak 💻 holiday-service-khaolak.com
Wonderland Tour 💻 m.facebook.com/KhaolakWonderlandTours
Green Biking Club (german, Englisch) 💻 greenbikingclub.com

Examples of guided tours:

Night Safari

You can book trips to the surrounding area of Khao Lak for example, in the *Sakai Bar* – the boss is also a tour guide for the *Khaolak Jungle Safari* and a real expert. Or you can go on a kayak night safari on the "little Amazon" after dinner, followed by a night hike through the jungle with a guide: 💻 khaolak-junglesafari.com/canoe-night-safari-only-by-us/ Or 💻 khaolak-adventures.de

Khao Lak: Rafting, Elephants and Turtles, approx. 5 hours

Elephant camp with bathing and feeding – Visit a waterfall (Sai Rung) – Bamboo raft ride through the rainforest – Visit the Sea Turtle Conservation Centre at Tap Lamu

Little Amazon tour, about 4 hours

Transfer and visit to Takua Pa Morning Market – Canoe ride on the Small Amazon – Visit to Sai Rung Waterfall. Back.

Khao Lak Temple Tour& Takua Pa Old Town, about 4 hours

Visit Khuk Khak Temple and guided tour – Kongkha Phimuk Temple with golden Chedi at Takua Pa with guided tour – Takua Pa Old Town with Sino-Portuguese houses, Chinese shrines and tea houses – Bath under a local waterfall.

Takua Pa historical and cultural tour, about 6 hours

Transfer and visit to a Chinese shrine – guided tour
Takua Pa Old Town – Visit to Takua Pa Market – Visit to Nam Kem Cultural Centre (locally run museum) – Visit to Taosor Cake Factory – Thai Lunch – Visit to Tsunami Memorial – Return.

Local Life / Local Tour Takua Pa, half day

Morning departure – Offering food to the monks – Breakfast: dim sum / noodle soup – Visit to a local school – Visit to a temple and chat with a monk – Thai lunch – Visit to the Saori Foundation.

Khao Lak Jungle Tour / offroad, about 8 hours

Drive on Takua Pa – Canoe ride through mangrove forests and wildlife spotting – Traditional Thai lunch at a lake – Offroad jungle drive through National Park (Sri Phangnga) in 4x4 – Short walk to a spectacular waterfall where you can swim – Visit a Buddhist temple.

Khao Lak Safari, about 8 hours

Elephant Bathing (no riding) – Bamboo Rafting – Turtle Breeding Centre – Thai Lunch – Waterfall – Tsunami Police Boat – Temple Visit.

Sri Phang Nga jungle tour, about 8 hours

Visit to Little Amazon and Canoe Ride – Visit to local market of Takua Pa – Sri Phang Nga Park and small walk to Tam Nang Waterfall and bathe under it – Thai Lunch – Visit to Romanee Hot Springs – Return on Khao Lak

White water rafting, waterfall hike, quad ride, about 9 hours

Transfer to Ton Pariwat Reserve near Phang Nga – Rafting – 30 minutes quad ride – Thai lunch – Short hike to Ton Pariwat waterfall, (swimming possible) – Coffee and tea break – return.

Phang Nga Bay, about 8-10 hours

Drive to a pier in Phang Nga Bay – Explore mangroves in a traditional longtail boat – Canoe tour among the limestone formations / into a cave – Visit to Khao Ping Kan (James Bond Island) – Visit to the floating village of Ko Panyee (possible with lunch) – Visit to the cave temple Wat Suwan Kuha with a large golden reclining Buddha. Some offer an early-morning tour, safely avoiding the crowds of tourists that usually attend.

Temple tour, about 9 hours

Explore Dragon Cave Temple – view from Wat Rat Upatham (Wat Bang Riang) – Wat Suwan Kuha: the cave temple with large reclining Buddha – feed monkeys – lunch at a Thai restaurant.

Phuket weekend market about 9 hours

Big Buddha Phuket Viewpoint – Visit to Naka Market / Phuket Weekend night market – Return trip.

Phuket Tour Sightseeing and Shopping full day

Visit a Cashew Nut Factory – Visit Gems Gallery Jeweller – Shopping at Central Festival Market – Wat Chalong – Kata Viewpoint – Patong Jungceylon Shopping Mall – Return

Patong Night half day (late night)

Pick up at hotel – drive to Patong – No Guide / Free Time in Patong – Depart 11.30pm from Junk Ceylon Mall and return.

Ao Tho Li

Makake at Little Amazon

Takua Pa

Monks at Phang Nga

Tam Nang, Si Phang Nga

AGAINST THE CULTURE SHOCK

A little bit of History: Khao Lak / Phang Nga

The area has been inhabited since early times: excavations on the island of Ko Kho Khao (Ban Tun Teuk Ancient City) show that there was an important port here, a **part of the Thai Silk Road**. Persian glass beads and Chinese artifacts from the Tang Dynasty (907-618 BC) were found at this trading hub, as well as what is probably the oldest trace of fired roof tiles in Thailand.

Established around 1809 under **King Rama II of Siam** (now Thailand), **the Phang Nga Province** was repeatedly attacked by Burma. The area became economically important when rich deposits of tin were discovered in the ground. These were mined by Chinese guest workers. Many of these workers stayed and today form an essential part of the population with their own traditions. This is best seen in Phuket Old Town and Takua Pa Old Town with their Sino Portuguese style buildings and Chinese temples.

A consequence of the **tin mining** are the many small lakes around Khao Lak, which were open-pit mines, now filled with water. After the mines on land were exhausted, tin mining shifted to the sea. Along the entire coastal region off Khao Lak, mining ships were still at work day and night in the 1980s, mining the stones and sand washed out by the rivers and sieving out the tin. It is said that thanks to this grinding Khao Lak has such fine sand. Today, especially in La On on Nang Thong Beach, you can find entire patches that are almost black with tin. A mining ship engine is on display in the Takua Pa Park, and the iron hulls from the deranged ships were used to build the Boon Soong Iron Bridge across the Takua Pa River in 1968.

Tourism discovered Khao Lak relatively late – and for a long time it was overshadowed by the more famous Phuket. In 1987, the Germans Gerd and Hans were the first to open a small bungalow complex on Bang Niang beach (today: Gerd and Noi Bungalows). Others followed – the destination changed from a pure backpacker's stopover to today's loved destination, or rather several places next to each other on the coast. Richard Doring was the first to mention Khao Lak in a travel guide (the Loose for southern Thailand). Today he lives and works in Khao Lak. Khao Lak has become a popular resort for tourists from Scandinavian countries, as well as from Germany. English guidebooks neglected the region for a long time (actually still today).

In December **2004**, during the greatest boom, **the tsunami** hit. It completely devastated the coastal area and claimed many lives. Reconstruction in the months that followed was difficult but was tackled by the surviving population and the help of numerous friends of Khao Lak from other countries.
Today you hardly see any of it anymore, even if the event left many mental scars. With building regulations, protection of the nature parks and committed local shops and accommodation, Khao Lak ensures that it does not just become a party- and mass-tourism destination.
From 2020 to the end of 2021, tourism collapsed again due to the **Covid pandemic**. A visit was only possible for local tourists. As a result, many providers in the tourism sector had to give up – the beautiful area is now slowly recovering. Today almost everything is up again and ready for visitors.

Do's and Don'ts in Thailand

Respect for the royal family: never insult the king who is highly revered. (And do not destroy money with his image).
Respect for Buddha: do not climb on Buddha statues, do not buy and export Buddha statues or images either.
The soles of the feet should never be turned towards someone, as this is considered very rude.
Thais should **never be touched on the head** (not even kids!), since the soul is located there.
The left hand is considered unclean (that is also the one you use to wash yourself on the toilet), so when you hand someone money / a gift / some food, always do so with your right hand.
Touching in public or openly showing physical contact (except for holding hands) is not welcome.
Be mindful of monks. Some are not allowed to touch women. As a woman you therefore ask a man to give the alms or put it on the ground.

The Wai is the Thai greeting. A foreigner is not expected to return it, especially since it is not easy to carry it out correctly with all of its deeper meanings. How low the head is bowed, or the hands are lifted depends on your own status and that of the person opposite. It is safer for a tourist to just smile and nod.

Thais usually address each other by **their first names**– which means that your own transfer or tour reservations will occasionally not be found when searching under your family name. Thais mainly talk to each other using **nicknames**, which they often received as babies.

Occasionally you will be asked **personal questions** that seem almost indiscreet. A typical question would be "How much you earn?" – This is pure sympathy and curiosity. You can answer it well with something like: "I do not know myself," or "It's enough for us"...

Gräng Jai describes a typical Thai trait and means: be considerate of others, do not make any claims, show restraint. Mutual sympathy and a polite approach are very important. That is why many Thais don't like to say "No" when a positive answer is expected – just not to disappoint.

Confrontations are avoided, so that both sides do not lose face. That is why you shouldn't publicly denigrate the country and criticize people. If you really must criticize, remain friendly and balance it with praise and ... smile a lot.
Thus in Thailand a smile opens doors – a smile helps you to get over so many (of your own) mistakes.

Public holidays

Few countries have more holidays than Thailand. Thai festivals and holidays are often very boisterous affairs – even Buddhist celebrations that you might not expect. Most are colourful and often elaborately celebrated. On public holidays, all government offices and banks are closed. If the holiday falls on a Saturday or Sunday, the following Monday is also a day off. Most holidays and festivals are religious, some regional festivals commemorate important events in the country's history or have to do with the royal family. Because of the large proportion of Chinese people living in the country, typical Chinese festivals are celebrated. The religious festivities are based on the lunar calendar and therefore, the dates change every year. The Thai lunar year ends with the last full moon in November and begins with the following new moon. A list of the current dates can be found here: 💻 timeanddate.de/feiertage/thailand

During religious (Buddhist) holidays, the sale and serving of alcohol is prohibited (until 1 minute after midnight) – this applies to restaurants and bars and often hotels.
The national anniversaries, on the other hand, take place on the same date every year because they are based on the Western calendar. According to the traditional Thai lunar calendar, time in Thailand begins with the year of Buddhas death. Thus, "our" year 2024 (after Christ's birth) is the year 2568 after Buddha's death.

January

First January / New Year: Nationwide, official holiday. It is celebrated in most hotels with a gala dinner and formal dress code. Public "Making Merit" takes place in front of the community centre in Mueang and Takua Pa: Monks and Buddhists gather at the temples to pray, sing, meditate together and listening to sermons on how to live a good life.
Chinese New Year: Nationwide, not a public holiday. Lasts 3 days. Most important celebration for the 12-15% of Chinese living in Thailand. Greatly celebrated with fireworks and dragons for example in Takua Pa or in the old town of Phuket.

February/March

Makha Puja: Buddhist holiday, based on the Thai lunar calendar. National holiday. On this day, 1250 monks came together without invitation to hear a sermon from Buddha.
Loy Rüa: Feast of the sea nomads. Phuket / P.hang Nga / Surin. Wooden miniature boats (about 2.5 meters long) with sacrificial offerings are exposed into the sea to appease the spirits of the seas. The festival takes place twice a year: at the beginning and at the end of the monsoon season.
February 14 – Valentine's Day: Not a public holiday
Thao Thep Krasatri & Thao Sri Suntorn: Feast in Phuket. The two sisters (Muk and Chan) were able to prevent the Burmese by means of tactics and tricks and perseverance from taking Phuket in 1785. Their statues form the Heroines Monument at the large roundabout on Phuket. On their feast day, the monument is decorated with lush flower garlands and flowers, and incense sticks are burning.

April

April 6 – Chakri Memorial Day: Nationwide, official holiday. It commemorates the accession of Rama I. Founder of the Chakri dynasty. Candlelight processions and general folk festival.
13-15 April – Songkran: also called water festival. Nationwide, official holiday. Thai New Year. The people on Thailand's streets splash water at

each other. Since Thai people then visit their relatives, public transport is often fully booked / overcrowded.

May

Visakha Bucha: Nationwide, holiest Buddhist holiday. In the evening, there are light processions in all the temples in order to commemorate the birth and enlightenment of Buddha.
May 1 – Labour Day: Bank holiday, national, official holiday.
May 5 – Coronation Day: Yasothon, former King Ramas IX / Bhumipol, who died on October 13, 2016. He was the longest reigning king and since 1992 the longest reigning monarch in the world. Because of his unifying and stabilizing power, he was very popular.

July

1st of July – middle of the year: public holiday, bank holiday, all banks in the country are closed.
Asalha Puja / Asanha Bucha: not a public holiday. Buddhist holiday. It recalls the Buddha's first public sermon.
Vassa: Beginning of the three-month rainy season retreat according to the Thai lunar calendar. Buddhist holiday, not a public holiday.
Khao Panza: Buddhist holiday, beginning of the fasting period and the monks' rainy season retreat. Processions with flowers and candles in the temples. Not a public holiday.
Buat Naag: Ordination of the monks, Buddhist holiday, no public holiday. Traditionally, every Thai male should enter the monastic order for some time before marriage. Nowadays, it doesn't matter so much when this happens or for how long, yet it is a celebrated step.
Por Gate: Phuket / Takua Pa. Feast of the hungry ghosts of the Thai-Chinese population. On that day, the Infernal Father opens the gates, so that the hungry spirits can return to their families who can do something for their own karma by offering food to the spirits. Celebrated mainly in the family. The red turtle cakes served with fruit and incense sticks as an offering are well known in Phuket.

August

August 12 – Mother's Day: Birthday of the former Queen Sirikit, national, official holiday. It celebrates Queen Sirikit and the many charities she has already rendered to her people. She is referred to as the Mother of the Land and Mother's Day has been celebrated in Thailand on her birthday since 1950.

September

Sart Thai: Remembering the deceased, Buddhist holiday, not an official holiday. In Thai Buddhism, death is not only viewed as a cycle of life, but it is believed that all the merits of the deceased family members somehow serve the surviving relatives. On this day, the images of the deceased are cleaned at home or at the urn graves, decorated with fresh flower garlands, lit candles and incense sticks and prayers are held.

Loy Rüa: Phuket / Phang Nga. Feast of the sea nomads. (See February)

Chinese Vegetarian Festival: Late September / early October on Phuket and Taku Pa. It lasts for 9 days and serves the inner cleansing of body and mind. Participants fast and dress in white. People walk over broken glass and glowing coals and some deliberately pierce parts of their bodies with sharp objects, including their cheeks (although that is not practiced in Takua Pa as pronouncedly as in Phuket). Fireworks on the last day. Not an official holiday

October

Ok Phansa Day: End of the three-month rainy season, Buddhist holiday, not a public holiday

October 23 – Chulalongkorn: Death of King Chulalongkorn (Rama V.), commemoration day, not a public holiday.

November

Thoth Kathin: donation of robes to monks. Buddhist holiday, not a public holiday.

Loy Krathong: Festival of Lights on the full moon day. Homage to the goddess of water (Mae Khinhkhe), boatmen with flowers, burning candles and offerings are placed on the water of rivers and lakes throughout the country. Not a public holiday.

December

5th December – Father's Day: Birthday of the previous king, Bhumibol Adulyadei, also national day. Official holiday.

December 10 – Constitution Day: Change to constitutional monarchy. Official holiday. On December 10, 1932, Thailand, then called Siam, received its first constitution and thus successfully managed the transition from absolute monarchy to a constitutional one without civil war and bloodshed.

December 31 – New Year's Eve: official holiday.

Papaya Salat

Tom Kha Gai

Mango Sticky Rice

Thai Cooking Courses

Eating in Thailand

Thai food is a mix of Chinese, Indian and European influences that have merged over time to its own national cuisine. Thai food is tasty and doesn't make you fat. There is a lot of rice – actually the Thai expression for "have a meal" literally means "eat rice" ... but the additions and spices make the food so tasty.

Kaeng

These are different "Curry"-dishes. However, they do not contain curry powder but are made with a spicy paste as a base. Galangal or ginger with kaffir lime leaves are used for this paste, along with fresh chilies and shrimp paste, which are all mashed in a mortar until a homogeneous paste is formed. There are red and green Kaeng dishes with different types of meat or fish or tofu.

Tom Kha Kai

Sweet chicken soup with coconut milk, galangal, lemongrass and chili. The coconut softens any spiciness. Tom Kha Kai is also a Kaeng dish and one of my favourite foods that can also be enjoyed in a less spicy way. Instead of chicken it may contain seafood and various vegetables, depending on the cook.

Tom Yam

Hot and sour shrimp soup: spicy. With fish sauce, shallots, lemongrass, lime juice, galangal, tamarind and chili. Classically with shrimp, but there are also versions with other fish and seafood.

Som Tam

Papaya salad (spicy), a kind of salad made with chopped and mashed green (unripe) papaya, onions, tomatoes. With lime, long beans, roasted peanuts, salt, palm sugar and chili, seasoned with fish sauce. Shrimps are often included (mostly dried, sometimes also fresh). It is usually very spicy (really!) and slightly tart.

Pad Thai

Noodles with vegetables and meat, the national dish of Thailand. This is a one-plate meal that combines the four flavours: hot, sour, salty and sweet. It contains dried chilies, lime, fish sauce and cane sugar. The noodles are fried with egg, tofu and small, dried shrimp. Bean sprouts, chives and chopped roasted peanuts are served with it – often separately for individual seasoning.

Phat Kaphrao

A single-plate meal with minced meat (pork or chicken or beef, but also shrimp) with Thai basil – the stronger and more aromatic version of the one known here. Chili, garlic and soy sauce are added, all fried in a wok and served with rice.

Satay skewers

This dish originates from Indonesia and Malaysia. These are skewers of grilled spiced meat, served with a sauce. The meat on the skewers is mostly chicken but can also be fish or beef or pork. However, the spice mixture always contains turmeric, which gives it the typical yellow colour. It is frequently served with a peanut sauce dip.

Tempura

Vegetables and shrimp fried in a light batter. The dish originates from Japan or India and contains various vegetables (small corncob, onion rings, beans, papaya) or shrimp or fish that is cut into pieces and freshly dipped in a light batter and then deep-fried.

Squid with pepper and garlic sauce

This dish can be ordered in the simplest local Thai restaurants and consists of various kinds of meat, fish or squid with a sauce of dark roasted garlic and pepper, served with rice.

Table manners

Thai attitude to food is simple: if you are hungry, you eat. Our three main meals a day don't exist as such in Thailand; most Thai people eat little, but often. Although you may have breakfast, lunch and dinner, in between you can have a bowl of pasta, a fried snack or some sweets at any time. Eating is simply a pleasure.

Originally Thai food was eaten with the fingers – which is still the case today in some regions and with some dishes. But today you normally use fork and spoon. Most of the time there are no knives and you won't need one because the food is made in bite-sized

pieces. The fork is used to slide something onto the spoon – the spoon then goes to the mouth.
Chopsticks are not part of Thai cuisine and are only used in Chinese restaurants or to eat Chinese and Vietnamese noodle dishes. Then you hold the spoon in the left hand and the chopsticks in the right.
A peculiarity is that the various dishes ordered in the restaurant usually do not arrive at the same time, but staggered and not necessarily in the order that you might expect (because you have chosen a starter). Thais usually share everything when they eat together, so everyone starts when it arrives.

Toilets

While the toilets found in the hotels and restaurants are almost exclusively western-style toilets, the ones outside are sometimes not. And there may be no toilet paper. Do not panic, you will still get clean – the Thais just use another system. As a beginner, it is advisable to take off all your clothes below the waistline to prevent accidents. With some practice you can keep your pants / skirt / underpants on later and just pull them down quite a bit, but at the beginning it is really better to take them off. Then crouch over the hole (facing the door, knees towards the ceiling) and let it run. Physiologically this is a better position than sitting on the loo, even if it is very unusual for us.
After business wash yourself with the (left!) hand and water. The water either comes from a hose or bucket with a ladle which you can find in every Thai toilet. With the right hand you draw/spray the water, with the left one you wash yourself thoroughly. Provided you use enough water, this is not a grisly affair. Rinse the toilet well with the water as you finish. If there is toilet paper – or if you brought some – use it to dry yourself. The toilets are not designed to flush the paper though – there is a bin, where you can dispose of it. Although 1-2 leaves usually go down, do not try to flush more! This often also applies to regular toilets – you will find corresponding signs.
Then thoroughly wash your hands and get dressed – that's it.

Electricity

Thailand uses sockets (and plugs) of the Types A, B, C. Older outlets are Type A, modern outlets are a combination of Types B and C. If you are from the UK or USA you will need a power plug adapter in Thailand.

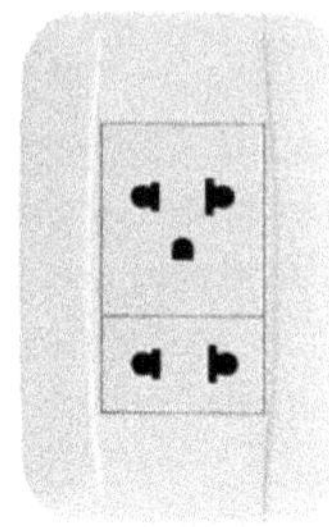

The main voltage in Thailand is 230 Volts as it is in Europe. For tourists from the USA, where they use 120 Volts – there may be problems, or they may need a converter. Have a look at the chargers for laptops, tablets, smartphones, cameras. If it says INPUT: 100-240 Volt, 50/60 Hz – that means that these devices can be used in the specified line voltage range around the world – also in Thailand.

Noteworthy here are the myriads of cables you see hanging everywhere, unfortunately also in front of the most beautiful sights in Thailand. Unlike in Europe, where the power supply of houses is mainly underground, the electrical cables in Thailand hang on poles above ground. Every house seems to have at least one cable going to the mast. To save costs, the homeowners in many regions are allowed to put up power cables themselves. So you can frequently see entire families working together to hang cables from large cable drums onto existing poles. Safety is often disregarded – and occasionally accidents occur when a pole is under current. In the countryside power outages occur when the network is overloaded.

Telephone, Roaming, Internet

Thailand is not a third world country when it comes to **cell phones/mobile phones.** Many Thais sport the latest phone models and the connection is good almost everywhere (the only exception is in the midst of the Khao Sok National Park at the northern end of Cheow Lan Lake or out on an overnight diving trip). However, for most foreigners it is not a good idea to use their phones with the SIM card from home to make calls or use the Internet, because you may quickly accumulate high bills due to expensive roaming fees.

You best get a Thai **SIM card** right after arriving in Thailand. At Phuket airport, just before the exit, you will find several providers (DTAC, AIS, True Move, True Online). If you present your passport (take a copy with you), you will receive a card and it will be topped up straight away. There are special tariffs for holiday makers: AIS Traveller SIM, True Move H Tourist SIM, True Online Tourist SIM. These tourist SIM cards are only valid for 90 days and then expire. To use the card, simply put it in your cell phone and activate it using the phone number shown on the card packaging. The sales outlets at

the airport and in 7-Eleven shops will help you set it up. If necessary, you can top up the card later: you can do this in all 7-Eleven shops or cell phone shops (called "top up") or alternatively online.
A new, elegant option are **eSIMs,** digital SIM cards that can be loaded onto compatible devices. You can find providers online and purchase a one-time prepaid plan for a specific number of days and data volume (but usually no free minutes), or you can book a package. For example, Nomadapp offers this for many countries: 💻 edelweiss.getnomad.app or Airolo 💻 airalo.com/de

Internet:

In the hotel they offer free WiFi for guests – access is provided in the form of a password at reception. There are now more and more restaurants with free WiFi. The password for access can be found on the menu or posted on the wall. When using such public networks, you should follow certain security rules, as they can be used as access to your own device and sensitive data can be intercepted. Never do online banking or online shopping and use httpS sites wherever possible.

Money

You don't need to bring Thai currency (baht) from home, as you can get it easily in Thailand. There are **exchange offices** at the airport in Phuket and in Khao Lak. Almost all Thai banks have a branch and counters in Khao Lak, most in the centre (La On), while the TMB has one in Bang Niang. Tips for exchanging money: Midday is better than afternoon or evening. The larger the amount you exchange in baht, the better the rate. It's better to give large bills. Caution: Banknotes for exchange should be in top condition. Torn, dirty, or badly crumpled notes will often be rejected. The cheapest exchange bureau is currently (2026) at the Pinocchio restaurant in Bang Niang.

You can withdraw money from **ATMs** using Visa, Mastercard, and Eurocheque cards. A fee (usually a flat rate of 250 Baht) is charged for this. Tips: When withdrawing, it's better to withdraw larger amounts. The flat fee is added to each withdrawal. Always decline DCC: if the ATM asks whether to convert to US Dollar $ or Pounds £, decline, as you'll otherwise get a worse exchange rate. Always have the transaction processed in Baht/the local currency. There's a withdrawal limit of 20,000-30,000 Baht per transaction. ATMs normally dispense 1,000 Baht notes. A good advice for getting smaller bills is to enter only 9,900 THB at the ATM, rather than round amounts like 10,000 baht. You will then receive at least 1 x 500 and 4 x 100 THB, and you won't have to pay with a 1000 THB note for a few bananas. Convenience stores like 7/11 and Lotus are also good places for changing large notes (1000s) into smaller ones – preferably if you buy something small.However, ATMs in Thailand have a peculiarity compared to those at home: after selecting the amount of money you want to withdraw, the machine first dispenses that amount, then asks about a receipt, and only then does it release your card. This once led to us leaving without our card. Luckily, it was very early in the morning, and the machine retracts the card after about a minute. With some local assistance, we even managed to get it back from the bank; otherwise, the only option is to have it blocked.

Hotels also do have ATMs or change money, but usually at a worse rate – but they are open after 9 pm

Bargaining

Except in shops with fixed prices (like the 7-Eleven) where you can see the price tags on the boxes, you are expected to negotiate the price in Thailand. This is especially true for the markets, but also for a large part of souvenir shops, tailors etc. This is an art, but if you do it with a smile it is much more pleasant and you usually have more success.

You should always first negotiate the price of one piece and then you bargain it further down it by taking several of them. Be prepared: the seller may quote a starting price that is up to five times higher than what it should be – especially if he suspects an inexperienced buyer. When asked what kind of hotel you are in, better tell them that you are staying with a local friend or have been here for some time – then you are more likely to get "normal" rates. Look carefully at the piece you want to buy and if you find a flaw you should point it out (this does not detract from mutual respect). Then bravely make a first counter-offer of one-fifth or a quarter of the price that was quoted, and then (after the seller has stopped jumping up and down and rolling his eyes), the real price negotiations can start. Keep smiling and remember this is all a game! Unless you really want the piece, you should not go over half the price of your first bid (and that's often more than what you should "pay"). By the way: just walking away when your own offer has been accepted is simply bad manners.

Tipping

Tipping is not generally expected in Thailand and is not mandatory. It is considered a gesture of gratitude for particularly appreciated service, not an obligation. In tourist areas like Khao Lak, it is more common and expected than in very rural areas.

Tips are given in the local currency: Thai Baht (THB). Dollars or Euros are impractical for staff. Coins are considered impolite. Give tips discreetly and adjust the amount depending on the region. The tip should always be proportionate to the bill. Many restaurants and tour operators have a "tip box" whose contents are shared among all employees. In hotels and upscale restaurants, a 10% service charge is usually already added to the bill, so a tip is not expected.

Examples:
Top restaurants: 5-10% of the bill if service is not already included.
Mid-range restaurants: Round up or 20-50 Baht.
Street food: Not expected, but you may round up. Tour guide: Day trip 100-200 Baht per person
Multi-day tour: 200-300 Baht per day per person
Taxi with a clock: Round up the fare
Tuk-tuk or taxi with negotiated price: Not mandatory. Round up the fare.
For long distances or exceptional service (luggage, advice): 50-100 Baht
Spa and massage: Top salons: Not mandatory, but appreciated for exceptional service
Traditional massage, small spas: 50-100 Baht per hour as a gesture

Health

It is worth visiting the pharmacy prior to a trip to obtain advice and information. You can also look up a lot of info on sites like 💻 nc.cdc.gov/travel.

The recommendations given here are for information purposes only and do not replace a consultation with a doctor or pharmacy!

Medication for travel

Even though you can buy many prescription drugs in pharmacies over the counter in Thailand, it is always advisable to have your regular medication with you. Pack enough for the whole stay. It is well-known that up to 30% of medicine in Asia is fake – even in pharmacies.

Mosquito repellent (like Sketolene) can be bought locally. By the way, well known "Balms" (such as Tiger balm) not only help with muscle pain, but also with mosquito bites. The basic equipment to take with you should include a strong disinfectant, dressings for minor injuries, painkillers and possibly something against athlete's foot. Remedies for diarrhea are also recommended.

Vaccination recommendations

These basic vaccinations are **recommended for everyone**:

Diphtheria and *Tetanus* (refresh every 10 years), *Polio, Measles, Hepatitis A*

Recommended for special situations / risk groups (e.g. long-term stays, backpacking and / or adventure trips or for bikes / bike tours):

Hepatitis B: transmitted through blood or sex.

Rabies. transmission by dogs, cats, monkeys, bats and forest animals. Children are considered particularly at risk. After being bitten or scratched, unvaccinated people have to be taken to hospital within first 24 hours for emergency vaccination / active immunization. After that it's too late (and rabies is nearly 100% lethal).

Typhoid fever: transmitted through infected water / food.

Japanese Encephalitis: transmitted by mosquitoes.

Not necessary for Thailand:

TBE, Yellow fever (only when entering from a yellow fever area), meningococci.

Health Risks

Khao Lak with its warm and humid climate poses some health risks that are not so well known in our areas, such as:

Sunburns:

Use sunscreen. This is especially important here because of the proximity to the equator. Sunburn is not only acutely uncomfortable but may have long-term effects – it promotes the development of skin cancer. For Thais, white skin is still an ideal of beauty and they do not understand the tanning craze of the Europeans. They protect themselves from the sun with long-sleeved clothing, hats and umbrellas. And you will find in most personal care product in Asia some skin-bleaching agent (even in deodorant!).

Gastrointestinal problems:

Although we have never had problems in Thailand even if we ate at night markets and in very small local stalls, this needs to be mentioned. The most common cause of gastrointestinal complaints is bad, raw or inadequately cooked food. Melons appear to be problematic (also in fruit shakes and fruit salads) if they are cut open and left lying around for too long. Meat should be well done. If you can select your fish/seafood yourself, make sure that the eyes are clear and not sunken in.
The water that comes out of the tap in Khao Lak is not drinkable but can be used for brushing teeth (although some hotels also provide extra water for this).

Mosquito bites and mosquito-transmitted diseases:

Mosquitos especially come out at dusk, but some species also bite during the day, so always use strong mosquito repellent, possibly local products, if they are already immune to the one you have. The bites should not be scratched, because that leads to infections and outright holes in the skin.
Chikungunya fever: This is a mosquito-transmitted viral disease appearing in southern Thailand. The symptoms are high fever with joint pain and tenderness. After 1-2 weeks most people recover, but occasionally permanent joint problems remain.
Dengue: This is also a mosquito-transmitted viral infection. It has non-specific symptoms such as head-, joint- and limb-pain, fever, occasionally a rash. In some cases, it takes a more serious course with bleeding complications and derailment of blood pressure. Then it is potentially life threatening and must be treated in a hospital. If dengue is suspected, you should neither take aspirin nor ibuprofen for the fever, but only acetaminophen / paracetamol.
Malaria: With this mosquito-transmitted disease there is no problem in Khao Lak. Introduced cases of the mosquito-borne disease come from northern Thailand.
Zika: Thailand is considered a country where transmission of the virus via mosquitoes may be sporadic, although no case of the

dreaded malformations in newborns is known. Pregnant women or those who want to become pregnant in the next 6 months should consult their doctor before travelling to Thailand.

Animals

Unrestrained (wild) dogs should not be fed or caressed. Hookworms can frolic in their fur and with the dog droppings, these hookworms get into the sand, that is why you shouldn't walk barefoot on beaches with many dogs. The minute worms penetrate the body over the skin and migrate to the lungs via the blood, as larvae they are coughed up and swallowed, and the adult worm in the intestine sucks blood form its host. Because of the loss of blood, long after returning home you get anaemia, fatigue, depression and stomach problems. If hookworms are suspected, a doctor should be consulted and an anthelmintic prescribed.

Monkeys can bite pretty badly (as dogs and cats) and the wounds often become infected. A visit to a doctor is absolutely necessary. You also should be vaccinated against tetanus and possibly rabies after a bite (you only have 24 hours for that!). It is best to avoid any contact.

Jellyfish are occasionally to be found in the water. Most are so small that you cannot even see them and only feel when you have been stung. They are annoying, but usually not dangerous. Rarely there may be poisonous jellyfish, where a touch can leave severe pain, skin rashes and even scarring. The Portuguese Man of War and the Box Jellyfish are the most dangerous. Upon contact, it helps to pour vinegar over it (maybe take some from home, you cannot get it there), wash it with water and go to the doctor if no improvement occurs. Thais use a paste of the green Vine with the violet flowers which can often be found on the beach to treat jellyfish stings.

Sea urchins are found primarily on rocks in the water. Whoever steps on one gets the thin spikes in the sole of the foot, where they can break off and cause severe pain. A doctor should remove the spines – or, if none is available, you can try to use a paste of Papaya: its enzyme papain softens the skin, so that the spines come out by themselves the next day.

Ever since Steve Irwin died of a **stingray** sting people know how dangerous they can be. A sting leads to severe pain and being stung in the abdomen and face is dangerous. Pakarang Beach is known to have stingrays, so it is advisable there to go in the water with caution and slippers only.

Swimming, snorkelling and scuba diving is great, but one principle applies here as elsewhere else: nothing should be touched in the sea. For nature's and for your own safety.
In lakes and ponds small parasites causing **schistosomiasis** may live. They get into the water with human faeces. where the larvae penetrate the skin an itchy rash develops, and can later cause an acute febrile illness with possible organ involvement, which can be dangerous. A physician should be consulted in case of symptoms. With early treatment the prognosis is good.

This may all sound a bit disconcerting, but in all the years we did not experience any of these problems – except for the small harmless jellyfish in the sea and mosquitoes in the evening. We have eaten everywhere, have been in many bodies of water (flowing and standing) and never suffered any negative consequences.
Caution is always important: Stay away from animals, eat where the Thais eat and protect yourself against mosquito bites – then not much can happen.

Food allergies and special diets in Thailand

Peanut Allergy: Peanut oil is used for cooking, and whole or crushed peanuts are found in Papaya Salad, Pad Thai, Massaman Curry, and Satay marinade.
Gluten: The protein is found in wheat, oats, barley and rye. They are ingredients in bread, muesli, pastries and ice cream. Rice dishes will do, but the soy sauce used to flavour them may contain gluten. There is gluten-free soy sauce.
Lactose and dairy products: Many Asians cannot tolerate this either, so there are lots of alternatives such as almond or soy milk or coconut milk. However, some products with coconut milk also contain regular milk: ice cream, Thai-style coffee with milk.
Seafood: Shrimp (prawns) in particular are found in many dishes – many curries contain shrimp paste.
Vegetarians / Vegans: Instead of salt, fish or oyster sauce is often used for seasoning. Fried Rice always contains eggs.

It is advisable to make notes with the allergy information in English and Thai and only to eat in restaurants where you can indicate your allergies.

Stop Sign

Cashew Nut on the Tree

Frangipani

Ketchup and Maggi

Pineapple

Orchidee

Doctor / Hospital / Clinic

Those who get sick in Khao Lak have several **doctors** to choose from. Some of them also make hotel-visits. As in many small towns in Thailand there are **first aid stations and small clinics.** However, the equipment and hygienic conditions are not up to European standards and as a tourist, you will be quickly taken to larger hospitals in Takua Pa or on Phuket in case of serious problems– where there are various hospitals that are very well equipped.

Unfortunately taxi drivers (but also hotels) like to recommend and bring you to the places where they benefit the most. There were some clinics that can only be described as rip-off clinics in Khao Lak. They demanded outrageous prices for (sometimes unnecessary) tests, examinations and treatments and occasionally wanted payment in advance. They are closed now – it remains to be seen whether there will be new ones.

In the event of an emergency, contact the **Andaman Hub Medical Network in Bang Niang**. The small clinic is located in a blue building at the upper (northern) end of the reservoir at the 4. ✆+66 76 48 67 99

Siam International Clinic: A small, new clinic located directly on Highway 4 between La On and Bang Niang, with a glass front into the waiting room. They offer free pick-up and hotel visits 24 hours a day. Open daily from 9 am to midnight. Also available via WhatsApp: ✆ +66 96 778 8450 💻 siaminternationalclinic.com/siam-international-clinic-khaolak

Andaman International Clinic: Another new, small clinic located on Highway 4 in La On. 🕒 Open 24 hours a day. Hotel visits available. andamaninternationalclinic.com and WhatsApp ✆+66 62 2680030

Takecare Doctor Khaolak Clinic, located at Highway 4 in La On. A chain clinic with branches in Phuket, Krabi, etc. 🕒 Open 24/7. ✆ +66 94 315 9495 💻 doctorkhaolak.com

Dr. Chusak is a long-established pediatrician and general practitioner. He speaks English and makes house calls. His clinic is located in Ban La On near the entrance to The Sands Hotel. 🕒 5:30 pm–8:30 pm. ✆+66 76 48 57 38 or +66 81 968970 (emergencies) 💻drchusak.com

Clinic Dr. Amornrut is located in Bang Niang at Main Road 4, north of Bang Niang Market. ◷ Open daily from 5-8 pm. ✆+66 83 647 7053

Khao Lak ENT Clinic - Ear, Nose and Throat Specialist in Khuek Khak ◷5-7 pm 💻 facebook.com/KhaolakENTclinic ✆+66 889 727 3099

Takuapa Hospital: 39/2 Moo 1 T. Bang Naisri, Takua Pa, ✆+66 76 584 250., 24 hours emergency, 209 Beds. **Emergency: 1669**.
Phuket International Clinic: ✆+66 76 210 935

Ambulance in Bang Niang: **1719 or 1699**
If you have an accident on the road (for example as a motorcyclist) you will probably be loaded into the back of the car by some helpful Thais and taken to hospital.

Decompression chambers are needed in diving accidents. In Khao Lak, thanks to caring dive guides, they apparently have never had a fatal accident. The nearest decompression chamber is located on Phuket: in Phuket Town: SSS Hyperbaric Chamber Network Phuket

Medical treatments are usually cheaper in Thailand than in Europe, and therefore health tourism has developed in some areas, especially for dental treatments. Many dentists on Phuket have adapted to foreign patients, speak English and have international standards.
It is still advisable to have **adequate insurance**.

Dentists in Khao Lak

The Dental Clinic is a recommendation for acute dental problems. 5/55 Moo 7, Petchkasem Road (in the Book Tree House still in La On) +66 99 619 4141 💻 facebook.com/khaolakdentalclinic

Dental Home 28/34 Moo 7, Petchkasem Road ✆ +66 89 588 8558 💻 facebook.com/khaolakdentalhomeclinic

Pharmacies

Khao Lak has many pharmacies, mostly in La On and Bang Niang. In the pharmacies, which are visited by both locals and tourists, you can seek advice on health problems and get most medications that you also can get in Europe – some with different names / packaging – and various others that would require a prescription at home such as antibiotics. These pills are often not sold in the packaging, but in a small plastic sleeve with just the medication name and dosage on it. Packaging inserts are completely missing most of the time. It is not recommended to stock up your long-term medication here because of possible counterfeit medicines. Experience has shown that it is also a good idea to check the expiry dates when purchasing. This also applies to cosmetics.

Phetkasem Foundation – formerly Khao Lak Rescue

The Phetkasem Foundation is a first aid organization that provides assistance in the event of accidents or other incidents such as animal rescue and snake removal.

In contrast to Europe, there are no laws in Thailand that require you to provide first-aid as a passer-by and there are no state-subsidized services here. Instead, there are privately sponsored organizations with volunteers as staff, relying on revenue and donations. Many of the volunteers were trained abroad and work here seasonally. The approx. 15 employees of Khao Lak Rescue have other full-time jobs, from crane operators to hotel employees, but were trained in first-aid by the hospital in traffic matters by the police. They are often the first to arrive at the scene of an accident. In the case of critically injured people, they call the ambulance of the hospital in Takua Pa for support. The doctor remains in the hospital in Thailand and does not come with the ambulance. Transport to the hospital is always free. They gladly accept donations for their organization.

The station is in Bang Niang. Telephone (for emergencies) 1669 or ✆+66 83 176 5873

Traffic in Thailand: A Survival Guide

In Thailand you **drive on the left side of the road**, so cars have the wheel on the right. If you are not used to this perhaps you should apply a "keep left" sticker on the wheel – However, the biggest problem to remember this is on wide and lonely roads ... which are rare in Thailand.

Expect everything, anytime: other drivers often behave erratically, are changing lanes without looking or indicating, run over red lights or stop on short notice, or turn abruptly onto the street. At night, many people drive without any functioning light and on the wrong side of the road. Be attentive and ready to brake, especially at intersections and the entrance of side roads.

The emergency lane next to the road is often used by motorcycle and bicycle riders as well as those small, mobile stalls that are simply too slow for the normal road, by cars to avoid collision with other cars overtaking on the other side, or if someone is waiting in the middle of the road to make a U-turn to the right.

There are **traffic lights** on some crossings in Thailand – on the way up north from the airport in Phuket there are two with a countdown, to signal the seconds until the next phase (green or red). At most traffic lights a left turn is permitted if the road is free, even if the lights are red. Some Thais do not stop at all or go early, when the traffic light is still red.

U-Turns: Now also in Khao Lak! Thanks to the main road leading up to Takua Pa, which is now separated throughout by a bold green median strip, it is no longer so easy to turn or turn around. The only possibility to do this now is at the marked U-turns, some of which are far apart. Unfortunately, the ones in Khao Lak are only partially adapted to local conditions – so you won't necessarily find them at important junctions. In Bang Niang and La On there are U-turns with traffic lights, otherwise you have to be careful, because vehicles can always be parked there (usually in the middle of the street) and some can't wait and just turn off.

Overtaking: Slower vehicles will be overtaken, even if it is not safe. This is done on the right or left, and sometimes on the track of the oncoming traffic, which then must dodge. You must therefore expect a suddenly oncoming car or van at any time. It is always a good idea to keep to the far left especially in front of hilltops.

Right of Way: The same rules apply as in Europe ... many people just do not stick to it. Larger cars in particular often take the right of way and where there is a gap, someone surely pushes in. You must be equally unscrupulous, or you will barely be able to turn into traffic.

Pedestrians and Crosswalks: Pedestrians are at high risk in Thailand, especially if they assume Thais will be as considerate as drivers are in Europe. Crosswalks or not: they don't always stop when someone wants to cross the street – even if they're already on it!

For **motorcyclists: wear a helmet**. Yes – you will see a lot of (local) people not wearing a helmet, and it is hot, but this is not only an important protection for you, but also required by law. Even if the police are less interested in the tourists than the locals, this is one of the things that are checked at the police stations and checkpoints, and you can see many Thais suddenly bring out a helmet there. The same goes for **wearing the seat belt in a car.**

Traffic is controlled at the **Police Checkpoints** but otherwise the police seem to have little interest in it. Motorists are less checked than motorcyclists – except for the dangerous days between Christmas and New Year and around Songkran when people are drinking and driving and the number of accidents and fatalities rise up – this time is also called "the 7 Days of Danger". Police check the driver's license, valid insurance, helmet, and seat belt.

Fines must be paid immediately at the police station or at temporary pay stations. You get a receipt – which amusingly makes you "immune" to the same offense for the next 24 hours. That means you don't have to pay again even if you still don't have a helmet on.

Parking: curbs painted in red and white mean: do not park here. If you find a chain on your bike, it was probably the police. To get rid of it, you go to the nearest police station and pay 400 baht. Then you just have to find the policeman who has the key to the chain lock.

Drinking and driving: Thailand has a maximum blood alcohol limit of 0.5 mg (0.2 mg if you have not had your license for 5 years yet). Checks are seldom, but those caught are facing unpleasant consequences: prison in a mass cell and a bail of 20'000 baht to get out again. The final fine will be determined at court (between 2'000 to 10'000 baht). And if you fall into the hands of a corrupt police officer it can get even more expensive.

Gas stations are not open 24 hours a day. most close after 8 pm. At the gas station you do not fill up yourself but ask the staff. Just tell them the mix you want: Diesel 91 (Normal) or 95 (Super) and either "Full" or the amount for which you want to fill up. Your car rental company will tell you what to fill up with, or you can find it on the tank lid.

Road maps: At the rental station you only get some very rough and inaccurate tourist maps. You can buy a good "Road Map of South Thailand" in the 7-Eleven. On smartphones Google Maps helps greatly, as do some apps – although Scout, which I have used successfully elsewhere, is still not detailed enough here.

In Case of a Traffic Accident

You occasionally hear horror stories of what could happen after an accident in Thailand. This is often based on the assumption that the tourist, no matter what happened, is guilty because: "If the tourist had not been there, then the accident would not have happened." That is no longer necessarily so, but it is always a good idea to look for some Thai speaking help (for example from the rental agency or the Tourist Police) in order to clarify the matter.

Procedure:

- Leave the vehicles how they are until the police arrive. (It's quite possible that the other party involved is fleeing the scene of the accident, so a photo of their car with number plate is helpful).
- There are no warning triangles here: a couple of tree branches put down on the road serve the same purpose. So be careful when you see these – although they often lie very close to the car.
- Call the owner of your car (the rental agency) who will send a damage assessor for your insurance.
- Stay calm and wait.
- The rental agency usually provides a replacement car.

With motorcyclists it must usually be negotiated on the spot about who pays how much (due to lack of insurance). Most of the time you (and not the rental agency) have to pay. It is usually cheaper to have the repairs done yourself because the owner might charge a higher (probably inflated) price for it.

Emergency numbers:

Emergency numbers:
Police 191 (Thai only)
Tourist Police 1155
Ambulance 1699 (transport, animal problems, Thai only)
Phetkasem foundation/Khao Lak Rescue +66 83 176 5873
Fire department 199

i lert U – The Tourist Police app has been available since 2024. You can set it up at home, but it will only work in Thailand. It allows you to contact the tourist police quickly and easily. You can write a message and maybe send a photo from the app. This will then show the police the exact location from where you sent it.

Entry / Exit

***** Please check the current rules before each visit – they change frequently** ***
Information on entry requirements for Thailand can be found on the website 💻 immigration.go.th.

For stays in Thailand lasting up to 30 days*, UK and US nationals do not need a **visa** prior to arrival (neither do those from Australia). You need a valid passport, that must be valid for at least six months beyond the entry date as well as a confirmed onward or return ticket. Children need their own passport.
If you intend to stay in Thailand for more than 30 days*, you will need a visa issued by a Thai diplomatic mission before entering Thailand. For stays of up to 60 days, a tourist visa is required. A "non-immigrant visa" entitles you to a maximum stay of 90 days. Tourists and non-immigrant visas are extended in practice by 30 days. A visa can and must be renewed only at the Thai Bureau of Immigration or at border crossings. The next border for a "visa run" is up in Ranong. Local travel agencies often sell fake documents that cause problems when leaving the country.
* The time has been extended from 30 to 90 days, but this may change back again.

Since May 1st 2025, there is an important new entry requirement for Thailand: the TM6 **Thailand Digital Arrival Card (TDAC)**. The card must be completed (in English) within three days of entry. You will then receive a confirmation email with a QR code, which you must present to the immigration police. They will ask for personal information: full name, nationality, telephone number, email address and passport information, as well as travel information: flight number, purpose of travel and address in Thailand (hotel or residential address). 💻 tdac.immigration.go.th/arrival-card

Cash on entry: Travelers who enter Thailand without a visa must carry the equivalent of at least 10,000 baht a family at least 20,000 baht with them upon entry. The minimum amount can be shown in any currency.
A bank statement, or subsequent withdrawal is not possible. If you do not stay longer than 30 days for a holiday in Thailand (i.e. without a visa, only with an entry stamp) and do not re-enter more than once in a row (i.e. make a visa run) this shouldn't be a problem as this is rarely controlled – but if there is a control, it can ruin the holiday. It's also worth having cash with you when exchanging money as currency exchange offices usually offer better exchange rates and do not charge fees as high as the ATMs do.

Customs regulations

Currency

Foreign visitors can import and export foreign currencies without limits (amounts over $ 20,000 should be declared). The national currency (baht) can also be imported freely, but only up to a maximum of 20,000 baht per person without prior authorization. Caution is advised against counterfeit money that is in circulation. It is recommended to exchange money only in authorized bureaux de change.

Counterfeit goods / product piracy

The purchase of counterfeit branded items such as watches, computers, software (even pirated copies of movies, music, etc.), clothing, etc. as well as the import of such goods to your home country is prohibited for copyright reasons. Thailand is well known for its many fakes. It is irrelevant whether the tourist is aware that something is counterfeit or not. If you are caught, the goods will be confiscated by customs, destroyed and the trademark owner informed, who may initiate legal action against you.

Antiques / Buddha statues

The export and import of certain antiques are only allowed with the permission of the Fine Arts Department of the National Museum in Bangkok. A reputable business will get you this permission. The export of Buddha figures, whether old or new, is prohibited for non-Buddhists.

Souvenirs

The export of certain leather products and ivory as well as their import into Europe or the US are subject to the Washington Convention. It is strongly recommended to inform yourself about such purchases. For Thailand, there is a detailed list of animals and plants, that are not allowed to be exported. See 💻 artenschutz-online.de (protection of species on holiday). This list includes corals, crocodiles, turtles, snakes, tarantulas, giant clams, elephants, scorpions, butterflies, seahorses, monkeys, bears, and among the plants: aloe, ginseng, cacti, orchids, pitcher plants.

Miscellaneous

Obscene objects or images as well as pornographic material are prohibited. Also prohibited are goods with a Thai flag as well as fake royal or official seals.

Food / Medicines / Tobacco

Allowed are *cigarettes* up to 200 pieces, cigars up to 50 pieces or *tobacco* up to 250 g, as well as up to 4 litres of *wine* or 1 litre of *spirits* - but liquor with more than 40% alcohol is banned in Thailand and the import will be punished. Apparently, up to 16 litres of *beer* can be imported into Thailand.

E-cigarettes (including IQOS) and accessories and hookahs are banned throughout Thailand!

The import of *meat or sausage products* has been strictly prohibited since the BSE crisis.

Anyone who wishes to import *medicines*, or food supplements needs a permit from the Thai Food and Drug Administration. Medication for personal use are normally allowed for a period of 30 days, but caution is advised with strong analgesics and other medicine that fall under the Narcotics Act. The import of all types of *narcotics* is prohibited.

The **exemption for duty-free goods** when returning to Europe is 430 euros. For the US it is 800$ and AUD900 for Australia.

Power banks and rechargeable batteries on the plane

Laptops, smartphones and tablets are permitted on board of airplanes only in hand luggage, although lithium batteries are not without risks.

The same applies to power banks. A maximum of two external lithium batteries (power banks) are permitted per passenger. They may not be used or charged during the flight. In addition the nominal power must be clearly written on the battery. A maximum of 100 watt-hours (Wh) or 27,000 mAh **are** permitted per battery. Illegible or unlabeled batteries were frequently confiscated during baggage checks at airports in Thailand. Since the beginning of 2025, following a fire on a South Korean plane involving a battery, stricter rules have been introduced by many Asian airlines, including Thai Airlines and Singapore Airlines. Use and charging during flight is prohibited and will be subject to inspection. They should be wrapped separately in plastic or insulation.

Drones

Recreational drones are allowed in Thailand (upon registration). For most camera drones you need 2 permits plus insurance:
-By the National Broadcasting and Telecommunications Commission (NBTC). They are responsible for the frequencies used by the drone. NBTC: 💻 anyregis.nbtc.go.th/sign_up/foreigner
-By the Civil Aviation Authority of Thailand (CAAT), which registers all drone pilots. CAAT: ✆+66 25 68 8815 💻uav@caat.or.th
Insurance for drone flights is also necessary and the certificate should be carried with you. Drone model and serial number must be visible on it and the validity in Thailand. The insured amount must be at least 1 million THB (approx. 30,000 euros).
The registration process is described here; the site also offers a registration service: 💻 stefaninthailand.de/anleitung-drohne-registrieren-in-thailand

Update 2026: Drone flying is prohibited on the border between Thailand and Cambodia. In the rest of the country, the drone ban has been largely lifted, except in Koh Kood.

Restrictions for flying a drone: The maximum flight altitude is 90 m in uncontrolled airspace. Stay 9 km away from airports and respect other people's privacy. You may approach a maximum of 50m from people, vehicles and buildings and it is not allowed to fly over towns and villages – if you do, permission should be obtained in advance. Flights are only allowed during daylight hours. A minimum age of 20 years applies

Thai for Tourists

It is always good to know a few words of the local language – and this is well received. It is not a requirement, but it improves every contact and sometimes you receive a better price when negotiating. With English you get very far (especially in tourist places like Khao Lak and Phuket), but it is worth to learn some expressions:

Important: at the end of almost every sentence you say **-ka** (if you are a woman) or **-krab** (if you are a man) to be polite

Hello/Good day – sa-wade-krab (for men) / sa-wade-ka (for women)
Goodbye: La gon-krab (m)/ la gon-ka (f)
Yes: Chai-krab (m) / -ka (f)
No: Mai Chai-krab (m) / -ka (f)
Thank you: Kop-kun-krab (m) / -ka (f)
Please: Mai ben rai-krab (m) / -ka (f)
Excuse me: Khor thot
No problem / It doesn't matter: Mai Pen-Rai
Good bye: La-gon-krab (m) / -ka (f)
Good: Dee
Bad: Mai-Dee
The bill, please: Keb-Tang-krab (m) / -ka (f)
Where is the toilet?: Hong nam Yu Nai-krab? (m) / -ka (f)
Not spicy: Mai pet
Very spicy: Pet pet
How much? Tau tai krab? (m) / -ka (f)
Cheap: Took
Pricey: Pang
I: Phom (Mann), Tschan (Frau)
My name is: Phom tschü (Mann) / Tschan Tschü (Frau)
I would like: Ao
I have a problem: Chan-Mee-Pan-Ha-krab (m) / -ka (f)
I want to go to..: Phom bpai-krab (m) / Tschü bpai-ka (f)
Temple Wat
Waterfall: Nahm Dtok
Island: Ko
Road: Soi
Cave: Tham
Market: Dtalaad
Sea: Thalee

Afterword

Dear readers, dear travellers, you are holding the 7th edition of the travel guide for Khao Lak in your hands. The book is a surprising success story for us: It started, after numerous visits to beautiful Khao Lak, when we were (once again) looking for something to do with the family and were annoyed that there was no travel guide for Khao Lak. Of course, you can find almost any information after a shorter or often longer search on the Internet – but that is quite impractical on site and generally very time-consuming. Especially if you don't know what to look for. I'm not a writer, but somehow the idea of writing our own guide came up. And when this was well received by our friend Jin from the Sky restaurant ("I'm sure you can do that.") – we started a first attempt in 2016 with a still fairly simple self-published book on Amazon. (My wife helped a lot). "Discovering Khao Lak – for individual travellers, tourists and families" was so well received that we dared to expand and completely revise it – in order to bring it to bookstores with its own ISBN in 2017. This is "Discovering Khao Lak Compact". A Khao-Lak travel guide made by non-professional enthusiasts with the aim of making the stay easier for visitors and bringing them closer to this beautiful piece of earth.

A travel guide like this needs a lot of work to keep it up to date, especially in a popular travel destination where there are frequent changes. It was therefore revised and further supplemented after our visits in 2018 and 2019. The next update was planned for 2020... and then came the new corona virus. For two years, travelling to Thailand was virtually impossible. As soon as we could, we came back – and ... it was nice as always. But a lot has changed. Service providers such as restaurants and tour operators had to give up and close due to a lack of visitors. After our visits in 2023 and now 2024 we can now report: many are back, others are new. We found new and beautiful places again, partly untouched by mass tourism.

Since 2024 our travel guide has faced considerable competition. Amazon is practically flooded with cheap and quickly made "travel guides" generated by artificial intelligence. As someone who has put a lot of time and effort into their books, this is incredibly annoying. Despite their highly professional-looking descriptions, these books are virtually useless. They are filled with platitudes, incorrect and outdated information and translation errors. I have looked at several... for travellers, these books are a complete waste of money.

And for dedicated self-publishing authors, they are a nuisance, because they undermine trust.

You have certainly noticed that the pictures in "Discovering Khao Lak" are in black and white – which is unusual for a travel guidebook. I also think that's too bad! – Thailand has so many beautiful photo opportunities. But you can admire the pictures from the book and many more on our **Instagram** account, and all in colour: **@khaolakkompakt**

We are always happy to receive feedback on the book content or recommendations for new attractions or excellent restaurants at ruco.kobi@gmail.com.

If you liked the book or if it was useful to you, we would be happy about a review (for example on Amazon).

The maps in the travel guide were done by us and serve as a rough overview. You can find the points we cover in the book here: On **Googlemymaps**: bit.ly/klentdecken

We wish you a nice holiday – and we're sure, you'll have it in Khao Lak!

Ruedi and Corinne Kobi

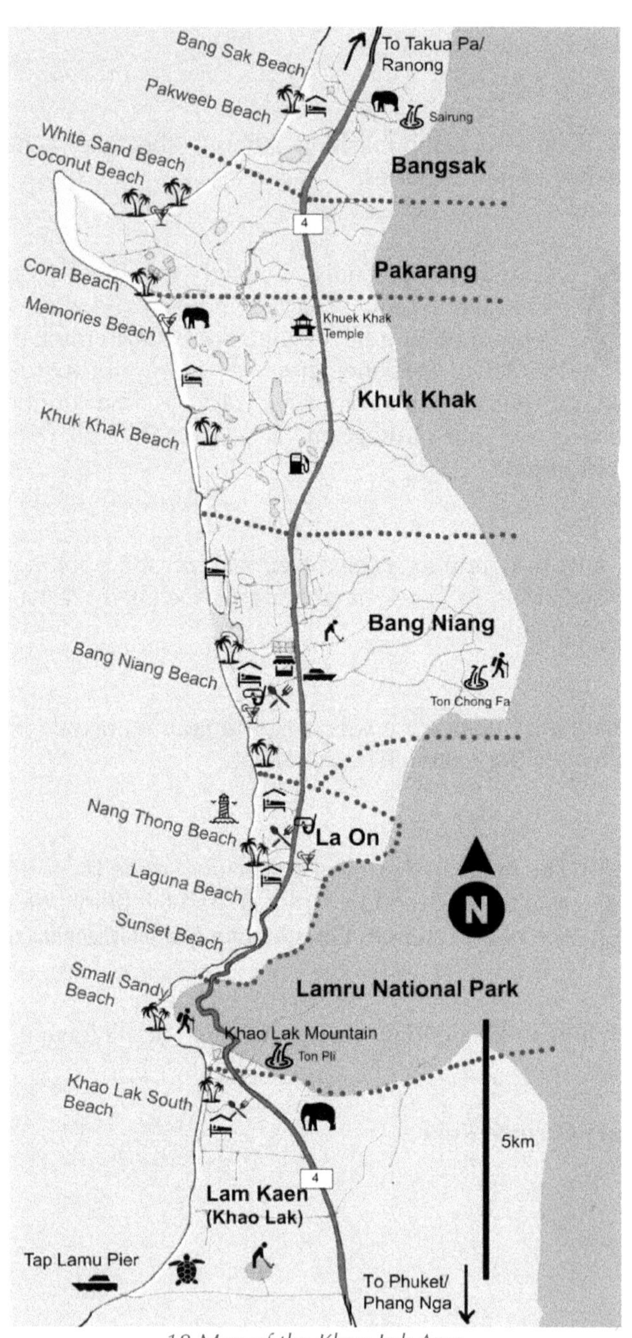

18-Map of the Khao Lak Area

www.ingramcontent.com/pod-product-compliance
Ingram Content Group UK Ltd.
Pitfield, Milton Keynes, MK11 3LW, UK
UKHW022002190726
13853UKWH00004B/1685